Birdfinding
in the Montreal Area

D1250307

Pierre Bannon

Translated by Margaret Pye

*Illustrations by Sylvain Tanguay
and René Roy*

The Province of Quebec Society for the Protection of Birds
and
Centre de conservation de la faune ailée de Montréal

Legend

═⟨20⟩═	: AUTOROUTE
─⟨132⟩─	: NUMBERED HIGHWAY
───────	: SECONDARY ROAD
─ ─ ─ ─	: WOOD ROAD
-------	: TRAIL
+─+─+─+	: RAILWAY
─ · ─ · ─	: PARK OR SANCTUARY BOUNDARY
· ─ · · ─ ·	: POWER TRANSMISSION LINE
·· ── ·· ──	: PROVINCIAL BORDER
▬▬▬▬▬	: INTERNATIONAL BORDER
⌒⌒⌒	: WOODLAND
──x──	: FENCE
●	: CITY / TOWN / VILLAGE
P	: PARKING LOT
⊢	: GATE
≋≋≋	: SWAMP OR PEAT BOG
⑩	: OBSERVATION SITE OR POINT OF INTEREST
⋞	: PLATFORM OR LOOKOUT

AUTHOR'S NOTE

Some of the sites described in this guide are on private property. Their inclusion in this book does not constitute an invitation to visit such property at will. Visitors should obtain permission before venturing onto any site located on private land.

Cover photo :
Normand David

Texts :
Pierre Bannon

Contributors:
Marika Ainley, Bob Barnhurst, Chuck Kling, Gaétan Duquette, Raynald Fortier, Lucie Giroux, Denis Henri, Guy Huot, Daniel Jauvin, Claude Lavoie, Barbara McDuff, Mabel McIntosh, Elsie Mitchell, François Morneau, Richard Pelletier, Desneiges Perreault, Michel Sainte-Marie.

Review Committee:
Gaétan Duquette, Michel Robert, Normand David, Richard Yank

Cartography:
Pierre Bannon, Sylvain Tanguay

Illustrations:
Sylvain Tanguay, René Roy

Word Processing and Secretarial Assistance :
Softcity: Michelle Kusters; Claudette Blanchard, Diane Bannon

Type-setting :
Bip, studio de photocomposition inc.

Publishers :
The Province of Quebec Society for the Protection of Birds and
Le Centre de conservation de la faune ailée de Montréal

Distribution :
Centre de conservation de la faune ailée de Montréal

Acknowledgments :
The following people have also contributed in various ways: Ken Thorpe, Steve Charlton, Peter Smith, Eric Tull, Sharon David, Michel Gosselin, Danielle Gagnon, Johanne Bérard (Montreal Urban Community Development Plan). We are most grateful for their invaluable assistance.

ISBN 2-9801098-2-7
© Centre de conservation de la faune ailée de Montréal 1991
7950, rue De Marseille, Montréal, Qc. H1L 1N7   Tel.: (514) 351-5496

Legal deposit first quarter 1991
Bibliothèque nationale du Québec
National Library of Canada

Printed in Canada

The Province of Quebec Society for the Protection of Birds

The Province of Quebec Society for the Protection of Birds (PQSPB) is a nonprofit organization of birdwatchers who are mostly from the Montreal area. Founded January 4, 1917, the PQSPB is by far the oldest birdwatching club in the province of Quebec.

The PQSPB has two main, complementary objectives. The first is to instill in its members – and the general public – a knowledge and appreciation of birds. The second is to protect bird life and bird habitat. Educational and recreational activities such as field trips, talks on birds and public expositions are some of the means whereby the Society endeavours to achieve its first objective.

In pursuing its second objective, the protection of birds and their habitat, the PQSPB must often take an active stand in conservation matters. Private donations have enabled the PQSPB to participate in the acquisition and management of essential bird habitat and thereby make a direct contribution to nature conservation.

The publication of this site guide represents the fruition of a long-cherished project, one that brings the Society closer to achieving its twofold purpose. Besides furthering the educational aims, the book will create public interest in the valuable bird habitat in our area and thus contribute to its protection in the years to come.

Le Centre de conservation de la faune ailée de Montréal

Founded in 1981 during the creation of a bird pavilion at Terre des Hommes, Le Centre de conservation de la faune ailée de Montréal is today Canada's main distributor of natural science material. Besides serving the public, the Centre supplies specialized businesses, garden centres, educational and scientific institutions. Books, recordings, bird feeders, bird seed and binoculars are among the many items it offers.

Besides publishing works related to the field of natural science, the Centre designs and markets nest boxes and bird feeders.

Daniel Coulombe
Director

From the same publisher

– L'observation des oiseaux dans la région de Montréal.
Map and table of 37 sites, by Daniel Coulombe

– Food preferences of birds at feeders.
A table of birds and bird foods in poster form.

– How to Live with Urban Wildlife.
Book by David Bird

– Birds around the House and Feeder Birds.
Two colour posters by Ghislain Caron.

– Birds of the Deciduous Forest and Birds of the Coniferous Forest.
Two colour posters by Ghislain Caron.

– Toxic Plants.
Two colour-photo posters, designed in collaboration with the Montreal
Botanical Gardens.

– Birds in Their Habitat and Birds of the Field.
Two colour posters by Ghislain Caron.

– Insect Orders and Our Butterflies.
Two colour-photo posters designed in collaboration with the Montreal
Insectarium.

– Les sons de nos forêts. (Wild Sounds of the Northwoods)
Audio cassette and booklet on 111 species of birds and several frogs,
toads and mammals of Quebec, Canada and the northern United States,
by Lang Elliot and Ted Mack.

TABLE OF CONTENTS

III

INTRODUCTION

We are surrounded by birds. Even the most unobservant Montrealer has probably noticed flocks of "honkers" flying over the city on a fine April day or watched "sea gulls" squabbling over picnic scraps.

More observant city dwellers will notice that at certain times of the year – spring and fall – migrating birds invade every patch of green space, sometimes in the very heart of the city. But the chorus of bird song arising from a thicket on a morning in May is likely to be lost in the din of traffic, before the songsters can even be spotted.

Birdwatchers in the suburbs are more fortunate. They can lure as many as 20 species of birds to their windows in winter, simply by providing the proper food. And with careful observation, suburban birdwatchers can see about 50 different species during the course of a year, right in their own neighbourhood.

People in city or suburbs who enjoy watching birds will soon want to know more about the bright-plumaged creatures found in their field guides to the birds of North America. There are over 800 species, 465 of which are found on the eastern half of the continent.

Over the last few years 359 species of birds have visited the Montreal area; 275 of these are sighted each year and 189 nest. This means that a birdwatcher can see a sizable proportion of the birds of the eastern North American continent here in the Montreal area.

But the question is where to go to see all these birds, since not all come to feeders or venture into suburban gardens. It is in answer to this question that this book has been written.

Over the years, birdwatchers have been visiting certain birdwatching sites in the Montreal area regularly, and some of these have acquired an excellent reputation. Fifty-five such sites have been selected, and these are the subject matter of this book. Twenty-two are found in Greater Montreal and are readily accessible by car and, in most cases, by public transportation. The 33 remaining sites are more distant but can be reached in less than 90 minutes from downtown Montreal. All the sites can be visited in a short one-day trip.

This guide gives a thorough description of each site, including the type of habitat and the birds found there. A detailed route is suggested, to help the birder find species of particular interest.

This is a book for all bird lovers living in or visiting the Montreal area. Binoculars and a field guide are all you need as you set out to discover the wealth of bird life at our doorstep!

Chapter 1

Discovering the Montreal Area

The area covered by this guide encompasses about 13,000 km². It is bounded to the south by the U.S. border, to the west by the Ontario border, to the north by the Laurentian foothills and to the east by the Yamaska River. Lake Saint-Pierre, situated at the northeast end of this area, has also been included. At the centre is Montreal, the largest city in the province of Quebec.

The area lies in a valley 100 to 150 km wide, through which the St. Lawrence River flows. North of this valley, just 50 km from Montreal, the Laurentian Mountains rise to an elevation of 300 m. The southern part is bounded by the Adirondacks, in New York State. These mountains are crossed by a valley north of Lake Champlain, where the Richelieu River flows north to the St. Lawrence. This southern escarpment rises to over 300 m and is 60 km from Montreal.

The relatively flat topography of this valley is broken by some of the Monteregian Hills. These are, from west to east, the Oka Hills, Mount Royal, Mount Saint-Bruno, Mount Saint-Grégoire, Mount Saint-Hilaire and Rougemount. Rigaud Mountain stands to the west of Montreal.

Situated in the southernmost part of Quebec, the Montreal lowlands have a sub-humid continental temperate climate that is much less severe than that of the rest of the province.

The mean annual temperature is 4.4 °C, -10.8 °C for January and 21.1 °C for July. Extreme temperatures rarely exceed -25°C in winter and 32 °C in summer. The frost-free period lasts from 125 to 150 days of the year, or about 4.5 months. The Montreal area has the longest average foliar period in the province, almost 200 days. Budding generally begins in late April, and defoliation is usually complete by early November. Annual precipitation ranges from 85 to 105 cm, with an average of about 7.5 cm per month. Total snowfall is 2.0 to 2.5 m between November and March, but the snow cover rarely exceeds 50 cm. Rain-and snowfall can last for several hours or even a few days on occasion, except during the summer months, when precipitation normally takes the form of brief thundershowers.

Although this area is only one per cent of the total area of Quebec, it contains over half the population of the province, three million inhabitants in all. This enormous demographic pressure and the fact that the area contains the best agricultural land in Quebec has had unfortunate consequences for the natural environment. Several sites, described later in this book, could be adversely affected in the not-too-distant future.

The habitats and their bird life

Woodland habitat

The Montreal area, as defined for the purposes of this book, is part of the upper St. Lawrence forest region, which comprises the lowlands of the upper St. Lawrence River Valley and the lower Ottawa River Valley. This area corresponds roughly to the domain of the sugar-maple hickory stand. The dominant forest cover is comprised of sugar maple, American beech and several other tree species that are at their northern limit. Softwood species are relatively uncommon. The primeval forest that once covered most of the area has almost disappeared, having given way to agriculture and urbanization. The wooded areas found here today are stands of regrowth in various stages of development, and these cover only 15 per cent of the territory. Seen from the air, the area around Montreal looks like a patchwork of fields and small, isolated woodlots.

There is no question that forest species nesting in the Montreal area have suffered from deforestation. Some researchers maintain that forest destruction is the reason certain species are no longer found in the area.

The species of woodland birds that nest around Montreal are those that do not need large forested areas. Typical of these are Northern Flicker, Eastern Wood-Pewee, Great Crested Flycatcher, Black-capped Chickadee, White-breasted Nuthatch, Wood Thrush, Red-eyed Vireo and American Redstart. It is also very apparent that edge species such as American Robin, Rose-breasted Grosbeak, Brown-headed Cowbird, and Northern Oriole have encroached upon these woodland habitats. Forest interior species such as Veery, Black-and-white Warbler, Ovenbird and Scarlet Tanager that typically nest in the northeastern deciduous forest are not very common in these woodlots.

Large tracts of woodland still, however, cover most of the Monteregian Hills, except for Mount Royal. Also, there is more forest cover in areas where the soil is not suitable for agriculture. Fine stands of forest subsist near the Canada-U.S. border, between Huntingdon and Hemmingford. This is also true of the Lachute area (north of Montreal) and certain sectors northeast of Montreal on either side of the St. Lawrence (Bois de Verchères, Contrecœur, sectors in Mascouche, L'Epiphanie, Lanoraie). From the ornithological point of view, these sectors are probably among the most diversified in Quebec. In fact, many woodland species that nest in Quebec have their highest density here, in the south of the province, and some of them breed only here, which makes the Montreal area an especially interesting one. The Eastern Screech-Owl, Red-headed Woodpecker, Blue-gray Gnatcatcher, Yellow-throated Vireo, Golden-winged Warbler and Cerulean Warbler are in this group.

Open habitat

Over the past two centuries, more than 80 per cent of the territory has been cleared for crops, pasture and housing. Some of this land, especially land on the outskirts of Montreal that is destined for industrial use, will often lie unused for several years. This type of habitat has encouraged reproduction of species that favour shrubby fields. Researchers have noted that most of the species that prefer very open habitat and uncultivated, abandoned land have benefited from deforestation; new species have even established themselves in the Montreal area because of these habitat changes.

Species typical of very open habitat such as the Barn Swallow, Tree Swallow, Bobolink, Eastern Meadowlark and Savannah Sparrow are very common throughout the Montreal area. This is also true of species characteristic of abandoned fields and edge habitat such as Gray Catbird, Brown Thrasher, Cedar Waxwing and Common Yellowthroat. Eastern Kingbird, Yellow Warbler, Song Sparrow, Red-winged Blackbird, Common Grackle and American Goldfinch also abound in both these habitats.

Other species that favour these two types of habitat nest only in this part of Quebec; although also found outside the province, they are of particular interest to Quebec bird listers. These birds are Upland Sandpiper, Gray Partridge, Willow Flycatcher, Northern Rough-winged Swallow, Northern Cardinal, Rufous-sided Towhee, Field Sparrow, Grasshopper Sparrow and House Finch.

During migration and in winter, raptors such as the Red-tailed Hawk, Rough-legged Hawk and Snowy Owl are often found in the cultivated and uncultivated fields, where they find an ample supply of food.

The St. Lawrence River

The Montreal area is traversed from southwest to northeast by one of the largest watercourses in North America, the St. Lawrence River. The topography of the surrounding lowlands is such that the river has expanded in some places into broad stretches of calm water; these are lakes Saint-François, Saint-

Louis and Saint-Pierre. Another large body of water is the Lake of Two Mountains, situated near the confluence of the Ottawa and St. Lawrence rivers. Altogether these four lakes cover an area of 700 km².

There are 33,000 hectares of submerged and emergent aquatic vegetation on the shores and in the shallows of these lakes. This represents 60 per cent of the aquatic vegetation found along the St. Lawrence and constitutes essential feeding and breeding grounds for waterfowl and other water birds.

In the spring, more than 120,000 Canada Geese, 75 per cent of all those noted in the St. Lawrence system, and 60,000 Snow Geese spend a few weeks in the flood plain of Lake Saint-Pierre, while 55,000 scaup stop to feed on the submerged aquatic vegetation around Lake Saint-François. In the fall, it is mainly the scaup that visit the Upper St. Lawrence, while the Canada Geese are almost totally absent from this area. Almost 165,000 scaup, 90 per cent of the scaup reported on the St. Lawrence, stop to feed on the submerged vegetation bordering the lakes in the Montreal area, especially lakes Saint-François and Saint-Pierre.

The Upper St. Lawrence is also characterized by several groups of islands: the Iles de la Paix, the islands off Boucherville, Varennes, Contrecoeur and Sorel-Berthier and several islands situated in the western part of Lake Saint-François. These islands and the emergent vegetation surrounding them are the breeding grounds of several species of ducks, geese and marsh birds. Seventeen waterfowl species nest in the Montreal area, the most unusual being the Canada

Goose, Redhead, Lesser Scaup and Ruddy Duck. Other marsh birds nesting in the area are Least Bittern, Green-backed Heron, Common Moorhen, Wilson's Phalarope, Little Gull, Black Tern and Sedge Wren. This is the main breeding area for these birds, which is another reason the Montreal area is of particular interest to bird listers in the province.

There are several heronries in the area. The Berthier Island heronry has 850 nests and is the largest known heronry in the world. Heron Island in the Lachine rapids has 300 Black-crowned Night-Heron nests, which makes it one of the largest colonies of this species in eastern North America. Since 1985, a few Great Egret nests have been found on Dickerson Island in the western part of Lake Saint-François. This is the only place in Quebec where this species breeds, and it is the northernmost colony on the eastern half of the continent.

This brief description of the habitat and bird life along the St. Lawrence would not be complete without mentioning the Ring-billed Gull. This species, which nests here in huge colonies, is most prevalent along the St. Lawrence. Several thousand birds nest on the islands in the St. Lawrence, 20,000 pairs on Ile de la Couvée in Brossard and almost 15,000 pairs on the islands between Boucherville and Contrecoeur.

Birdwatching as a recreational activity in the Montreal area

We hope that the following pages will help the reader discover the variety of activities that the study of birds can offer and to understand why it is such an absorbing pastime for so many people.

The Birdwatching Clubs

The first birdwatching club with members mostly from the Montreal area was the Province of Quebec Society for the Protection of Birds. This group came into being over 70 years ago, in 1917. It was not until the 1980s that other clubs appeared in the area. Since then, birdwatching has become an extremely popular pastime, to the point where there are now more than a dozen clubs in the area. These clubs are listed in the Appendix.

Birdwatching clubs offer their members a number of activities, the main one being field trips. By taking part in such trips, beginners learn to identify the local birds and discover the most interesting sites. Members receive newsletters that keep them abreast of activities and local bird sightings. There are monthly lectures to keep them informed on a host of ornithological topics. Birdwatchers can also take part in special projects such as the Christmas Bird Count, the Quebec Breeding Bird Atlas Project, Project FeederWatch and a variety of nest box programmes. They can work on preparing exhibits or become involved in habitat conservation. In short, there is something for everybody.

Seasonal Activities

Birdwatching activities vary according to the season.

Spring

The migration periods are the favourite seasons of the birdwatcher, as they bring species into our area that are not normally seen at other times of the year. This is especially true for the spring migration. Migration begins early, with some birds such as Horned Larks arriving on their nesting grounds in mid-February; other species may still be migrating in early June. Birds of prey and wildfowl usually pass through in March and April, and passerines arrive mostly in May. Even the most persistent birders would have difficulty finding more than 70 or 80 species during the three winter months, but in May they can find twice this number in a single day. On May 23, 1981, a team of four birders identified 140 species! Such a project requires a lot of planning to ensure that all the different types of habitat are visited in the shortest time possible. Only during the last two weeks in May can such a large number of species be seen in such a short time.

Forest fragmentation is responsible for the declining numbers of certain woodland nesting birds in this area. Fragmentation has been most extensive around Montreal and actually works to the birdwatchers' advantage during the spring migration. At this time, migrating woodland birds gravitate to the small isolated woodlots in large concentrations and are much easier to observe. This phenomenon is particularly prevalent in urban and semi-urban woodland.

Summer

Most birds nest in June and July, although some species, such as crossbills, nest during the coldest months of the year. The Great Horned Owl begins incubating at the end of February; by the beginning of April, all the owls that nest here have begun their breeding season. They can be identified by their calls, most often heard on still nights during the full moon. Night field trips to find local nesting owls at this time of year can often bring surprising results.

The nesting period reaches its peak in June and July. This is the time to study the behaviour of nesting birds – their breeding displays, songs, territorial defence, nurturing of young. The Montreal area has 189 nesting species, the largest number in Quebec. Some of the best sectors have nearly 100 or even 120 within very small areas. At this time of the year, many birders participate in breeding bird survey programs sponsored by national organizations such as the Canadian Wildlife Service. These projects establish the distribution of nesting species and provide year-by-year monitoring of their populations. Summer is also a good time to photograph birds.

Autumn

The fall migration extends over a very long period and even overlaps the breeding season. By mid-July, some species have already completed their reproduction cycle and are beginning their long journey towards their winter quarters. Other species, however, leave only in November and sometimes at the beginning of winter, when they are forced southward by inclement weather.

Although the Montreal area does not offer much shorebird habitat, over 30 such species can be observed here. They are normally seen between mid-July and mid-October, mostly along the St. Lawrence River and on the islands between Montreal and Lake Saint-Pierre.

Migration in the fall is much less spectacular than in spring. The birds gradually become less active, and once the leaves have fallen in October, the woodlands are almost totally devoid of bird life. At this time, the migration of raptors, wildfowl and gulls is much more interesting. Many of these birds linger until the beginning of winter, much to the delight of birdwatchers.

Winter

Although Montreal has a rigorous climate in winter, this is an extremely interesting season for the birdwatcher. It is the only time you can observe northern species such as the Iceland Gull, Glaucous Gull, Snowy Owl, Northern Shrike, American Tree Sparrow, Lapland Longspur, Snow Bunting, White-winged Crossbill and Common Redpoll. Other, less common northern visitors are Gyrfalcon, Northern Hawk-Owl, Great Gray Owl, Boreal Owl, Three-toed Woodpecker, Black-backed Woodpecker, Gray Jay, Boreal Chickadee, Bohemian Waxwing, Pine Grosbeak and Hoary Redpoll. It has been established that with a little perseverance a birder can see 80 species or more in the Montreal region between December 1 and February 28. In the winter of 1987-88, when the weather was particularly mild, the author identified 104 species between December 1 and February 29. Some of these species, however, were late migrants still present at the beginning of December.

Many birdwatchers make a point of taking part in the Christmas Bird Count at the beginning of winter. This activity usually takes place on a Saturday or Sunday between December 14 and January 3. It consists of counting all the birds found within a circle 25 km in diameter. In 1987, almost 1,500 such sites were inventoried across North America by more than 40,000 volunteers. Since 1900, the results from these counts have been compiled and published. This helps ornithologists to monitor changes in species distribution and abundance throughout North America. About 60 species are seen in the Montreal area during this count.

Other winter birdwatching activities include Snowy Owl counts and the winter waterfowl census. The Montreal area, especially the Lachine Rapids in the St. Lawrence, has the greatest numbers of ducks wintering in fresh water in Quebec. The duck census has been conducted during the first two weeks in February for the last eight years. According to this census, 19 duck species have wintered here on at least one occasion. The regularly wintering species are Common Merganser (about 1,500), Common Goldeneye (1,000), Mallard (500), American Black Duck (400) and Northern Pintail (20). The less common wintering species are Canada Goose, Wood Duck, Green-winged Teal, Gadwall, American Wigeon, Canvasback, Ring-necked Duck, Greater Scaup, Lesser Scaup, Harlequin Duck, Barrow's Goldeneye, Bufflehead, Hooded Merganser and Red-breasted Merganser. These species only winter occasionally and in very small numbers.

Bird feeding stations provide an activity that is accessible to all. Beginners and experts, young and old, can enjoy watching birds from their own homes. This subject has been dealt with in a number of books, and it would be superfluous to describe it here. Suffice it to say that there are 50 species in the Montreal area that come to feeders. But even the most ideally situated feeding station will not attract more than 20 or 30 of these. The feeding station provides an opportunity to become thoroughly familiar with certain birds and their behaviour. Many people have taken up birdwatching from having observed birds at their feeders.

Chapter 2

The Birdwatching Sites

This chapter, which constitutes the main body of this book, gives a detailed description of the 55 best birdwatching sites in the Montreal area. The sites have been grouped into six sectors, according to their location. Each sector is designated by a letter from A to F:

Sector A : Montreal and Suburbs (22 sites)
Sector B : West of Montreal (7 sites)
Sector C : Southwest of Montreal (7 sites)
Sector D : The Richelieu Valley (7 sites)
Sector E : The St. Lawrence River, from Montreal to Lake Saint-Pierre (7 sites)
Sector F : North of Montreal (5 sites)

These sectors are shown on the map of Montreal and part of the Laurentians.

The description of each site is preceded by a map showing where the site is found in relation to the Island of Montreal. Each site is identified by the letter designating the sector to which it belongs and a number; for example: D2 refers to Mount Saint-Hilaire, which is found in the Richelieu Valley.

The sites are presented in a similar format, which comprises seven sections, and all are accompanied by maps. The first five sections give a short overall view of the site :

The Montreal Area

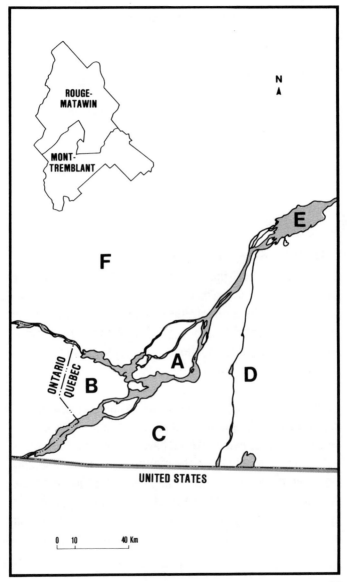

- What to look for : lists the main groups of birds to be found and the species of particular note.

- Where: gives the location in relation to downtown Montreal. Distance and travelling time are given as well.

- How to get there : tells which roads to take from Montreal or other locations.

- When to go : gives the time of year, the best time of the day and the time required to cover the site.

- Special information.

The last two sections are much more detailed. Under "Site Description" you will find characteristics of the habitat and the bird communities found there. The section "Suggested Route" guides the visitor through the site and indicates the main points of interest. The most common birds in the Montreal area are not, as a rule, mentioned unless they have particular relevance.

Many of the sites, especially those in the metropolitan region (Sector A) are fairly small public areas with a good network of trails. Few, however, have any facilities for visitors – less than half of those in the metropolitan region and only a quarter in the other areas. Other sites, especially the more distant ones, cover extensive areas. These are usually visited by car, with many stops along the way to explore areas near the roadside. Caution should be exercised when birding in this fashion, even though the suggested routes are along little-travelled roads. These routes should be taken early in the morning, before there is too much traffic. If you park beside the road, even where there are few cars, make sure your vehicle is well over on the shoulder, in accordance with the highway code. Many areas along these roads are private property, and you should ask permission before entering.

When choosing a birding site, a number of factors can come into play: the distance to be travelled, the number of people visiting, the species of bird you are looking for, the season. The first four sections will help you in this choice, and you can also consult chapters 3 and 4, where the sites are listed according to season and type of bird.

Montreal and Suburbs

Montreal and Suburbs

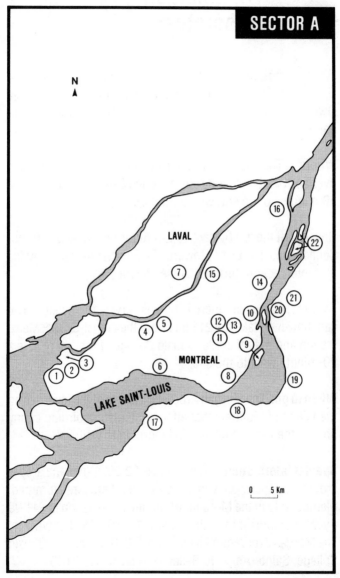

N

LAVAL

MONTREAL

LAKE SAINT-LOUIS

0   5 Km

The Morgan
Arboretum

What to look for : Hawks, owls, many nesting passerines. *Special species :* Cooper's Hawk, Great Horned Owl, Barred Owl, Pileated Woodpecker, Scarlet Tanager, Northern Cardinal, Indigo Bunting.

Where : The Arboretum is located on the West Island and overlaps Sainte-Anne-de-Bellevue and Senneville. It is within 30 minutes of downtown Montreal.

How to get there : *By car :* Follow Autoroute 40 west (Trans-Canada) and take Exit 41 towards Chemin Sainte-Marie. At the first intersection, turn left to the entrance.

By bus : At present, there is no bus service to this site. You can, however, take the 211 bus from the Lionel-Groulx Metro station and get off at MacDonald College. From there, it is a 20-minute walk to the site.

When to go: The Morgan Arboretum is one of the few sites on the Island of Montreal that affords interesting birding at any time of the year. It takes a full morning to visit.

Special information : Admission is $2.00. When the area is crowded, mostly in winter, only members are admitted. Membership in the Morgan Arboretum Association is $41.00 a year. For more information call: (514) 398-7811 or write to: The Morgan Arboretum Association, P.O. Box 500, MacDonald College, Sainte-Anne-de-Bellevue, Québec H9X 1C0.

Site description : The Arboretum, which is affiliated with MacDonald College of McGill University, was established in 1945. It was intended primarily to be used for research and teaching in the fields of forestry and arboriculture. The Arboretum covers 218 hectares, 80 per cent of which is wooded. It encompasses natural woodland as well as plantations of a variety of indigenous and exotic tree species. When the adjoining woodlots are included, the total forest cover is 230 hectares, the largest on the Island of Montreal. The characteristic forest types are the sugar-maple hickory stand and beech stands. There are large stands of eastern hemlock. The Arboretum is a good place for hiking, cross-country skiing, snowshoeing, horseback riding and nature study.

About 185 different birds have been reported here, some 80 of which nest. In June, when the nesting season is at its peak, an experienced birder can identify 70 species in a single day. Surprisingly enough, several forest interior species are found here; in fact, Ovenbirds and Scarlet Tanagers are very common. It is also one of the few places on the Island of Montreal where, during the nesting period, one can find such species as Red-breasted Nuthatch, Golden-crowned Kinglet, Philadelphia Vireo, Black-throated Green Warbler, Black-throated Blue Warbler, Blackburnian Warbler and Northern Waterthrush. The dozen nesting warblers on this territory make it unique on the Island of Montreal. At least five nesting woodpeckers, including Yellow-bellied Sapsucker and Pileated Woodpecker inhabit the forest, and these are occasionally joined in winter by Three-toed and Black-backed Woodpeckers. In winter, the conifer plantations provide shelter for the various species that visit the feeders. Fruit trees attract fruit-eating birds such as Bohemian Waxwing and Pine Grosbeak.

The edge habitat and abandoned fields north and east of the Arboretum contribute to the variety of bird life. Here you can find Eastern Bluebirds, Brown Thrashers, Warbling Vireos, Northern Cardinals and Indigo Buntings.

Raptors are also frequently observed in the Arboretum. Great Horned, Barred and Northern Saw-whet Owls have nested, and Boreal and Great Gray Owls have been sighted in winter. The Red-shouldered Hawk, Sharp-shinned Hawk and Cooper's Hawk, which has been classed as vulnerable in Quebec, probably nest in the Arboretum as well.

In autumn, the Arboretum is an excellent site for observing the hawk migration. Turkey Vultures and Bald and Golden Eagles are sighted here every year. Broad-winged Hawks are the most abundant. An average of 500 to 600 of these birds are normally counted every year in early September, but in 1981 there were 8,388, of which 2,753 were sighted on September 12. The hawks funnel over the Arboretum, which lies between the Lake of Two Mountains to the west and Lake Saint-Louis to the east, to avoid flying over these large bodies of water.

Suggested route : The numerous hiking trails in the Arboretum give access to a variety of habitats, mostly forested. You can easily spend a whole day in spring or summer and still not fully explore the area. Your choice of itinerary will depend on the amount of time you have.

The Morgan Arboretum

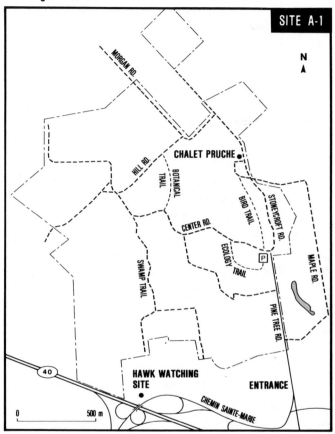

The Ecology Trail and the Bird Trail are located near the parking lot and can each be completed in less than one hour. The Ecology Trail is 0.3 km from the parking lot and can be reached via Centre Road. This trail, which is at its loveliest in spring and summer, first goes through a sugar-maple beech stand and a plantation of red pine and eastern larch. It then leads to a small clearing and ends in a mixed forest where you can admire very mature specimens of eastern white pine and eastern hemlock. Many passerines, Scarlet Tanagers in particular, nest along this trail. Great Horned Owls usually hide their nest in a tall eastern white pine. Red-shouldered Hawks and Cooper's Hawks patrol the sector, most frequently in the spring. The trail ends at a field behind the parking lot.

The Bird Trail is most interesting in winter. It is located between the parking lot and Chalet Pruche to the north. The area includes a landscaped zone with tall conifers, ornamental shrubs, fruit trees and bird-feeding stations. In winter, the fruit trees attract Pine Grosbeaks and Bohemian Waxwings, and sometimes owls visit the coniferous plantings near Chalet Pruche. The common species of owls have been observed here over the years and also the more northern species such as Great Gray Owl and Boreal Owl, whose occurrence is cyclical.

In summer, you might take the time to follow the loop formed by Centre, Hill and Stoneycroft roads. Beech stands and the sugar-maple hickory stand are the main forest cover along this 3-km trail. The Botanical Trail is a short, self-guided trail that links Centre Road to Hill Road. It goes through a diversified habitat that supports a variety of plant life. There are Black-throated Blue Warblers here. South of Centre Road are plantings of red pine and Norway spruce which are about 30 or 40 years old. Red-breasted Nuthatches and Golden-crowned Kinglets nest here. Centre Road will also take you to the Swamp Trail, which goes south through rather wet habitat dominated by American beech and eastern hemlock. Barred Owls probably nest in this area, and passerine species are numerous.

Morgan and Maple roads, on the north and east sides, lead to open habitat where the most common species are Gray Catbird, Yellow Warbler, Common Yellowthroat, Bobolink and Red-winged Blackbird. East of Pine Tree Road, you will find Stoneycroft Pond. There are a few water birds here, and the pond is surrounded by nest boxes, mostly occupied by Tree Swallows but occasionally by House Wrens and Eastern Bluebirds.

Following the fall hawk migration over the Arboretum is a thrilling experience for hawk watchers. The best site is at the south boundary of the Arboretum, near Autoroute 40. It is not necessary to enter the Arboretum to get to it. Take Exit 41 and, instead of going towards Chemin Sainte-Marie or Sainte-Anne-de-Bellevue, take the service road back to Autoroute 40. Just before you get to Autoroute 40, stop and park. The site is at the top of the small hill on the right.

The Arboretum is close to the Ecomuseum and the Raptor Research Centre of MacDonald College. Both are of interest to birdwatchers and are open to visitors.

The Ecomuseum was set up on the initiative of the St. Lawrence Valley Natural History Society. It describes itself as a living museum with the primary objective of developing understanding and appreciation of the natural world of the St. Lawrence Valley. Once the project is completed, there will be flight cages for passerines, waders and ducks. The Ecomuseum is located at 21,125 Chemin Sainte-Marie, just east of the Arboretum. Tel : (514) 457-9449.

The MacDonald Raptor Research Centre is an organization devoted to the protection of birds of prey. The Centre offers lectures and guided tours by appointment only. It is possible, however, to see captive Bald and Golden Eagles and Great Horned Owls on the grounds outside the Centre. When leaving the Arboretum, you can get to the Centre by taking the road to the MacDonald campus. The Centre is on the left after the overpass crossing the railroad. Tel : (514) 398-7929.

Ruffed Grouse

L'Anse-à-l'Orme
Regional Park

What to look for : Shorebirds, migrating passerines. *Special species :* Great Horned Owl, Bohemian Waxwing, Northern Cardinal.

Where : Located in the northwest part of the Island of Montreal, a 30-minute drive from downtown.

How to get there : *By car :* From downtown Montreal take Autoroute 40 west (Trans-Canada), Exit 49 and Chemin Sainte-Marie west. A right turn onto Chemin de l'Anse-à-l'Orme will take you through the park.

By bus : From the Côte-Vertu Metro station take bus 215 to Fairview and transfer to bus 206 westbound to l'Anse-à-l'Orme.

When to go : Each season has its own special appeal at this site but, like most sites in the Montreal area, it is best in spring and summer. It can be visited in one to three hours.

Site description : The park overlaps four municipalities (Sainte-Anne-de-Bellevue, Pierrefonds, Kirkland and Senneville) and is one of the Montreal Urban Community's network of regional parks. It is a narrow strip of 61 hectares that includes the area around Ruisseau de l'Anse-à-l'Orme and some of the bay itself, which is on the east shore of the Lake of Two Mountains.

At the present time, the only place in the park where you can bird is from Chemin de l'Anse-à-l'Orme, which is not a particularly pleasant site because of the heavy traffic. There are, however, quieter birdwatching spots adjacent to the park.

These areas may well be acquired by the Montreal Urban Community to extend the park. Two such sites are in Sainte-Anne-de-Bellevue at the south end of Chemin de l'Anse-à-l'Orme. You will find paths here that lead through the area. This rich habitat is a stopover for migrating birds and nesting grounds for many woodland species.

The Montreal Urban Community has not completed work on the park except for the parking lot near Gouin Boulevard that provides access to the Lake of Two Mountains and a launching area for sailboats. Here, the silty banks near the mouth of Ruisseau de l'Anse-à-l'Orme attract large numbers of shorebirds at the end of summer.

Suggested route : The first two sites mentioned below are outside the present limits of the park.

The first site is a long strip of land along the west side of Chemin de l'Anse-à-l'Orme. The woods, dominated by red ash, are interspersed with fields and abandoned land. From Chemin Sainte-Marie, drive 0.7 km along Chemin de l'Anse-à-l'Orme and stop on the left side of the road. Here you will find a bridge over Ruisseau de l'Anse-à-l'Orme. A trail runs along the stream to the right and then goes west under the Hydro-Québec power lines. This trail, which is heavily overgrown in summer, goes past a cedar grove, through dense

L'Anse-à-l'Orme Regional Park

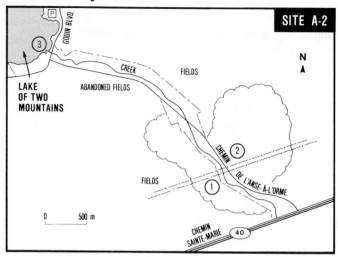

shrubbery under the power lines and ends in the middle of fields surrounded by superb hawthorn hedgerows. There are fruit trees everywhere here, and it is not unusual to find Bohemian Waxwings and American Robins near the stream in winter.

The second site is a wood of about 50 hectares on the east side of Chemin de l'Anse-à-l'Orme. Drive 1.0 km from Chemin Sainte-Marie and stop on the right side of the road just under the power lines. Follow the trail east under the lines for about 200 m, then take the left fork that goes into the woods. Along with the species normally found in the deciduous forests of southwestern Quebec, you can find Red-shouldered Hawks, Great Horned Owls and Pileated Woodpeckers here.

The third site is the shoreline along l'Anse-à-l'Orme, which is a stopover for many species of migrating shorebirds in August. You can observe up to ten species here: Semipalmated Plover, Killdeer, Greater Yellowlegs, Lesser Yellowlegs, Solitary Sandpiper, Spotted Sandpiper, Sanderling, Semipalmated Sandpiper, Least Sandpiper and Short-billed Dowitcher. Occasionally there are Stilt Sandpipers, Wilson's Phalaropes and Red-necked Phalaropes. In August, there are Great Blue Herons and several small flocks of Blue-winged Teals in the shallow waters of the bay. To get to this site, turn right on Gouin Boulevard at the end of Chemin de l'Anse-à-l'Orme and stop on the left side of the road after about 100 m. You can also drive 0.4 km further and park in the Montreal Urban Community parking lot.

Cap-Saint-Jacques Regional Park

What to look for : Ducks, nesting and migrating passerines. *Special species :* Eastern Screech-Owl, Great Horned Owl, Northern Cardinal.

Where : Cap-Saint-Jacques is in the northwest part of the Island of Montreal, at the confluence of the Lake of Two Mountains and Rivière des Prairies. It is less than 30 minutes from downtown Montreal.

How to get there : *By car :* The park is approached by Gouin Boulevard. From the downtown area, take Autoroute 40 west (Trans-Canada), Exit 49, Chemin Sainte-Marie west, Chemin de l'Anse-à-l'Orme and Gouin Boulevard right to Chemin du Cap-Saint-Jacques.

By bus : From the Côte-Vertu Metro station, take bus 64 to Gouin Boulevard and then take bus 68 to the last stop, which is near the park entrance.

When to go : Spring is by far the most rewarding season for birdwatchers, although summer is of interest as well, because of the 50 nesting species. One to three hours will give you ample time to visit this site.

Special information : You will need insect repellant in the woods in early summer and boots for the muddy trails in spring.

33

Site description : Cap-Saint-Jacques, which encompasses 345 hectares, is the largest of the Montreal Urban Community's regional parks and also the most scenic. From the deep recesses of its peaceful, shady coves one can see the distant Oka hills on the far side of the Lake of Two Mountains. The park was created in 1980 and opened to the public in 1985. It consists of two separate sectors. The largest covers 283 hectares in Pierrefonds on the Island of Montreal, along the Lake of Two Mountains. The second sector, which covers 62 hectares, is in the southwest part of Ile Bizard beside the Cap-Saint-Jacques rapids, at the source of Rivière des Prairies.

The park is crossed by a 28-km network of marked ski trails. Picnic areas are found along the network of pedestrian trails, and there is a large parking lot at the entrance.

Thirty per cent of the park is comprised of cultivated or recently abandoned fields; 30 per cent is abandoned farms and another 30 per cent is fragmented woodland, mainly dominated by sugar-maple hickory and silver maple stands. Over 400 plant species have been inventoried.

This site is a migratory stopover and nesting ground for more than 100 species of birds. The most common species in summer are Eastern Wood-Pewee, Great Crested Flycatcher, White-breasted Nuthatch, American Robin, Yellow Warbler, American Redstart, Song Sparrow, Red-winged Blackbird, Brown-headed Cowbird and Northern Oriole.

Studies conducted in 1987 show that the nesting bird population is comprised of a large number of grassland and

Great Gray Owl

edge-dwelling species, many of which have penetrated into the woodland areas. The researchers discovered that species characteristic of the central part of the northeastern deciduous forests of North America are not very common in the park. These two factors, the intrusion of edge-dwelling and grassland species into the woodland habitat and the small number of forest species, indicate that forest fragmentation has affected the bird life in this park, as it has in a large part of the Montreal area.

Suggested route : The numerous trails go through a variety of habitats. There is a special 2.2-km trail for observing wildlife and birds; it leads to the shores of the Lake of Two Mountains, after first passing through fields, a sugar maple stand and abandoned fields. Along the trail is a wildlife station and a bird station with photographic exhibits of birds found in the park. As you come back from the beach, take the trail around the west part of the point. This goes through a sugar maple stand inhabited by Eastern Wood-Pewee, Wood Thrush, Red-Eyed Vireo, Black-throated Blue Warbler, American Redstart and other species common to the deciduous forest of southwestern Quebec. The pair of Eastern Screech-Owls can be attracted by playing a recording of their call at dusk.

Rue Charlebois leads to the eastern end of the park, which is mainly abandoned fields inhabited by Gray Catbird, Brown Thrasher, Yellow Warbler and Northern Cardinal. The small parking lots along Rue Charlebois provide easy access to the shores of Rivière des Prairies.

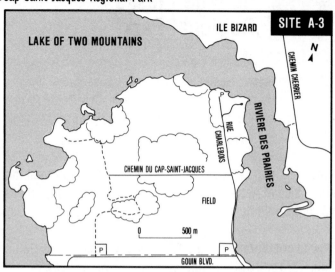

Sometimes Common Goldeneyes and Common Mergansers visit the Cap-Saint-Jacques rapids in winter. In May, you might see hundreds of swallows flying over the rapids; among these flocks are all the swallow species of southwestern Quebec. Diving ducks, such as the Hooded Merganser and Bufflehead, visit the aquatic vegetation at the foot of the Cap-Saint-Jacques rapids in April. A spotting scope is useful here, as the ducks are usually on the opposite shore, near Ile Bizard. You can get a closer look at them by going to Pointe-Théoret on Ile Bizard (not shown on the map). To do so, go east on Gouin Boulevard, turn left onto Jacques-Bizard Boulevard, left onto Rue Cherrier and drive 3.3 km to Chemin de la Pointe-Théoret.

Bois-de-Liesse
Regional Park

What to look for : Nesting and migrating passerines. *Special species :* Cooper's Hawk, Eastern Screech-Owl, Great Horned Owl, Pileated Woodpecker, Scarlet Tanager, Northern Cardinal.

Where : The park is situated on the Island of Montreal, on either side of Autoroute 13 along Rivière des Prairies. It is a 15- or 20-minute drive from downtown Montreal.

How to get there : *By car :* The park is approached by Gouin Boulevard and by Henri Bourassa Boulevard. Take Autoroute 40 west (Trans-Canada), Autoroute 13 north (Autoroute Chomedey) and Gouin Boulevard west (Exit 8 from Autoroute 13) to the parking lot (Pitfield sector). The south sector is approached by turning left on Henri Bourassa Boulevard (Exit 8 from Autoroute 13) and right onto Rue Etingin. From Autoroute 40, take Exit 62 and drive along the service road to Henri Bourassa Boulevard. Turn left onto Rue Etingin and leave your car at the end of the street.

By bus : Take bus 64 from the Côte-Vertu Metro station and transfer to bus 68, which stops near the park entrance. Bus 215 goes to the south sector.

When to go : The park is enjoyable at any time of the year, but is most interesting for birdwatchers in the spring. You will need only a few hours to visit this site.

White-crowned Sparrow

Special information : Insect repellant is virtually indispensable here in June.

Site description : The Bois-de-Liesse Regional Park, which covers 142 hectares, is one of the seven regional parks recently created by the Montreal Urban Community. The park is very much fragmented, being crossed by Boulevard Gouin, Autoroute 13 and the Canadian National railway tracks. It overlaps four municipalities: Dollard-des-Ormeaux, Saint-Laurent, Pierrefonds and Montreal. There are two sections, which lie on either side of the railway tracks.

The north section (Pitfield sector), which is between Rivière des Prairies and the railway tracks, is approached by Gouin Boulevard. This section comprises a house featuring English architecture and a riverside area along Gouin Boulevard. One part of the south section is abandoned farmland – a habitat mix of fields, hedgerows, small wooded areas, clumps of bushes and vacant lots. The other part is wooded and covers more than one-third of the park area. This woodland is known as Bois-Franc. It is composed of mature deciduous stands such as sugar maple and American beech. Until recently, less than half of Bois-Franc was included in the park. In 1990, however, the Montreal Urban Community acquired another section of this wood so that now 80 per cent of the area is protected. Unfortunately, a former project for constructing an intermunicipal road has resurfaced. This would divide the woods into two sections and considerably alter the composition of the present bird communities.

Another interesting feature of the park is the long stream, Ruisseau Bertrand, which crosses the park in a south-north direction to empty into the Rivière des Prairies. Regrettably, this stream collects the overflow from storm sewers that drain the nearby highways and industrial sectors and is very polluted.

The park facilities still have not been completed; for the time being, the main activities are hiking and skiing. Over 130 species have been observed in the park; 50 of these nest here. The birds found in summer are mostly land birds. On a good morning in June, an experienced birder can identify 40 species in a few hours.

Bois-de-Liesse Regional Park

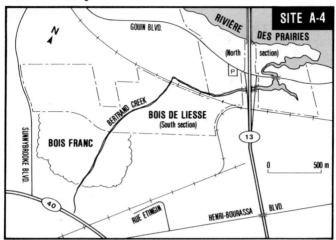

Suggested route :

The north sector : There is a short path on either side of Autoroute 13 that goes through abandoned fields dominated by common buckthorn. The black fruit of these bushes remain on the branches all winter, providing an abundant food source for fruit-eating birds such as the Bohemian Waxwing and American Robin.

Water birds are found in the riverside area. In spring, the flamboyant Wood Duck can be seen amongst them.

The noise pollution from Autoroute 13 is a major hindrance to birdwatching in this sector.

The south sector : This section is quieter and the birdwatching more interesting. The numerous cross-country ski trails can be used for hiking, but make sure you have the proper footwear, especially in spring. There is little underbrush, so the going is fairly easy.

A pair of Cooper's Hawks recently nested in this sector. This is one of the few sites in the Montreal area where this species has been confirmed as nesting. Many other hawks have been sighted in the park, and it may be that the Red-shouldered Hawk and Northern Harrier nest here as well. Of the several species of owls observed here, only the Great Horned Owl and the Eastern Screech-Owl nest. Belted Kingfishers nest along the Ruisseau Bertrand, and Pileated Woodpeckers frequent the mature diseased trees. Their presence is easy to detect because of the huge rectangular-shaped cavities they make when foraging for insects. This is a stopover for passerine species during migration, and many of these remain to nest. Besides the more familiar species found in summer, there are Veery, Wood Thrush, Black-throated Blue Warbler, American Redstart, Ovenbird, Scarlet Tanager and Northern Cardinal.

The abandoned fields east of the wood are inhabited mainly by Alder Flycatchers, Gray Catbirds, Cedar Waxwings, Yellow Warblers, Common Yellowthroats, Song Sparrows and Red-winged Blackbirds. Kildeers are also present and, with a bit of patience, you might see Common Snipes or American Woodcocks executing their aerial breeding display.

Bois-de-Saraguay
Regional Park

What to look for : Owls, woodpeckers, warblers. *Special species :* Wood Duck, Eastern Screech-Owl, Northern Saw-whet Owl, Red-shouldered Hawk, Pileated Woodpecker.

Where : The Bois de Saraguay is located at the northwest end of the City of Montreal along Rivière des Prairies.

How to get there : *By car :* The site is approached by Gouin Boulevard. It can be reached in less than 20 minutes from downtown Montreal by taking Autoroute 20 west or 40 west, Autoroute 13 north, Gouin Boulevard east and Joseph Saucier Avenue to Jean Bourdon Avenue.

By bus : From the Côte-Vertu Metro station, take bus 64 to Gouin Boulevard. Transfer to bus 68 and get off at Joseph Saucier Avenue.

When to go : Interesting sightings are made in all seasons, but the greatest number of species is found in spring, especially in May. The site can be visited in one to two hours.

Site description : This 97-hectare mature deciduous forest is probably the same type that our ancestors knew 300 years ago. It is the only forest within the limits of the City of Montreal that has remained in its primitive state. It is no doubt for this reason that the Quebec cultural affairs ministry declared it a natural site in 1981.

The Bois de Saraguay has a rich and diversified plant life, comprising 35 species of trees, 45 species of shrubs and 275 plant species. There are seven forest communities, the two main ones being the sugar-maple hickory and the silver maple stands. A total of 137 species of birds have been recorded here, 65 of them nesters. The most common nesting species are those characteristic of fragmented forest, edge habitat and clearings: Yellow Warbler, American Goldfinch, Indigo Bunting, Gray Catbird, Northern Oriole. It is interesting to note, however, that certain forest-interior species, such as the Scarlet Tanager and Ovenbird, still nest in small numbers in the Bois de Saraguay. Although rather small and totally isolated from any large forested area, it remains an interesting site for studying local woodland bird life.

Red-shouldered Hawks nest in this wood. In 1976 and 1979, a nest with young was found. This is probably the only site within city limits where this species has nested successfully in recent years.

The many dead trees in this mature forest attract woodpeckers. The spectacular Pileated Woodpecker is present throughout the year, and sometimes Black-backed and Three-toed Woodpeckers are found in winter. Other species such as Wood Duck and Eastern Screech-Owl use abandoned woodpecker holes or natural cavities to nest in.

The largest number of species is found during migration; the 23 warbler species recorded here were found at this time.

Bois-de-Saraguay Regional Park

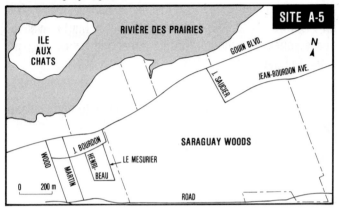

The Northern Saw-whet Owl is one of many sought-after species observed here. It frequents the cedars and hemlocks in the southwest part of the wood. It usually perches in a cedar during the day, and a great deal of patience is needed to find it. It is present in spring, from late March to late April, and in fall from late September to November. It has also been observed in winter.

Suggested route : At present there are few trails through the wood. You can park on Jean Bourdon Avenue and walk wherever you think you may find woodland species.

Edge species are mostly found along the south border of the wood and in the clearings beside the railway tracks. The quickest way to get to the railway tracks is by Martin Avenue. Leave your car at the end of this street and follow the path along the tracks.

Go along the edge of Rivière des Prairies to find wetland species.

Northern Saw-whet Owl

The North Shore of Lake Saint-Louis

What to look for : Diving ducks. *Special species :* Canvasback, Barrow's Goldeneye, Northern Cardinal, House Finch.

Where : This area overlaps three municipalities along Lake Saint-Louis: Lachine, Dorval and Pointe-Claire. It is between 15 to 30 minutes from downtown Montreal.

How to get there : *By car :* The suggested sites in these municipalities are approached by Highway 20. There are several exits from this road that will take you along Lake Saint-Louis – the exits to 32nd and 55th avenues in Lachine, the Côte-de-Liesse- Aéroport de Dorval exit and the Des Sources Boulevard exit in Dorval.

By bus : Bus 191 leaves from the Lionel-Groulx Metro station and goes along Lake Saint-Louis to Lachine and Dorval.

When to go : The parks along Lake Saint-Louis attract people when the weather is warm, but the birds prefer it during the cold weather of fall and winter. Usually this sector can be visited in a few hours.

Site description : Lake Saint-Louis is the result of a widening of the St. Lawrence River above the Lachine Rapids. Large numbers of diving ducks stop here during migration; many of these stay all winter, especially in the easternmost part of the lake, where strong currents prevent the water from freezing

The North Shore of Lake Saint-Louis

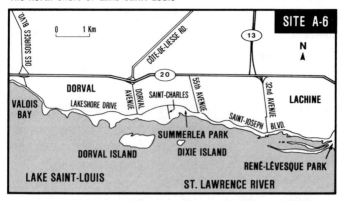

over. According to the Canadian Wildlife Service, over 30,000 scaup stop on the lake in fall, mainly in November. Not all are visible from the shore, although several hundred and sometimes even a few thousand can be seen.

Suggested route :

Valois Bay : Large rafts of scaup are seen here in the fall. Canvasbacks, which are rare in Quebec east of the Montreal area, are seen annually in large numbers. Take Des Sources Boulevard in Dorval and Lakeshore Road; the Valois Bay and Pine Beach parks east of Des Sources Boulevard are good vantage points for scanning the lake.

Saint-Charles Avenue : This street comes to a dead end along Lake Saint-Louis in Dorval. Here you will find yourself across from Dixie Island, where diving ducks congregate in large rafts, especially in winter. Canvasbacks and Barrow's Goldeneyes are seen here in late winter or early spring. To get there, take Highway 20 and Dorval Avenue south (Côte-de-Liesse - Aéroport de Dorval exit), turn left onto Lakeshore Road and right onto Saint-Charles Avenue (0.9 km). There is no parking at the end of Saint-Charles Avenue, so park along the nearest cross street, which is Ducharme Avenue.

Summerlea and Fort Rolland parks : These riverside parks are located in Lachine between Lake Saint-Louis and Saint-Joseph Boulevard, the scenic road that goes along the lake. Summerlea Park is especially interesting because it affords a view of the area around Dixie Island. Here too it is possible to see Barrow's Goldeneye, especially towards the end of winter. From Saint-Charles Avenue continue east on Lakeshore Road or take 55th Avenue in Lachine. Alternatively, these parks can be approached by 32nd Avenue, which also leads to Saint-Joseph Boulevard.

René Lévesque Park : This park, which is located on La Grande Jetée in Lachine, attracts gulls and shorebirds at the beginning and end of summer. It also affords a splendid view of the river, at the entrance to Lake Saint-Louis. To get to it, take Saint-Joseph Boulevard from 32nd Avenue, Chemin du Musée and Saint-Patrick Street.

Terra Cotta Park (not shown on the map) : This is a natural woodland, located in Pointe-Claire. It comprises a stand of very mature trees and a sector of much younger trees which are still in the shrub stage. A brook runs through the woods. The Eastern Screech-Owl is found here in all seasons, as are some of the more colourful passerines such as the Northern Cardinal and House Finch. In May, several of the neo-tropical migrating birds stop here; the most unusual birds to have been sighted here are Yellow-breasted Chat and Carolina Wren. To get to the park, take Autoroute 20 west and Exit 53 (Des Sources Boulevard). This exit has two lanes; take the one that goes to Cardinal Avenue and turn right onto Donegani Avenue at the lights. Drive 1.7 km, turn right onto Coolbreeze Street and go to Windward Crescent. The entrance to the park is on the left, across from Windward. Leave your car near the entrance.

Dorval Airport (not shown on the map) : North of Dorval Airport are abandoned fields inhabited by a number of species, one of which is the Gray Partridge, a permanent resident. These fields are overgrown with tall plants that attract seed-eating birds during migration and in winter. Several sparrows spent the winter here in 1988-89 – American Tree Sparrows, Song Sparrows, White-throated Sparrows, Dark-eyed Juncos and even a White-crowned Sparrow – and these in turn attracted a Cooper's Hawk. This area, part of the Saint-Laurent industrial zone, is only awaiting new investors before it disappears. To get to it, take Autoroute 40 (Trans-Canada), Henri Bourassa Boulevard (Exit 62) and Rue Halpern to the right. Go west, or right, on Chemin Saint-François (0.6 km) until you find a place where you can enter the field.

Ile Jésus

What to look for : Wildfowl, raptors, passerines.

Where : Ile Jésus is located just north of Montreal. It is only a few minutes from downtown Montreal.

How to get there : *By car :* From Montreal, take one of the many bridges over Rivière des Prairies. Autoroutes 13, 15 and 19 and three other highways all give access to Ile Jésus.

By bus : The area is serviced by the Société de transport de la Ville de Laval (STL). For information call: (514) 688–6520.

When to go : Interesting finds are made here throughout the year but, like most sites, it is best in spring and summer. It takes several visits to explore all the interesting parts of the island.

Site description : Ile Jésus, which comprises 242 km^2, is surrounded by Rivière des Mille-Iles, Rivière des Prairies and the Lake of Two Mountains. Laval, the second largest city in the province after Montreal, is located on this island. Laval was incorporated in 1965 when 14 municipalities on Ile Jésus merged. Today the population is about 300,000.

For two centuries, Ile Jésus was devoted exclusively to agriculture. In the early 1900s, tourists discovered the island, and it proved to be an excellent resort area. Since the beginning of the 1960s, rapid development of the island has caused a considerable loss of wildlife habitat and today only a few sectors on the east side remain unspoiled. A few cultivated and fallow fields and some woodland in various stages of regeneration subsist, and a few forest fragments such as the Bois de l'Equerre and the Bois Papineau are found in the central part of the island.

About 200 species of birds have been observed on the island. The Quebec Breeding Bird Atlas Project (1984–88) shows that 120 of these are probably still nesting on the east side.

Suggested route:

The east side of Ile Jésus : From the Metropolitan Autoroute (40), take Papineau Avenue (Highway 19), cross the Papineau-Leblanc Bridge and turn immediately onto Lévesque Boulevard east. East of Duvernay, where Rivière des Prairies widens, many water birds can be seen during the spring migration. The river is easily viewed from Lévesque Boulevard, especially in the Saint-François sector. The river between this sector and the eastern tip of the island only partially freezes in the winter, and this draws ducks, such as Common Mergansers, and gulls, including Iceland and Glaucous gulls. The Berge du Vieux-Moulin Park *(Site 1)* in Saint-François and the Berge Olivier-Charbonneau Park *(Site 2)* at the eastern tip of the island are also excellent vantage points for scanning the river. As you approach the eastern tip of Ile Jésus, you will see a group of islands known as the Archipel du Moulin *(Site 3)*. These islands attract dabbling ducks in the spring. With a spotting scope you can see American Black Duck, Mallard, Northern Pintail, Northern Shoveler and American Wigeon around the island. The broods of young ducks that in summer inhabit the emergent vegetation along the shores are an indication of the value of this habitat. Now in the hands of real-estate promoters, its future is precarious, however.

The agricultural areas and the woodland on the east end of the island are crossed by several kilometres of roads that are interesting to explore by car or bicycle, especially in spring and summer. The best ones are Montée Masson, Boulevard Sainte-Marie, Avenue des Perron, and Rang and Montée Saint-François.

Boulevard Sainte-Marie crosses a peaceful area of the countryside dotted with swampy pools and forest regrowth. One site particularly worth exploring is the large stand of cedar. This area, known as Bois Saint-François *(Site 4)*, is of unquestionable ecological value. Several avian communities inhabit this site, including birds of prey.

Bois Papineau and the nature centre : Bois Papineau *(Site 5)* is located on Boulevard Saint-Martin at the junction with the Papineau Autoroute. When coming from Montreal, take Exit 7 from the Papineau Autoroute. This natural woodland, part of which was recently lost to residential development, has a total of 103 species observed over the years. At the Laval nature centre *(Site 6)*, which is used for outdoor activities, there are stands of conifers and shrubs where several species can be found during migration. Northern Mockingbirds have nested here. From Boulevard Saint-Martin, turn right onto Boulevard Lesage and left onto Avenue du Parc, where you will find parking lots along the road.

The Bois de l'Equerre : In all, 106 species of birds have been recorded on this site *(Site 7)*, which is best known for its owls.

Ile Jésus

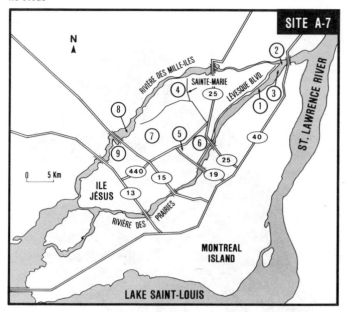

Great Horned Owls are present throughout the year, and Northern Saw-whet and Long-eared Owls are seen in spring, fall and sometimes in winter. These two species spend the day hidden in the cedars that are found throughout the woods. The quickest way to get to the Bois de l'Equerre from Montreal is to take Autoroute 15 north (Laurentian Autoroute). Turn right onto Autoroute 440 (Autoroute Laval), left onto Industrial Boulevard north, left onto Chemin de la Petite-Côte and right onto Rang de l'Equerre. Park along Rang de l'Equerre, except in winter when there is too much snow.

Long-eared Owl

Rivière des Mille-Iles : Rivière des Mille-Iles still has several unspoiled islands. This sector is now accessible to the public, thanks to the organization Eco-Nature, which offers guided excursions and boat rental. The Rivière des Mille-Iles Park *(Site 8)* is at 345 Boulevard Sainte-Rose (tel: (514) 662-4941).

The wooded shoreline west of Autoroute 15 *(Site 9)* is an interesting birding spot, despite the human habitation. The feeders maintained by the residents definitely contribute to the diversity of bird life, especially in winter. Explore this area by taking the dead-end streets running north of Boulevard Sainte-Rose. To get there, take Autoroute 15, Exit 16 onto Boulevard Sainte-Rose west (left). The first three streets west of the Autoroute are, in order, Boulevard de Lisbonne, Rue Vauquelin and Boulevard Mattawa. A small bridge connects Boulevard de Lisbonne to Ile Locas, which has a mature woodland inhabited by several forest species. At the end of Rue Vauquelin, a path goes east along the river, first through open habitat interspersed with shrubs and then through a stand of mature silver maple. In spring, there are Northern Cardinals and sparrows, including Fox Sparrows. Barred Owls are seen occasionally in the maple stand in winter. Boulevard Mattawa goes through a wet wooded section dotted with swampy pools to an attractive residential area. Explore the woodland around the little bridge, and you may find a Wood Duck or a Red-shouldered Hawk. A little further on, across from Rue Yamaska, is a winding path that leads to swampy areas along the river.

The Lachine Rapids and Islands

What to look for : Herons, ducks, gulls and terns, shorebirds, several irregular species. *Special species :* Eurasian Wigeon, Little Gull, Franklin's Gull, Laughing Gull, Common Tern, Arctic Tern, Caspian Tern.

Where : The Lachine Rapids are across from Ville LaSalle on the western part of the Island of Montreal, about 20 minutes from downtown.

How to get there: *By car :* This site is approached by Boulevard LaSalle, which runs along the river. You can leave your car at the parking lot at the corner of 6th Avenue and Boulevard LaSalle. When coming by the Champlain Bridge from the South Shore, take the Wellington exit, turn left onto Wellington and left onto Boulevard LaSalle at the next traffic lights. The parking lot is 5 km from this intersection. When coming by the Décarie Boulevard (Autoroute 15), take the La Vérendrye exit and La Vérendrye Boulevard south. Drive 4.5 km and turn left onto Bishop Power Boulevard and left onto Lasalle Boulevard. From here go to the municipal parking lot on 6th Avenue. You can also park on the west side of LaSalle Boulevard or on the cross streets.

By bus : Take bus 110 from the Angrignon Metro station to the corner of Central and Bishop Power streets. From here you can walk to LaSalle Boulevard.

When to go : Surprising sightings are made at this excellent location throughout the year. It may take anywhere from a few minutes to several hours to cover the area.

Site description : Ville LaSalle unquestionably enjoys the most attractive setting of any of the Montreal Urban Communities. It lies along the Lachine Rapids, one of the finest natural sites along the St. Lawrence. The flow rate of the rapids is sometimes as much as 12,000 m^3 per second. This turbulence purifies and oxygenates the water, which is why the rapids are considered to be the lungs of the St. Lawrence. They also have historical significance. Lying as they do on the main navigable route to the Great Lakes, the rapids form a natural barrier that forced the early explorers to stop and establish a post which later became Montreal. Strangely enough, no provincial or federal legislation has ever been enacted to ensure protection of this site. The long-term future of the rapids therefore remains uncertain, particularly as the area was recently the subject of a costly feasibility study on the construction of a hydroelectric dam there. Although the project does not seem to threaten the rapids for the time being, it may very well resurface because of the increasing demand for electricity.

The Lachine Rapids are caused by a 12-m slope in the river bed between the east end of Lake Saint-Louis and Verdun, a distance of about 10 km. Several islands and islets, covered with unusual vegetation, lie in the rapids. The largest, Heron Island and Ile aux Chèvres, have the greatest number of rare plant species in the Montreal area. In several places the wooded parts are dominated by sugarberry, a tree species rare in southwestern Quebec. These islands and part of the rapids are a migratory bird sanctuary where hunting is prohibited.

Because of the variety of water species that can be seen in all seasons, the Lachine Rapids are a remarkable birdwatching site. Over the last few years, a hundred or so species, most of them water birds, have been sighted from the LaSalle shoreline.

Because of its size, the Great Blue Heron is the most striking species to be seen here. Its feeding habits also make it easy to observe. There are about 30 Great Blue Heron nests on Heron Island, and these can be easily seen with a spotting scope from the shore. The Black-crowned Night-Heron is never as much in evidence as the Great Blue Heron because of its nocturnal habits. Yet it is much more abundant, as indicated by the 300 nests recently counted on Heron Island. This is one of the largest colonies in eastern North America. Herons have remained remarkably faithful to this site; the heronry was described by Champlain in 1611.

Thirty species of ducks visit this area. They include the Eurasian Wigeon, which is seen regularly in spring and summer. Ducks are also observed in the rapids throughout the winter. This is the only place in Quebec where such large concentrations of wildfowl can be seen in fresh water during the winter months.

The rapids are an excellent site for gulls and terns. This is the only known nesting site of the Little Gull in Quebec.

The Lachine Rapids and Islands

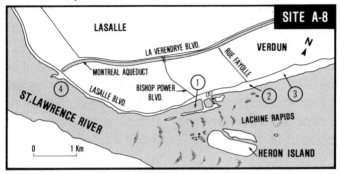

Franklin's and Laughing Gulls are seen occasionally, and Arctic and Caspian Terns are seen every year in migration. A colony of Common Terns has established itself in recent years on the rocky island at the foot of the rapids.

This is not ideal shorebird habitat, so it is surprising to note that 18 such species have been observed here, mainly on the rocky islands and the floating mats of vegetation that form during the summer on the calmer waters below the rapids.

The Double-crested Cormorant and Osprey are species commonly seen near the rapids. The list of unusual species observed here is impressive; it includes Long-tailed Jaeger, Common Black-headed Gull, Black-legged Kittiwake, Forster's Tern, Marbled Godwit, Ruff and Bald Eagle.

Suggested route :

Terrasse Serre Park (Site 1) : Just across from the parking lot, a little below an old abandoned dam, is a stand of willow.

Ducks frequent this area all year long, except in January and February. During the summer, broods of ducklings are seen, most of them Mallards and American Wigeons. A little upstream from this site, in the middle of the rapids, is a road leading to a pier that runs parallel to the shore. During the winter months, a number of dabbling and diving ducks rest on the small island to the right of this pier. If you visit the area at dusk, you will see several hundred ducks flying in to roost for the night.

Ducks are particularly abundant in the fall, in the willows at the extreme left of the pier. This whole area is also an excellent site for winter gulls such as the Great Black-backed, Iceland and Glaucous Gulls. Sometimes a Harlequin Duck is seen here.

The foot of the rapids (Site 2) : This is probably the site that is most interesting in summer. You can walk to it by following the river downstream. You can also park on the west side of LaSalle Boulevard near Rue Fayolle, if you want to get there more quickly.

There are benches along the river where you can sit and scan the rapids with a spotting scope. Some of the small rocky islands about 300 m from the shore draw a number of species. One of these was the nesting site of the Little Gull. Common Terns and several species of ducks also nest here. The islands are also a staging area for some unusual larids – Franklin's Gull, Caspian Tern, Arctic Tern, Forster's Tern – and for shorebird species as well. The most interesting period is

June (late May and early June for Arctic Terns). In w..
there are numerous gatherings of dabbling and diving ducks.

Verdun (Site 3): If you continue downstream towards Verdun, you will find a place where the water is less turbulent. This site is interesting in early spring when it is visited by ducks. The Eurasian Wigeon comes here every year. In summer, a floating mass of vegetation forms; ducks raise their young there and migrating shorebirds are attracted to it as well.

Upstream from Terrasse Serre Park (Site 4) : There are several riverside parks between the old dam and Lachine where the rapids can be viewed. Gulls, especially Ring-billed Gulls, gather by the thousands here to feast on the mayflies that abound in spring and summer.

Nuns' Island

What to look for : Waterfowl, owls, migrating passerines, several irregular species. *Special species:* Red-throated Loon, Gray Partridge, Solitary Sandpiper, Long-eared Owl, Northern Saw-whet Owl, Rusty Blackbird.

Where : Nuns' Island is a 300-hectare island in the St. Lawrence River across from Verdun. It is a 5- or 10-minute drive from downtown Montreal.

How to get there : *By car :* From the Island of Montreal, go south on Décarie Boulevard (15) or the Bonaventure Autoroute. Just before the Champlain Bridge, take the Nuns' Island exit onto Ile des Soeurs Boulevard. When coming from the South Shore, take the Champlain Bridge.

By bus: Take bus 168 to Nuns' Island from the McGill Metro station or bus 12 from the LaSalle Metro station.

When to go : Interesting species can be found at all times of the year. The site can normally be explored in a few hours.

Site description : Like several other sites in the Montreal area, Nuns' Island is losing its value as wildlife habitat. The island's destiny was irrevocably altered in 1962 when the Champlain Bridge was built, opening it to residential development that began in 1966 and has continued unabated ever since. In addition, landfill has significantly altered the island's appearance. The islets at the southwest end of the island and the lush emergent vegetation that surrounded them are now lost forever.

Nevertheless, its proximity to the city makes Nuns' Island a favourite haunt of Montreal birders. Scarcely a week goes by without one setting foot there. The island still has a variety of habitats: overgrown landfill, a 28-hectare wood, a pond with a small area of emergent vegetation, the St. Lawrence River on all sides. The diversity of habitat explains why 260 bird species have been recorded within this small area during the last two or three decades.

The woods, which are dominated by silver maple and red ash, are undoubtedly the island's centre of interest. Large numbers of migrating passerines pass through here along with species that favour moist bottomlands, such as the Solitary Sandpiper, Northern Waterthrush and Rusty Black-bird. Owls visit during migration and in winter, and this is probably the best spot in the Montreal area for Northern Saw-whet, Long-eared, Great Horned and Boreal Owls. Wood-peckers are abundant in winter months; look for the occasional Three-toed or Black-backed Woodpecker. Pied-billed Grebes raise their young on the small pond southwest of the woods each summer. At the southwest end of the island, in the clumps of reed-grass and eastern cottonwood that cover the landfill, are found the occasional Short-eared Owl, migrating Palm Warbler or Gray Partridge, which is a permanent resident. Several species of dabbling ducks continue to nest here.

Great Gray Owl

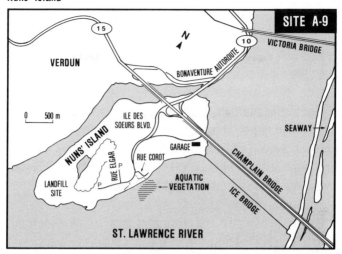

The island is well known for its colonies of Purple Martins and Cliff Swallows. The martins nest in bird houses erected along Ile des Soeurs Boulevard, and the swallows build hundreds of nests under the Champlain Bridge.

The St. Lawrence lies on a major waterfowl flyway. Every year its waters attract a good variety of diving ducks and other aquatic species, including Red-throated Loon, Horned Grebe, Red-necked Grebe and Brant. Over the years, the list of birds found on Nuns' Island has been swelled by a number of irregular species.

Suggested route : There are two parking areas near the woods and the pond. The first is in front of the Elgar shopping centre, and is approached by turning right onto Elgar off Ile des Soeurs Boulevard. The other is at the end of Ile des Soeurs

Boulevard. From either spot, it is only a short walk to the many paths that cross the woods. Between fall and spring, investigate all the vine tangles (see map) for roosting owls. They are so well camouflaged that they can escape the notice of even the most experienced birder.

The landfill site to the south of the woods is being continually altered and is becoming less interesting. A walk along the shore, however, will inevitably reward you with diving ducks in spring and fall. The rocks off the south point are frequented by a large flock of Double-crested Cormorants.

There are two other excellent sites from which to view the river. To get to the first, the District of Vancouver West Park, leave your car on Rue Corot, just after the left turn in the road. Behind this park is a vast area of submerged vegetation that attracts hundreds of dabbling ducks in late summer and early fall. Shorebirds also feed on the floating mats of vegetation in late summer. To get to the second site, which is behind Champlain Pontiac Buick Cadillac Inc., park on Ile des Soeurs Boulevard and walk to the river. A number of unusual sightings have been made here.

Nuns' Island Woods

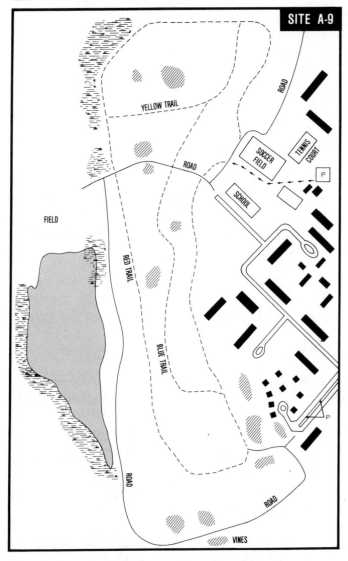

SITE A-9

Downtown Montreal and Ile Sainte-Hélène

What to look for : Falcons, diving ducks, woodpeckers. *Special species :* Peregrine Falcon, Gyrfalcon.

Where : This familiar site is located on the Island of Montreal, along the St. Lawrence River.

How to get there : *By car :* Downtown Montreal and the area around the port can be reached via Notre-Dame Street. Ile Sainte-Hélène can be reached via the Jacques Cartier or the Concord Bridge. Take the Bonaventure Autoroute to get to Cité du Havre.

By bus: The Port of Montreal is a few minutes' walking distance from the Champ de Mars and Place d'Armes Metro stations. Ile Sainte-Hélène is on the Longueuil Metro line.

When to go : This site is most productive in winter.

Site description : Besides the downtown area and Ile Sainte-Hélène, this site includes the Port of Montreal and Cité du Havre. The Port of Montreal has a number of warehouses and grain elevators. The most common species here is the Rock Dove, and a study conducted by the Centre de recherches écologiques de Montréal shows their numbers in the Old Port may well exceed 2,000. The neighbouring downtown section is taken up by skyscrapers.

Falcons, and especially the Peregrine Falcon and Gyrfalcon, are what draw birders to this site. Peregrine Falcons are frequently observed in downtown Montreal. A pair that nested on top of the Sun Life building every year for 17 years suddenly disappeared in 1953. This disappearance coincided with a severe decrease in the numbers of the Anatum sub-species in eastern North America. Subsequent studies revealed that the decrease was linked to the use of the pesticide DDT. The Peregrine's prospects have brightened, however, since DDT was banned in North America in the 1970s. Attempts to reintroduce the species through breeding in captivity have also been successful. In 1984, a pair nested on top of a building in downtown Montreal for the first time in 30 years, and peregrines are now being sighted more regularly in the downtown area throughout the year.

Another member of the falcon family that is occasionally seen here is the Gyrfalcon. This bird, which seldom appears in Montreal, is more likely to be sighted here than anywhere else in the area. The large population of Rock Doves provides an endless source of food for the Gyrfalcon during its winter visits.

The third falcon species, one that is frequently observed in the area, is the American Kestrel. This bird is usually found in open spaces, but for some reason it seems to like the habitat of tall buildings in the downtown area and the Port of Montreal.

Suggested route :

Cité du Havre and Ile Sainte-Hélène : From the Décarie Autoroute (Autoroute 15), take the Bonaventure Autoroute to Cité du Havre, exiting at "Autoroute Bonaventure-Centre

Ville". From there, exit at "Port de Montréal-Cité du Havre", turning right onto Pierre-Dupuy Avenue and heading toward the Concord Bridge. You can also take the Bonaventure Autoroute from University Street, at the Notre-Dame Street intersection. Just before the Concord Bridge, stop on the left along Pierre-Dupuy Avenue. With your spotting scope, scan the downtown buildings, particularly the Banque Nationale at Place d'Armes and the Stock Exchange at Victoria Square, the two most obvious buildings. The Peregrine Falcon often perches on top of these buildings, while the Gyrfalcon is most often seen in winter hunting along the wharves.

To reach Ile Sainte-Hélène, cross the Concord Bridge and immediately turn right towards the parking lot. The channel between Ile Sainte-Hélène and the Port of Montreal is often visited by waterfowl, mostly diving ducks and most often in late autumn and early winter. Hélène-de-Champlain Park, a wooded area in the middle of the island, attracts many passerines during the spring migration. In winter, the regularly sighted Downy and Hairy Woodpeckers and Northern Flickers are occasionally accompanied by Three-toed and Black-backed Woodpeckers. Ile Sainte-Hélène can also be reached from Montreal or from the South Shore by the Jacques Cartier Bridge.

Downtown and the Port of Montreal : Leave the Bonaventure Autoroute by the Wellington exit, turn right onto Wellington Street, right onto McGill Street and left onto Rue de la Commune. Several streets, including Bonsecours, lead from Notre-Dame Street to Rue de la Commune. You can scan the downtown buildings from Rue de la Commune, where the

Downtown Montreal and Ile Sainte-Hélène

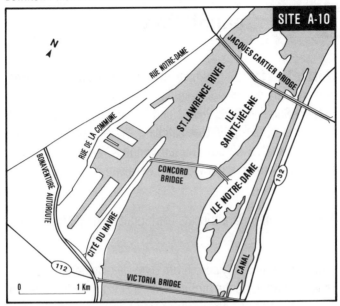

best site is probably Place d'Youville. Here you will have an excellent view of the Banque Nationale building, which is the black one on the left. You will notice Peregrine whitewash on the east side of the building.

You can only enter the Port by Bonsecours Street on the weekend. A 9-km street goes through the port facilities from Rue Bonsecours to Rue Boucherville (not shown on the map). You can enter or leave the port by Viau, Bossuet or Boucherville streets, which can all be reached from Notre-Dame Street. There are many places in the port where you can scan the river for diving ducks and gulls in fall and winter.

Summit Park

What to look for : Migrating passerines, including 33 species of warblers and several irregular species. *Special species :* Eastern Screech-Owl, Olive-sided Flycatcher, Yellow-bellied Flycatcher, Blue-gray Gnatcatcher, Gray-cheeked Thrush, Yellow-throated Vireo, Golden-winged Warbler, Orange-crowned Warbler, Palm Warbler, Cerulean Warbler.

Where : Summit Park is located on Mount Royal in Westmount.

How to get there : *By car :* From Côte-des-Neiges Road, take Belvedere Road up the mountain across from Remembrance Road. Turn right onto Summit Road and drive to Summit Circle, which goes all the way around the park.

By bus : From the Guy-Concordia Metro station, take bus 66, 165 or 166 to the corner of Côte-des-Neiges and Belvedere roads. From here it is a 15-minute walk to Summit Park. Bus 165 also stops at the Côte-des-Neiges Metro station, and bus 166 stops at the Snowdon Metro station.

When to go : May is the ideal time to visit Summit Park, especially if you arrive early in the morning, around 6:00 a.m. By June, only a few local nesting species remain. The fall migration, from August to October, is less spectacular than the spring migration but is interesting nonetheless. In spring, it is definitely worth your while to make several trips to the Summit and invest many hours of birding.

Site description : Summit Park, one of the best-known birdwatching sites in the province, is a small, natural wood located on Mount Royal in Westmount. This tiny green space, rising more than 200 m from the heart of urban Montreal, draws a spectacular variety and concentration of woodland birds during the spring and fall migrations. It has been said that Summit Park is to Quebec what Pointe Pelee is to Ontario.

The best time to go is early in the morning around mid-May, shortly after a warm air front has moved in from the south. There are hundreds of birds, mostly flycatchers, thrushes, vireos, warblers and sparrows, all singing together with incomparable effect. Birdwatchers should beware of stiff necks when trying to pinpoint the source of the songs floating down from the woodland canopy!

The warbler family is the best represented at Summit Park. A total of 33 warbler species has been observed over the years, and 24 species are seen every year. Colourful though warblers may be, their small size and restless behaviour make them a challenge to identify, especially for the novice birder. Beginners, however, will have no difficulty in identifying other such colourful species as the Scarlet Tanager, Rose-breasted Grosbeak or Northern Oriole. Veteran birders will be interested in the more sombre-hued but unusual species such as the Olive-sided and Yellow-bellied Flycatchers, Blue-gray Gnatcatcher, Gray-cheeked Thrush, Yellow-throated Vireo, Orange-crowned, Pine, Palm and Blackpoll Warblers. These are seen every year. With a bit of luck they might also see a Golden-winged or Cerulean Warbler.

Birders who want to increase their lists should go to the Summit, because more rare birds have been seen here than at any other site in the area. Every spring, unusual species are observed here, most of them brought from the south by favourable weather conditions. Some of these birds are several hundred kilometres outside their normal range. Some of the exceptional species seen in the last ten years are Chuck-will's-widow, Red-bellied Woodpecker, White-eyed Vireo, Prairie Warbler, Prothonotary Warbler, Worm-eating Warbler, Kentucky Warbler, Hooded Warbler and Summer Tanager.

Summit Park is also an excellent site for watching migrating hawks. Besides the more common species, such as Osprey and Broad-winged Hawk, are the occasional Turkey Vulture and Golden Eagle.

Very few species stay on the Summit to nest after May. Some that do remain are Great-crested Flycatcher, Wood Thrush, Northern Cardinal and Indigo Bunting. The most illustrious nesting species is the Eastern Screech-Owl, a permanent resident here. On a fine winter day, it can often be seen sunning itself at the entrance to a nest-hole with a southern exposure.

Summit Park

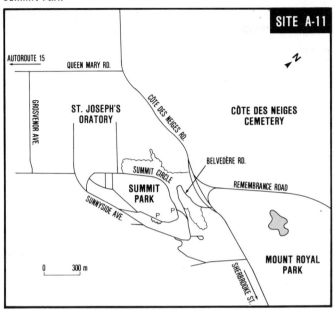

Suggested route : A great number of trails cross the park. On a good morning, the first migrating birds are already active before 6:00 a.m., mostly on the south slope. This area should be visited first, especially the clearing above the lookout. You should also check the nearby shrubs, as they attract species that live near the forest floor. Later in the morning, you can bird the north slope for species you may have missed earlier. The small muddy stream on this north slope may have a few surprises. The woods north of Summit Circle are also worth visiting.

After 10:00 a.m. the birds are quieter and gradually they disperse. If the weather is good, you can then concentrate on hawks. The lookout is best for this. In the evening, the birds become more active, but never to the extent that they are in the morning.

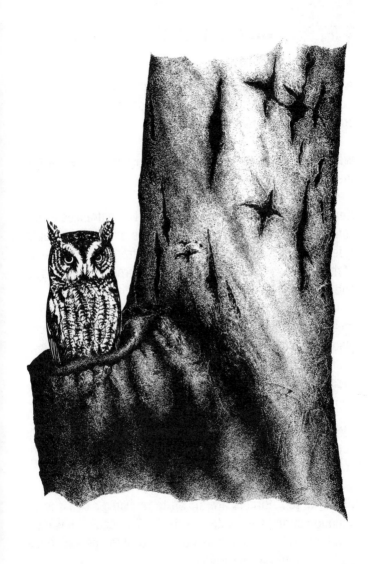

Eastern Screech-Owl

Mount Royal Cemetery

What to look for : Migrating and wintering passerines. *Special species :* Eastern Screech-Owl, Eastern Bluebird, Northern Mockingbird, Pine Grosbeak.

Where : This site is located on Mount Royal, in the heart of the City of Montreal.

How to get there : *By car :* There are two entrances to the cemetery, one on the north side and the other on the south side. The south entrance is approached from the east by way of the Camillien Houde Parkway, at the corner of Mont-Royal and Park avenues. From the west, take Côte des Neiges and Remembrance roads. There is a parking lot with parking metre opposite the south entrance. The north entrance can also be reached from the east, either via Mount Royal Boulevard and Forest Road or from the west by taking Côte Sainte Catherine Road, Rue Vincent d'Indy, Mount Royal Boulevard and Forest Road. You can park along Forest Road.

By bus: Take bus 11 from the Mont-Royal Metro station to the south entrance or bus 119 from the Edouard Montpetit Metro station to the north entrance.

When to go : Birders are drawn to this area all year long, although spring and winter are the best seasons. In winter, one hour will give you ample time to explore the site, but a spring outing will take longer.

Site description : Mount Royal has a relatively pronounced topography. The cemetery lies on an inclined plateau with a southeastern exposure and is flanked by hills on the north, east and west. The original vegetation has almost entirely disappeared except from the East Hill. There is a small wooded area here where the predominant tree species are red oak, sugar maple, American beech and white and red pine.

Paved walkways wind amongst the graves and lawns. Most of the bushes, trees and shrubs that line the paths and surround the burial plots are exotic, and the flower beds and ornamental plants appear to have been placed at random. The outstanding feature of the cemetery is the impressive number of ornamental crab apple trees. The fruit remains on the trees all winter long, providing an ample food supply for fruit-eating birds. When in bloom, the trees add to the charm of the site and at the same time attract insect-eating species.

More than 145 bird species have been counted in the cemetery. The birds are most abundant in the spring and particularly in May. Insect-and seed-eating passerines are numerous and include Palm and Orange-crowned Warblers, two species that are sometimes difficult to find. April is the time to watch hawks; Turkey Vultures and Golden Eagles have been sighted here. Sometimes a Northern Goshawk will fly over, to the terror of the smaller birds.

The three mimic thrushes are among the birds that stay to nest in the cemetery : Gray Catbird, Brown Thrasher, Northern Mockingbird. House Wrens and Indigo Buntings also nest in the cemetery, but the species that captures the attention of

Brown Thrasher

birdwatchers is the Eastern Screech-Owl. Nest boxes have been put up to encourage it to breed.

Fruit-eating birds visit the ornamental crab apple trees in winter. Up to 100 Pine Grosbeaks have been sighted in the cemetery at once. Other fruit-eating birds that may visit the area are the Bohemian Waxwing, Cedar Waxwing, American Robin and Northern Mockingbird. Unexpected sightings may occur at the beginning of the winter, before the severe cold sets in; Townsend's Solitaire, for instance, was found here in December 1967.

Suggested route : Be sure to take the time you need to explore this site thoroughly. The ornamental crab apple trees are

Mount Royal Cemetery

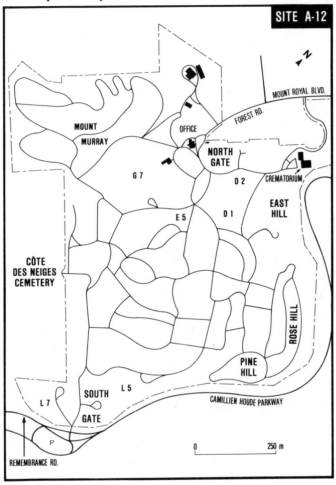

MOUNT ROYAL BLVD.

FOREST RD.

MOUNT
MURRAY

OFFICE

NORTH
GATE

D 2

CREMATORIUM

G 7

E 5

D 1

EAST
HILL

CÔTE
DES NEIGES
CEMETERY

ROSE HILL

PINE
HILL

L 5

CAMILLIEN HOUDE PARKWAY

L 7

SOUTH
GATE

0   250 m

P

REMEMBRANCE RD.

found mostly at D1, D2, G7 and L5. These are the areas that are best in winter.

In the summer, Pine Hill and Rose Hill are the best places to watch the mimic thrushes, especially the Northern Mockingbird. Two screech-owl nest boxes have been placed in tall trees, one along Forest Road to the right of the north entrance and the other on the East Hill near the crematorium. Watch for the owl at dusk, when it leaves its nest. Great Horned or Barred Owls will sometimes hide in the tall conifers in the E5 section in fall and winter. There are many conifers at the south entrance (Section L7), and it is not unusual to see crossbills there when pine cones are plentiful.

The area left of the north entrance can also be of interest in the winter. There is a stream here that never freezes over, where birds often come to drink.

Nest boxes were recently put up on Mount Murray where much of the woods has been cut down. To everyone's astonishment, a pair of Eastern Bluebirds decided to nest there in 1989. This is virtually the only place within the city limits where this species nests.

In any season, a visit to the cemetery can be combined with a trip to nearby Mount Royal Park (Site A13).

Mount Royal Park

What to look for : A great variety of migrating birds, particularly warblers; various wintering species and several hawks. *Special species :* Turkey Vulture, Northern Goshawk, Northern Cardinal.

Where : Mount Royal Park is immediately northwest of downtown Montreal. It is bordered to the northeast by Park Avenue, to the east by Pine Avenue, to the south by Côte-des-Neiges Road and to the west by the Camillien Houde Parkway.

How to get there : *By car :* Mount Royal Park can be reached from the east by the Camillien Houde Parkway at the corner of Mont-Royal and Park avenues or from the west by way of Côte-des-Neiges Road. A cycling path and a cross-country ski trail also afford access, along with numerous footpaths.

By bus: Take bus 11 from the Mont-Royal Metro station.

When to go : It is possible to bird on Mount Royal in any season, but spring is best, especially the first three weeks of May, because of the migrating birds. The feeding stations maintained by the Centre de la Montagne from December to April draw wintering species into close range. Owls are seen occasionally during this period, and hawks are sighted in spring and fall. Morning is without question the best time of day, and three or four hours are sufficient to cover the main points of interest.

Special information : Further information about Mount Royal Park can be obtained from the Centre de la Montagne (tel: (514) 844–4928). There are detailed maps available at the Centre offices, located on the second floor of the Chalet.

Site description : Mount Royal Park was created in 1874 and is one of the largest green spaces on the Island of Montreal. Rising 232 m above the busy streets of downtown Montreal, this oasis of greenery is easily accessible to a great number of birdwatchers. Although the park has lawns, recreational and other facilities, a good proportion of the 174 hectares is still characterized by red oak, sugar-maple hickory and other deciduous stands. These natural woods are complemented by many plantings of pine and spruce. Other characteristics are the ponds and wet hollows that occur throughout the area and the particularly accentuated topography of the east slope.

Because of its location in a highly urbanized area, Mount Royal Park does not attract many nesting species; only about 30 species nest here, aside from those common to urban habitat. Nonetheless, the park is large enough to attract a variety of migrating species, especially in spring. This is when you will find a good proportion of the 150 species that have been recorded on Mount Royal.

In the spring, insectivorous species are the most numerous and are found mainly in the wooded areas. Most of the nesting warblers of Quebec can be observed here, as well as most of the other species that nest in the area – vireos, flycatchers, kinglets, wrens, woodpeckers and nuthatches. Regular visits to this site will almost certainly lead to surprising discoveries, mostly of warblers that are normally found in more southern regions.

The spring migration also brings a number of seed-eaters to the forest habitats, Rose-breasted Grosbeaks, Purple Finches, American Goldfinches, Dark-eyed Juncos and White-throated Sparrows being the most characteristic. Three species found here that are at the northern limit of their range in eastern North America are Indigo Bunting, Northern Cardinal and Rufous-sided Towhee. The first two are known to nest here while the towhee has been observed on a few occasions.

The wooded areas in spring also attract omnivorous species such as Cedar Waxwing, Blue Jay and Scarlet Tanager. There are many thrushes: Wood Thrushes nest here and Hermit and Swainson's Thrushes and Veeries are relatively abundant during migration. The more open areas – woodland borders, bushes and landscaped areas – are habitat for Northern Orioles, Brown Thrashers, Gray Catbirds and various species of swallows and sparrows. The Northern Mockingbird, which is rare in the area, is seen regularly.

In winter, Black-capped Chickadee, White-breasted Nuthatch, Downy Woodpecker, Hairy Woodpecker, Common Redpoll, Dark-eyed Junco and Pine Siskin are the most frequently observed species. The Northern Cardinal, although not abundant, is nonetheless regularly sighted. Less frequently seen are Pine and Evening Grosbeaks, White-winged Crossbills and Bohemian Waxwings. Winter is also the time for owls; Eastern Screech-Owl, Great Horned Owl, Barred Owl and Northern Saw-whet Owl being the most likely sightings.

In the spring and fall, American Kestrels, Broad-winged Hawks and Sharp-shinned Hawks are the most frequently observed hawks. In fact, 15 of the 16 hawk species recorded in the area have been seen at this site. Turkey Vultures, Northern Goshawks and Ospreys are seen each year, and Bald and Golden Eagles and Peregrine Falcons are sighted sporadically.

Suggested route :

The northeast slope (Site 1) : This site can be reached on foot from Park Avenue or Mount Royal Boulevard. Located below the cliffs, this section is partially covered by a sugar-maple hickory stand. Numerous trails give access to the complete area. The site is interesting because of its variety of woodland species. Some that are rare or occasional in other parts of the area can be seen here: Winter Wren, Philadelphia Vireo, Solitary Vireo, Scarlet Tanager and Northern Cardinal.

There are a few clearings here, most of them low-lying wet areas, and sometimes birds that favour wetlands are found in these more open micro-habitats. Small as they may be, these clearings do occasionally produce such odd sightings as the Marsh Wren, seen in the spring of 1985.

The summit (Site 2) : The best way to get to the summit is to take the staircase leading to the Chalet. In this stand of red oak are coniferous plantings where you can see a wide range of woodland species during the spring migration : Northern

Mount Royal Park

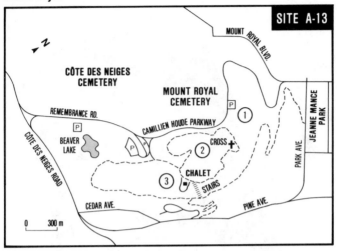

Cardinal, Rufous-sided Towhee and Indigo Bunting are only three of these.

There are also some relatively open areas that are good hawk watching sites. Vultures have been seen on various occasions above the picnic area behind the Chalet, and Northern Goshawks have often been sighted in various places at this site. Looking from the observatory over the downtown area will increase your chances of seeing hawks.

In the winter, Chemin des Calèches is kept open for pedestrians and is a good spot for studying birds that come to feeders. Northern Cardinals are unquestionably the main

Northern Cardinal

attraction, but regular visits may turn up other surprises. The fruit trees along the road are worth checking. The owls that occur in winter are most often spotted in this area.

The pond area (Site 3) : This area is located between the Chalet and the parking lot and is probably the best birding spot in the park. Several trails lead to the site, which is a wet basin bordered by various deciduous tree species and coniferous plantings. Many woodland species arrive in large concentrations during the spring migration. Several species that are rare and exceptional for the area have been observed, especially warblers. Rubber boots are needed in the flooded area, and keep an eye out for poison ivy, which is abundant around the pond.

In the winter, the birds are easy to see at the feeder not far from the pond, along a cross-country ski trail. Be careful not to get in the way of the skiers. You will find more or less the same species as at the previous site, except that Northern Cardinals are more likely to be present. A Northern Shrike was seen near the feeder in the fall of 1985.

House Finch

Montreal Botanical Gardens

What to look for : Wintering and migrating species. *Special species :* Gray Partridge, Bohemian Waxwing, House Finch, Northern Cardinal.

Where : The Montreal Botanical Gardens are located at 4101 Sherbrooke Street East. They are bordered to the south by Sherbrooke Street, to the west by Pie IX Boulevard, to the north by Rosemont Boulevard and to the east by Maisonneuve Park.

How to get there : *By car :* From the west end of the Island of Montreal, take the Metropolitan Autoroute east (Autoroute 40), and Pie IX Boulevard south. You can also take the Ville Marie Autoroute (Autoroute 720), Notre Dame Street and Pie IX Boulevard north. From the South Shore, take the Lafontaine Tunnel and Sherbrooke Street west to Pie IX Boulevard.

By bus : The Botanical Gardens are across the road from the Pie IX Metro station.

When to go : Winter and the spring are the best seasons. You need one or two hours to have a good look at the feeding stations.

Site description : The Montreal Botanical Gardens, a 73-hectare site, were created in 1931 by Frère Marie-Victorin, a botanist of international renown. There are about 30 specialized gardens and nine greenhouses for exhibits. The gardens are known all over the world and attract a lot of visitors.

Few bird species nest here, but over the years no less than 130 species have been recorded, mainly during the spring migration. For some years now, feeding stations have been maintained during the winter, which has made the site more interesting for birdwatchers.

Suggested route : The main attraction is a 2-km circuit along which 16 feeding stations are maintained in the winter. These species are found in large numbers: Dark-eyed Junco, Northern Cardinal, Common Redpoll, House Finch, Purple Finch, Evening Grosbeak, American Goldfinch, Pine Siskin, American Tree Sparrow and the occasional Hoary Redpoll.

Feeder no. 4 attracts birds because they can find shelter in the nearby pine shrubs.

A planting of ornamental crab apple trees near feeder no. 8 attracts fruit-eating species throughout the winter. This is a good spot for Northern Mockingbirds, American Robins, Bohemian Waxwings, Cedar Waxwings, and Pine Grosbeaks. House Finches seem to be attracted by the fruit in winter as well.

In winter, a flock of Gray Partridges is occasionally seen near the feeders early in the morning before visitors arrive.

The Montreal Botanical Gardens

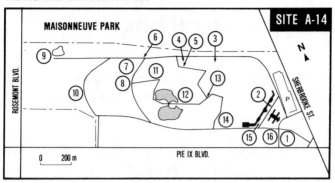

In spring, particularly mid-May, the shrubs and woods are alive with insect-eating passerines. This is the time to study flycatchers, vireos, warblers and sparrows. The ponds attract a few ducks, some of which remain to nest.

Ile-de-la-Visitation
Regional Park

What to look for : Mostly migrating birds: ducks and geese, gulls, passerines. *Special species :* Iceland Gull, Glaucous Gull.

Where : The park is located on the north part of the Island of Montreal along Rivière des Prairies. The site can be reached in less than 30 minutes from downtown.

How to get there : *By car :* From the Metropolitan Autoroute (Autoroute 40), take the exit marked "Rue Saint-Hubert - Avenue Christophe-Colomb - Avenue Papineau" and take Papineau Avenue north. Turn right onto Henri Bourassa Boulevard, left onto Rue de Lille, right onto Gouin Boulevard and left into the parking area.

By bus: From the Henri Bourassa Metro station, take bus 69 to Rue d'Iberville, and walk north for one block.

When to go : The most interesting seasons are spring, fall and winter. The trails can be covered in less than one hour.

Site description : The site is located in an urban area along Rivière des Prairies, between the Papineau-Leblanc Bridge and the Rivière des Prairies hydroelectric power station. This 30-hectare park was the first to be set up by the Montreal Urban Community. It was inaugurated in September 1983.

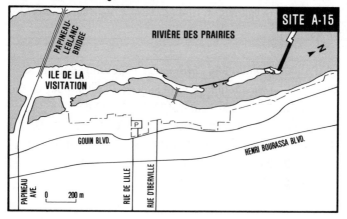

The park comprises Ile de la Visitation and a strip of land on the Island of Montreal.

The park is mostly open area interspersed with trees and bushes. It is used by cross-country skiers in winter and by fishermen, joggers and strollers in summer.

There are few nesting species here. Nonetheless, this island of greenery located in the midst of a heavily urbanized area, attracts large concentrations of numerous passerine species during the spring migration, especially in May. Several water birds are found on the river. A total of 122 species has been recorded for the park.

Suggested route : A short trail gives access to the main habitats of the park, and you will find a large variety of passerines, especially in May. These include woodpeckers, flycatchers, swallows, thrushes, vireos, warblers and sparrows.

In the fall, winter and spring, use a spotting scope to scan the water. You will find several species of diving ducks and other water birds upstream from the dam. In the winter there are Great Black-backed, Glaucous and Iceland Gulls. On the downstream side in late summer are small gatherings of shorebirds on the banks and rocks. You will also see Great Blue Herons and Black-crowned Night-Herons.

Bois-de-la-Réparation Regional Park

What to look for : Ducks and migrating passerines, particularly warblers. *Special species :* Green-backed Heron, Wood Duck, Solitary Sandpiper, Great Horned Owl, Willow Flycatcher, Loggerhead Shrike.

Where : The park is located at the extreme northeast end of the Island of Montreal, in the Pointe-aux-Trembles area, on land owned by the City of Montreal. It is a 30- to 45-minute trip from downtown Montreal.

How to get there : *By car :* The park is readily accessible via Sherbrooke Street. From the Metropolitan Autoroute (Autoroute 40) take Exit 87, Henri Bourassa Boulevard and Sherbrooke Street to the park entrance.

By bus : During the week, take bus 189 at the Honoré Beaugrand Metro station, get off at De la Rousselière Boulevard and walk eastward. During the weekend, take bus 187 and get off at 55th Avenue.

When to go : The park is best in the spring, but is also very interesting in the summer and during the fall migration. The morning is without question the best time. Two to three hour are needed to walk through the park, but during the peak of the spring migration you can easily spend five hours there.

White-throated Sparrow

Special information : There are trails in the park, but these do not always lead to the main points of interest. Choose waterproof footwear, especially in early spring, as the area is damp. Watch out for the poison ivy that lurks among the other vegetation.

Site description : The Bois-de-la-Réparation park is one of the few green spaces at the east end of the Island of Montreal that has remained in its natural state. Purportedly a conservation park, it is one of the network of regional parks belonging to the Montreal Urban Community.

This 94-hectare site is remarkable for its diversity of habitat. There are two sections: (1) the Bois de la Réparation, which is mostly a sugar-maple hickory ash stand; (2) the Bois de l'Héritage, which is much larger and comprises fallow fields bordered by shrubs, a sizable red maple grove and a number of ponds of varying sizes.

The variety of habitat attracts a considerable variety of birds. Recent checks have confirmed that about 164 species from 34 families have been observed over the years. This is one of the rare sites on the Island of Montreal where you can find such a variety of herons, ducks, waders, birds of prey and field and forest passerines in such a small area.

Herons are seen in large numbers. American Bitterns, Great Blue Herons, Green-backed Herons and the Black-crowned Night-Herons are often observed here.

There is a surprising number of dabbling ducks, considering the size of the ponds. The ducks are seen mainly during the spring migration, when the ponds have swelled from the melting snow. Mostly there are large numbers of Wood Ducks, Mallards, Northern Pintails as well as Blue-winged Teals, Northern Shovelers and American Wigeons.

Hawks include the Northern Harrier, which nests in the park, and Red-shouldered, Broad-winged and Red-tailed Hawks, which are frequently observed. Merlins are seen from time to time.

Rails and shorebirds are fairly numerous. Sora and Solitary Sandpiper are common during migration. Wilson's Phalarope, which is expanding its range in Quebec, was seen in 1989.

Great Horned Owls have been here for many years.

The Bois-de-la-Réparation Regional Park may be last nesting site in Quebec for the Loggerhead Shrike, whose numbers are declining in the northeastern part of the continent.

This is one of the better sites for warbler watching during the spring migration. It is not unusual to see almost 20 species at the peak of the migration. Eighteen species were sighted on May 21, 1985. In 1989, the Golden-winged Warbler was seen here.

Suggested route : Water birds – herons, ducks, shorebirds, rails – are found on the ponds in the abandoned fields along Sherbrooke Street *(Site A)*. Willow Flycatchers also visit the site in the summer. These fields and ponds are not within the park boundaries and thus are not protected.

The Bois de l'Héritage encompasses a number of waterways *(Site B)*. These often attract ducks (mainly Wood Ducks).

The sugar-maple hickory stands in the Bois de la Réparation and Bois de l'Héritage *(Site C)* draw the warblers, tanagers, thrushes and flycatchers normally found in the Montreal area.

Bois-de-la-Réparation Regional Park

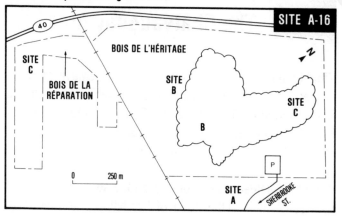

The Bois de l'Héritage has gravel trails that make walking easy. Birds are most plentiful around the woods and water.

Further north is the Rivière des Prairies Regional Park.

This is mostly open area with a few small ponds that attract nesting dabbling ducks. To reach this site, continue eastward on Sherbrooke Street and turn left onto Gouin Boulevard. You will find the park entrance on your left, just after you drive under the overpass on Autoroute 40.

The Châteauguay Area

What to look for : Nesting wetland species, owls and nesting passerines. *Special species :* Least Bittern, Green-backed Heron, Wood Duck, Virginia Rail, Sora, Common Moorhen, Black Tern, Eastern Screech-Owl, Barred Owl, Willow Flycatcher, Northern Cardinal, House Finch.

Where : Châteauguay is located on the southeast shore of Lake Saint-Louis, at the mouth of the Châteauguay River, less than 30 minutes from downtown Montreal.

How to get there : *By car :* Châteauguay is approached by Highways 132 and 138 west. From downtown, take Highway 20 west and follow the signs to the Mercier Bridge. From the south end of the Mercier Bridge, follow the signs to Châteauguay.

By bus: Public transportation leaves from Angrignon and Longueuil Metro stations (Autobus Léo Auger; tel: (514) 691-1000).

When to go : The greatest numbers of birds are found in the wooded and swampy habitats in spring and summer. The gatherings of dabbling ducks on the Châteauguay River reach their peak only in fall and winter. The numerous feeding stations maintained by local residents encourage several species to overwinter. Completing the suggested route will take several visits.

Least Bittern

Site description : The Châteauguay area is mainly characterized by 4 km² of swamp and flooded forest around the mouth of the Châteauguay River and along Lake Saint-Louis. Ile Saint-Bernard, a 235-hectare island at the mouth of the Châteauguay River, is representative of this extraordinary wetland. It comprises mature woodland, a field and a young stand of Trembling Aspen. There is also a huge marsh and a swamp where close to 200 Great Blue Heron nests were counted in 1987.

Châteauguay is surrounded by small wooded areas comprised mostly of deciduous trees. These ensure the presence of a diversity of woodland species. The nearby Kahnawake Mohawk Reserve, with its 30 km^2 of woodland, offsets the effects of forest fragmentation and explains the presence of the several forest interior species nesting in the Châteauguay woods. These are the species most affected by forest fragmentation in the rest of the area.

More than 100 species breed every year on this site. Wetland species are particularly predominant : Pied-billed Grebe, Green-backed Heron, Least Bittern, American Bittern, Wood Duck, Virginia Rail, Sora, Common Moorhen, Common Snipe, Black Tern, Marsh Wren. Land birds include Sharp-shinned Hawk, Red-shouldered Hawk, Gray Partridge, Eastern Screech-Owl, Barred Owl, Willow Flycatcher,Northern Rough-winged Swallow, Northern Cardinal, Indigo Bunting, Field Sparrow, House Finch and several more common species.

Among the irregular visitants reported at Châteauguay are Great Egret, Snowy Egret, Forster's Tern, Tufted Titmouse, Harris' Sparrow, and Yellow-headed Blackbird. The Tufted Titmouse is seen more often in Châteauguay than in any other part of the area, there having been four reports in the last few years. This bird, which nests in New York and Vermont, is steadily expanding its range and may eventually nest in the Châteauguay area.

The Châteauguay Area

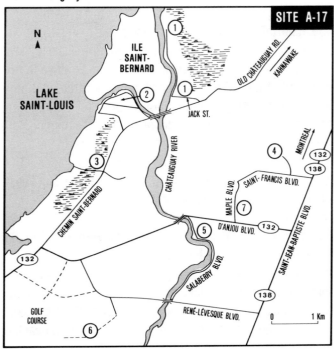

SITE A-17

Suggested Route :

The Johnson Point marsh (Site 1) : This 80-hectare marsh overlaps Châteauguay and Kahnawake. At the south exit from the Mercier Bridge, go right toward Châteauguay. Drive for 2.6 km to the Kahnawake exchange and turn right toward Kahnawake village. After 0.9 km, a left turn onto Old Châteauguay Road will take you through about 5 km of the wooded areas of the Kahnawake reserve. Soon after leaving the reserve, turn right onto Jack Street. The Johnson Point marsh extends north from here to the St. Lawrence River. After turning onto Jack Street, drive 300 m to a dyke that runs 1.5 km northward along the west side of the marsh to the St. Lawrence. This dyke prevents spring flooding in Châteauguay. You can park near the entrance to the dyke. To drive to the other end of the dyke, continue along Jack Street and turn right onto Salaberry Boulevard north. Drive for 1.3 km, turn right onto Higgins Street and continue on to the marsh. You can leave your car at the end of the street. To get to the dyke, go around the fence surrounding the pumping station. The species of interest here are the Green-backed Heron, Least Bittern, Marsh Wren and Swamp Sparrow.

The Marais de la Commune and Ile Saint-Bernard (Site 2) :

To get to this site, come back to the corner of Jack Street and Chemin Saint-Bernard and drive westward. Cross the Châteauguay River and take the first exit to D'Youville Boulevard along the river. D'Youville Boulevard and Rue Vinet skirt the Marais de la Commune on the left. Leave your car near the Ile Saint-Bernard Bridge and walk around the marsh. A platform on D'Youville Boulevard serves as a lookout. This 9-hectare cat-tail marsh, bordered by willow and young ash, is rich in bird life. There are Pied-billed Grebes, Least Bitterns, Common Moorhens, American Coots, Virginia Rails, Soras, one of the few Black Tern colonies in the Montreal area, Marsh Wrens and Swamp Sparrows. Along D'Youville Boulevard are Willow Flycatchers, which can be identified by their song. Some species disappeared from this site after the 1988-89 drought and consequent habitat degradation.

At the present time, Ile Saint-Bernard is not open to the public, although it may be in the near future. This island is of enormous ecological value; it is inhabited by about 80 species of nesting birds that include Great Blue Heron, Wood Duck and Barred Owl. In fall and spring, diving ducks gather on Lake Saint-Louis opposite the island.

Ruisseau Saint–Jean (Site 3) : From D'Youville Boulevard, come back to Chemin Saint-Bernard and go west toward Léry. Drive the 1.4 km to Ruisseau Saint-Jean and turn right just before the bridge. There is another, unused bridge, parallel to the first one, where you can park. Ruisseau Saint-Jean flows into a huge 200-hectare marsh along Lake Saint-Louis. Studies have shown this to be one of the most important spawning grounds of Lake Saint-Louis. You can walk for a short distance along the stream. The marsh can also be explored from an old dirt road running along Chemin Saint-Bernard. Green-backed Herons, Wood Ducks and Common Moorhens are frequent in this area. Northern Rough-winged Swallows nest under the bridge.

Woodbine Street woods (Site 4) : This sector overlaps Châteauguay and Kahnawake. From the Kahnawake interchange, drive along Highway 138 toward Châteauguay for about 4 km. Turn right onto Saint-Francis Boulevard and right again onto Woodbine Street and drive to Oliver Street. You can leave your car at the corner of these streets. You will find a narrow, muddy path through dense shrubbery that leads to a small stand of eastern white pine. Woodland birds are seen here throughout the year. The pines attract northern species in winter, and Northern Cardinals are very much in evidence because of all the feeding stations in the nearby residential areas.

The Châteauguay River (Site 5) : Once you are back at the corner of Highway 138 (Boulevard Saint-Jean-Baptiste) and Boulevard Saint-Francis, drive to D'Anjou Boulevard and continue westward to Laberge Bridge. Just before the bridge, turn left onto Salaberry Boulevard which goes south along the river. The section of river between the bridge and the dam, located upstream, never freezes in the winter. Hundreds of Mallards and American Black Ducks stay in this area, where they can feed undisturbed; Wood Ducks and Green-winged Teals have been reported wintering here. Mourning Doves and House Finches are among the species attracted to the feeding stations in the area. Take Haute Rivière Boulevard if you wish to observe the river from the west side.

The Fernand Séguin Ecological Centre (Site 6) : To get to this site, take D'Anjou Boulevard, René Lévesque Boulevard to the left and Rue Brisebois to the right. At the end of Rue Brisebois, go behind the Léo Crépin Arena to the small parking area at the entrance to the ecological centre. The centre is located in a sugar-maple hickory stand inhabited by several forest species typical of southern Quebec: Great Crested Fly-catcher, House Wren, Wood Thrush, Warbling Vireo. Eastern Screech-Owls have been heard at twilight. Several trails, one of which is self-guided, lead through the site. The ecological centre is not very large, but it is part of a vast 200-hectare area of forest that overlaps Châteauguay and Léry and surrounds

the Bellevue Golf Club. Trails lead from the centre to fallo
fields west of the golf course. On the east side they cross a
mature maple grove and a stand of eastern hemlock. Forest
interior species nest here: Sharp-shinned Hawk, Barred Owl,
Pileated Woodpecker, Scarlet Tanager. This sector can be
reached from René Lévesque Boulevard along a path just 0.4
km west of Rue Brisebois.

Howard S. Billings High School (Site 7): This school is located at the corner of Maple Boulevard and McLeod Street,
just north of D'Anjou Boulevard. For some years now, Brown-
headed Cowbirds have been roosting in the trees on Maple
Boulevard, opposite the school, in the winter. Every evening
up to 3,000 of them congregate there for the night. They
usually arrive between 4:00 and 4:30 p.m. In 1988 and 1989,
a Yellow-headed Blackbird was among these birds.

The LaPrairie Basin and Surrounding Region

What to look for : Wintering ducks, shorebirds, gulls and terns. *Special species :* Barrow's Goldeneye, Willow Flycatcher, Grasshopper Sparrow.

Where : The site is located in the municipality of Sainte-Catherine on the south shore of the St. Lawrence River, downstream from the Lachine rapids. It is about 30 minutes from downtown Montreal.

How to get there : *By car :* There are two routes from the Island of Montreal. The first is by the Champlain Bridge, where you take the first exit toward New York State (15 sud-132 est). From here take Exit 46 (LaPrairie-Boulevard Salaberry) and turn right onto Marie-Victorin Boulevard. Drive 5.2 km and turn right at the Sainte-Catherine locks. (Watch out for the 90 degree turn to the right on Marie-Victorin Boulevard at the second traffic lights.)

The second route is by the Mercier Bridge. At the south end of the bridge, take the left exit (LaPrairie-132 est), drive 6.5 km, turn left onto Rue Centrale and go to Marie-Victorin Boulevard. The Sainte-Catherine locks are a little farther on.

By bus: Les autobus Ménard (1-800-363-4543) provide public transportation from the Voyageur bus terminal (Berri-UQAM Metro station).

When to go : Fall, winter and early spring are the best times to visit Sites 1 and 2; Site 3 can be visited in spring and summer. You will need 1 to 3 hours to explore the area, depending on the season.

Special information : You will need a spotting scope to scan the water.

Description of the site : The LaPrairie Basin is a 40-km^2 stretch of water that has resulted from a widening of the St. Lawrence River downstream from the Lachine rapids. The LaPrairie shoreline, just southeast of this basin, used to be the best place in the Montreal area for watching shorebirds but was completely destroyed during the 1950s when the St. Lawrence Seaway was built. Few shorebirds now visit this area, except when floating mats of vegetation form that can support them.

The shallows of the basin are full of submerged vegetation and are regularly visited by waterfowl, mostly in fall and winter.

The Sainte-Catherine locks make it possible for cargo ships to by-pass the Lachine rapids. They are located at the southwest end of the basin. The embankment here affords a scenic view over the basin and the islands in the Lachine rapids. This is the best place to watch the birds that visit this section of the river. A little west of the locks is a very pleasant summer campground beside the rapids, across from Heron Island.

South of Sainte-Catherine, particularly in the municipality of Saint-Constant, the cultivated fields and numerous fallow fields attract species that favour open habitat. In summer, the species of interest here include Black-billed Cuckoo, Willow Flycatcher, Blue-gray Gnatcatcher and Grasshopper Sparrow.

Suggested Route :

The Sainte-Catherine locks and campground (Site 1) : Cross the lock, turn left and park your car along the road to the campground. If you scan the Baie des Canards with a spotting scope, particularly in November and December, you will find several species of dabbling ducks. As soon as there is ice in the bay, a good number of these leave the area, but many spend the winter beside the ice and in the open water of the rapids. The dabbling ducks are then joined by diving ducks such as Common Goldeneye and Common Merganser. The Barrow's Goldeneye usually only puts in an appearance at the end of winter.

Several species of gulls, including Iceland and Glaucous Gulls, are present in late fall and winter. Snowy Owls often stand watch over the ice, but they look so much like lumps of snow that they are easily overlooked. You can walk or snowshoe on the campground beside the rapids to get a better look at the ducks. This is also a good place to visit in the fall when several sparrow species are observed.

Several irregular species have been seen in the lock area over the years. On more than one occasion there have been Eurasian Wigeon, Harlequin Duck, Bald Eagle, Parasitic Jaeger, Lesser Black-backed Gull and Ivory Gull.

The LaPrairie Basin and Surrounding Area

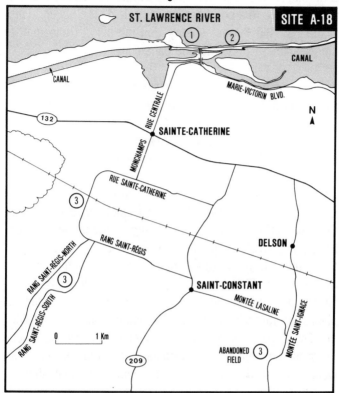

The St. Lawrence Seaway dyke and the Chemin du Fleuve (Site 2) : East of the locks is a road to the Victoria Bridge that runs nearly 15 km along the dyke between the Seaway and the river. There is a gate to prevent cars from entering, but bicycles are allowed. This can be an interesting drive, if there is not too much snow, particularly at the beginning of winter. Several species of ducks and other birds visit the open water at the edge of the ice in December. During the nesting season, you can cycle to a point across from Ile de la Couvée. This island has the largest colony of Ring-billed Gulls in the Montreal area – about 20,000 pairs.

The Chemin du Fleuve, which can also be reached from the lock, runs along the riverside below the Seaway dyke. Often it is blocked by snow in winter, but it can be interesting in late summer or fall when there are small gatherings of shorebirds on the riverside and on the floating mats of vegetation.

Saint-Constant (Site 3) : When you leave the Sainte-Catherine locks, go right on Marie Victorin Boulevard towards Rue Centrale. Cross Highway 132 and continue along Rue Monchamp to Rue Sainte–Catherine. Here you turn right. Cross the railway tracks and park on the side of the road (at this point called Rang Saint-Régis). The abandoned fields on either side of the road and along the railway track are excellent places for observing American Woodcocks at dusk and Willow Flycatchers and Black-billed Cuckoos in early summer. Towards the west is a wet woodland that you can reach by walking along the railway tracks. Blue-gray Gnatcatchers have nested here, and Northern Waterthrushes, Great Horned Owls and Eastern Screech-Owls also frequent the area.

Go south towards Saint-Constant, on Rang Saint-Régis, which crosses a river with the same name. You can either go straight to Saint-Constant or take a detour on Rang Saint-Régis north and Rang Saint-Régis south, both of which follow the Saint-Régis River. This route will take you through open habitat where you can see Northern Mockingbirds in summer and Horned Larks, Snow Buntings and Lapland Longspurs in winter. Gray Partridges are present year-round but are more easily observed in winter.

At Saint-Constant, turn right onto Highway 209 and then turn left immediately onto Montée Lasaline. Turn right again onto Montée Saint-Ignace and stop after 400 to 800 m. The fields on the right of Montée Saint-Ignace have several species that favour open habitat, in particular a colony of about five pairs of Grasshopper Sparrows found here in 1988.

Gray Partridge

Short-eared Owl

Brossard and LaPrairie

What to look for : Hawks, passerines. *Special species :* Rough-legged Hawk, Short-eared Owl, Blue-gray Gnatcatcher, House Wren, Willow Flycatcher.

Where : This site is located on the south shore of the St. Lawrence River, less than 20 minutes from downtown Montreal by car.

How to get there : *By car :* From Montreal, the site can be reached via the Champlain Bridge, the Eastern Townships Autoroute (10) and Taschereau Boulevard west.

By bus : The STRSM services this area. For information call: (514) 463-0131.

When to go : The best time to see hawks and owls is late fall and winter; spring is best for passerines. In winter, it will only take a few minutes to cover the interesting spots, but in summer you may need the whole morning.

Site Description : Brossard and LaPrairie are suburbs that have developed considerably over the last few years, with a consequent loss of valuable habitat. There are, however, some vacant lots and wooded areas at the outskirts that still attract birds. Further development could entail the loss of these sites. The abandoned land east of Brossard between the Eastern Townships Autoroute and Des Prairies Boulevard is excellent habitat for certain hawks and owls, especially during migration and in winter. When small rodents are plentiful, these fields become the favoured hunting ground of Rough-legged Hawks and Short-eared Owls. Snowy Owls, Red-tailed Hawks and Northern Harriers are also found there in the fall and sometimes in winter. During the nesting period, species that favour open habitat are numerous; the Grasshopper Sparrow, a species that is rare in southwestern Quebec, has been seen here.

The regenerating woodlands south of Des Prairies Boulevard are inhabited by woodland passerines, particularly during the spring migration, and this is one of the few areas where Blue-gray Gnatcatchers breed in Quebec. Other typical nesting species are House Wren and Wood Thrush.

Suggested Route :

Brossard :

Site 1: Part of this site may soon be turned into a golf course. From the Eastern Townships Autoroute (10), take Taschereau Boulevard west, turn left onto Rome Boulevard, right onto Niagara Street and left onto Nogent Street. Stop at the end of the street in the parking lot of the Centre d'accueil Champlain. Use a spotting scope to scan the fields for hawks. Late afternoon is the best time for Short-eared Owls, particularly in winter.

Site 2 : Go back to Taschereau Boulevard and drive westward to Des Prairies Boulevard (2 km), where you turn left. After

Brossard and LaPrairie

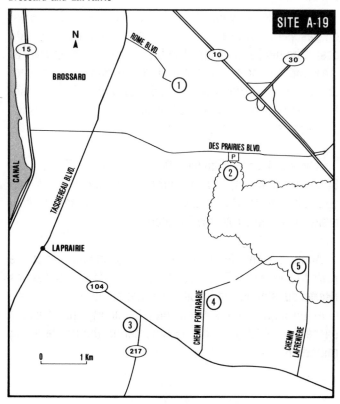

you pass the railway crossing, make a few short stops to study the fields on either side of the road. After you have driven 3.4 km, turn right into a parking area here. The adjacent wood has cross-country ski and snowshoe trails maintained by the municipality of Brossard. Blue-gray Gnatcatchers frequent the south end of the main trail.

LaPrairie :

This municipality has three points of interest. Drive west on Taschereau Boulevard, then turn left onto Highway 104 east (Chemin Saint-Jean). The first interesting stop *(Site 3)* is a wood that can be approached through a small parking spot at the corner of Highway 104 and Highway 217. There are trails here where you will find House Wrens, Wood Thrushes and Northern Waterthrushes in summer.

A little farther on Highway 104, 4 km from the Taschereau Boulevard junction, you will come to Chemin Fontarabie on your left *(Site 4)*. This road leads to fallow fields and shrubby areas inhabited by Willow Flycatchers.

About 6.2 km along Highway 104 is Chemin Lafrenière *(Site 5)* on the left. This leads to Hydro-Québec installations (Hertel substation and La Citière power station). A path here goes through swampy woodland inhabited by insect-eating passerines which are particularly numerous during the spring migration.

The Longueuil Shoreline

What to look for : A great variety of migrating species: herons, ducks, shorebirds, gulls and terns.

Where : This site is located along the St. Lawrence River in Longueuil. It can be reached in less than 15 minutes.

How to get there : *By car :* From Montreal, take the Champlain, Victoria or Jacques Cartier bridge and Highway 132 east or the Lafontaine Tunnel and Highway 132 west.

By bus : Take bus 17 from the Longueuil Metro station to Marie Victorin Park.

When to go : Summer and fall are the most interesting seasons. You can easily spend three hours, depending on how many birds are there.

Site description : It is easy to see that much of this habitat has been spoiled. It was severely encroached upon by the construction of Highway 132 in 1966, and the unrelenting traffic noise is a constant reminder of this disturbance. The site is nonetheless of undeniable interest to birders. In 1988, a boardwalk and a cycling path were laid between the river and Highway 132, thus restoring access to the St. Lawrence. The

4-km promenade, named after a former premier of the province, René Lévesque, goes between Marie Victorin Park and the Lafontaine Tunnel. Footbridges spanning Highway 132 provide safe access to the promenade.

Filling operations resulting from the construction of Highway 132 created a habitat of small islands and dykes that attracts ducks, gulls, terns and shorebirds. Dabbling ducks, sometimes in great numbers, raise their broods here. Early in spring, they build their nests a little further off shore, mostly on Ile Verte. This area is mainly a staging ground for gulls and terns, although Common Terns do nest here from time to time. Apart from the Ring-billed Gull, which is, of course, the most common gull in summer, there is the occasional Caspian Tern, and sometimes more unusual species such as Franklin's Gull occur.

The number of shorebirds in late summer and fall depends on the level of the water. When the water is low, they can be found in large numbers. When it is very high, the shorebirds are less numerous and are concentrated on a few islands of floating vegetation. Twenty or so species of shorebirds are sighted every year. These include Stilt Sandpiper, Wilson's Phalarope and Red-necked Phalarope. Sometimes less common species such as Whimbrel, Hudsonian Godwit and Western Sandpiper stop over.

Aside from the dabbling ducks in fall, there are diving ducks, Common Loons, Horned Grebes, Red-necked Grebes and Double-crested Cormorants.

Great Blue Herons and Black-crowned Night-Herons often come to feed along the shore, and sometimes birds from the south such as Great Egrets, Snowy Egrets and Glossy Ibises stop over briefly, particularly in spring and autumn.

The numerous shorebirds attract the Peregrine Falcon, sometimes seen hunting along the shore, mostly in autumn.

Suggested route : The most interesting birding is between Marie Victorin Park and Pointe du Marigot, where the dykes and small islands attract many species, particularly in late summer. This is where the most unusual sightings have been made. It is possible to walk along the dyke at Pointe du Marigot toward the middle of the river. A spotting scope is essential here as the birds are often far from the shore.

A footbridge over Highway 132 leads to Marie Victorin Park. To get to it, exit from Highway 132 onto Roland Therrien Boulevard and turn right immediately onto Rue Saint-Charles. Turn right at the next traffic lights onto Rue D'Auvergne then left onto Rue Bord-de-l'eau. The footbridge and a small parking lot are not far from here. When coming from the east on Highway 132, you will have direct access to Marie Victorin Park; simply follow the signs.

Another footbridge leads to the east side of Pointe du Marigot onto the René Lévesque promenade. From Highway

132, take Roland Therrien Boulevard and turn left immediately onto Marie Victorin Boulevard. The footbridge is 1.7 km to the east. You can leave your car in the small parking lot nearby. A third footbridge, located near the south entrance to the Lafontaine Tunnel, leads to the far end of the René Lévesque promenade.

The Longueuil Shoreline

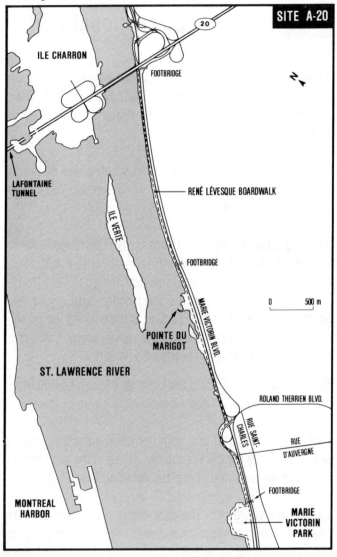

SITE A-20

ILE CHARRON

FOOTBRIDGE

LAFONTAINE TUNNEL

ILE VERTE

RENÉ LÉVESQUE BOARDWALK

FOOTBRIDGE

0   500 m

MARIE VICTORIN BLVD.

POINTE DU MARIGOT

ST. LAWRENCE RIVER

ROLAND THERRIEN BLVD.

RUE SAINT-CHARLES

RUE D'AUVERGNE

MONTREAL HARBOR

FOOTBRIDGE

MARIE VICTORIN PARK

Longueuil Regional Park

What to look for : Ducks, woodpeckers, passerines. *Special species :* American Woodcock, Great Horned Owl, Great Crested Flycatcher, House Wren, Wood Thrush, Yellow-throated Vireo, Warbling Vireo.

Where : This park is located on the south shore of the St. Lawrence River, 5 km from downtown Montreal. You can get there within 15 minutes.

How to get there : *By car :* Cross the St. Lawrence River via the Jacques Cartier, Victoria or Champlain bridge, take Highway 132 to Roland Therrien Boulevard and go to Curé Poirier Boulevard.   Turn left at the intersection and go to Rue Adoncour. At the last intersection is the parking lot and the visitors' centre. If you take the Lafontaine Tunnel, go west on Highway 132 to Roland Therrien Boulevard.

By bus : Take bus 75 from the Longueuil Metro station to the corner of Curé Poirier and Adoncour.

When to go : Spring and summer are the most rewarding seasons. Since the park is mostly visited in the afternoon, it is best to go early and spend the morning there.

Special information : The park offers group birdwatching hikes, mostly in spring and summer. For more information call (514) 646-8269 between 8:00 a.m. and 5:00 p.m. from

Monday to Friday. The visitors' centre has a permanent display on the wildlife found in the park.

Site description : The Longueuil Regional Park, which covers 185 hectares, is completely surrounded by residential areas. The area is mostly wooded with some open habitat. Sugar maple is the dominant tree species, and there are red oak, bitternut hickory, American beech, American elm and white ash.

Near the centre of the park is a large field, once cultivated, which is now overgrown. A thicket of hawthorn, sumac and gray birch has grown up at the edge of the forest. Three small marshes have somehow escaped being bulldozed. One of these, the Marais des Trois Lacs, is only partly bordered by trees, which makes for easier viewing.

The park has been developed considerably. There are three small artificial lakes, a community garden, cycling paths and ski trails, some of which are lighted, and a picnic area. Despite all this development, the park has remained largely unspoiled, which explains why more than 100 bird species are found there every year. Most of these birds are woodland or grassland passerines and are representative of the habitat. American Kestrels and Northern Harriers are the nesting hawk species. Other raptors are seen during migration. Great Horned Owls are sighted regularly, and Northern Saw-whet Owls have been seen several times, mostly in the fall. The swamps diversify the habitat and offer a consequent diversity of species. An experienced observer can easily sight more than 40 nesting species in a few hours in June.

The Yellow-throated Vireo, a rare breeding species, appears to have nested in the tall deciduous trees near the Marais des Trois Lacs during the last few years. The Yellow-billed Cuckoo, another unusual nesting bird in Quebec, has been seen here several times and probably nested in 1980.

A surprising count of 20 or so mammal species footnotes the list of birds. Even more surprising is the presence of white-tailed deer. During the winter of 1988, nine were counted.

Suggested route : The park has a network of over 14 km of paths and trails. The three lakes *(Site 1)* are not far from the visitors' centre. There are a lot of common species in this area in summer: American Robins, European Starlings, Common Grackles, Brown-headed Cowbirds and House Sparrows. Hundreds of Ring-billed Gulls wander about the lawns, while Killdeers and Spotted Sandpipers forage at the edge of the ponds. Purple Martins, Tree Swallows and Barn Swallows dart incessantly above the ponds after insects.

Beyond the ponds is the Marais des Trois Lacs, a cat-tail marsh *(Site 2)*. Great Blue Herons are often seen in the early morning or in the evening, American Bitterns and Black-crowned Night-Herons somewhat less often. American Black Ducks, Mallards, Northern Pintails and American Wigeons are the most common dabbling ducks; every year, a few pairs breed here. Virginia Rails and Soras are much more difficult to find. Swamp Sparrows and Red-winged Blackbirds are the most obvious passerines, and if you go too close to the nest of the latter you are likely to come under attack. In June, the

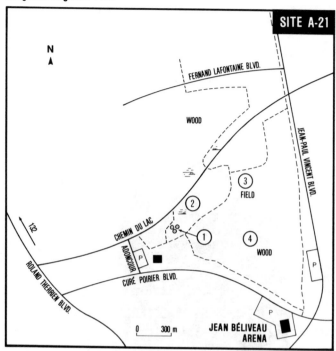

tall trees around the marsh are filled with the songs of Warbling Vireos and Northern Orioles.

Site 3 is the large field and surrounding shrubs. The most common species in spring and summer are American Woodcock, Alder Flycatcher, Eastern Kingbird, Gray Catbird, Cedar Waxwing, Yellow Warbler, Common Yellowthroat, Chipping Sparrow, Savannah Sparrow, Song Sparrow, White-throated Sparrow and American Goldfinch. American Kestrels nest in

Boreal Owl

the natural cavities in the lone trees. The open habitat is the place to watch high-flying hawks in migration.

The last sector, which is by far the most extensive, is the woodland *(Site 4)*. The species here belong to various families. Heard in the dawn chorus are Northern Flicker, Eastern Wood-Pewee, Least Flycatcher, Great Crested Flycatcher, White-breasted Nuthatch, House Wren, Veery, Wood Thrush, Red-eyed Vireo, American Redstart and Rose-breasted Grosbeak. The Great Horned Owl and Ruffed Grouse are more secretive, and it is only by chance that you will see them.

In winter, there are feeders near the visitors' centre and elsewhere in the park. These attract Mourning Doves, Downy Woodpeckers, Hairy Woodpeckers, Black-capped Chickadees, Evening Grosbeaks, Pine Siskins, Purple Finches and Blue Jays. The woods are worth covering at this time as well. In the winter of 1989, birdwatchers were surprised to find two Boreal Owls and one Northern Saw-whet Owl, which stayed for about a month.

Iles-de-Boucherville
Provincial Park

What to look for : Wetland species: ducks and geese, herons and bitterns. *Special species :* Great Blue Heron, Common Moorhen, Black Tern, Willow Flycatcher.

Where : The Boucherville Islands are on the St. Lawrence River near Montreal, only 10 km from downtown.

How to get there : *By car :* Take the Lafontaine Tunnel and Exit 89.

By bus : From the Radisson Metro station take South Shore Transit bus 61 (STRSM). It stops at the park.

By boat : A ferry runs between the René Lévesque promenade in Longueuil to Ile Charron, which is south of the park.

When to go : This site is most enjoyable between April and October, although winter can sometimes be interesting. It takes two to three hours to go around the island by bicycle.

Special information : The park is open every weekday from 8:00 a.m. until sunset. The cable ferry that goes to three of the islands operates from May to October inclusively, starting at

10:00 a.m. The ramp for launching boats is available every morning after 8:00 a.m. Bicycles and boats can be rented on Ile Sainte-Marguerite, but these services vary from year to year. For more information call: (514) 873-2843. A spotting scope is a must in this open habitat.

Site description : The 12 Boucherville islands are 8 km long in all and are located in the St. Lawrence River between Montreal East and Boucherville. The Iles-de-Boucherville Park, officially opened in 1984, encompasses five of these islands, which are, from south to north, Sainte-Marguerite, Saint-Jean, Pinard, de la Commune and Grosbois. In 1989, Ile Pinard was granted to a private business with the intent of having the land turned into a golf course; consequently it is no longer part of the park.

This is an extensive recreational park, where the main activities are picnicking, cycling, hiking and canoeing. The park is heavily used, especially on summer weekends.

The islands are characterized mainly by extensive grasslands and broad channels filled with aquatic vegetation. There is only one sizable wood, on Ile Grosbois, to break the monotony of the landscape. Corn was grown on the islands long before the park was created and is still grown extensively on some of them.

The large amount of aquatic vegetation in the Chenal du Courant is what makes this an attractive birding site. During the nesting period, there are several species of dabbling ducks, the most common being Northern Pintail, Gadwall and American Wigeon. A study has shown that most nests are found on Ile Saint-Jean. The Chenal du Courant, located near this island, is where the many ducklings that hatch during the summer are raised.

The other species that inhabit the Chenal du Courant during the summer are Pied-billed Grebe, American Bittern, Least Bittern, Great Blue Heron, Green-backed Heron, Black-crowned Night-Heron, Virginia Rail, Sora, Common Moorhen, Spotted Sandpiper, Common Snipe, Common Tern, Black Tern, Marsh Wren and Swamp Sparrow.

Unlike lakes Saint-François, Saint-Louis and Saint-Pierre, the Boucherville Islands and the other islands in the Montreal-Sorel section of the St. Lawrence do not attract huge gatherings of ducks during the migration. A few hundred birds are reported in May and October.

The diverse habitat of fields, shrubs and the few wooded sectors support an equally diverse avian community. More than 160 species have been observed here. Blackbirds are attracted to the cultivated fields: American Crows, European Starlings, Red-winged Blackbirds and Common Grackles. The nesting raptor species are Northern Harrier, American

Mallard

Kestrel and Great Horned Owl. Ospreys, Rough-legged Hawks, Snowy Owls and Short-eared Owls are seen fairly commonly in winter or during migration.

Suggested route : The island can be visited on foot or by bicycle, the latter naturally being more efficient. There are

18 km of footpaths and 22 km of cycling paths. Canoeing is another good way to explore the park and is particularly rewarding in the Chenal du Courant. During the summer, there are organized canoe trips in many of the channels of the park. These are highly recommended for beginners.

Ile Sainte-Marguerite : There is a pond near the park entrance, behind the administrative building *(Site 1)*. The pond is inhabited by a few species of nesting ducks and is a migratory stopover for Pied-billed Grebes, Green-winged Teals, Virginia Rails and Soras.

On Ile Sainte-Marguerite, as on the other islands in the park, only the west shore (across from Montreal) is of interest to birdwatchers *(Site 2)*. Usually there are no water birds on the east shore (across from Boucherville). From the west shore, which is off the trail, you can see diving ducks in spring and dabbling ducks in the aquatic vegetation on the west part of Ile Saint-Jean. Great Blue Herons, Ospreys and Common Moorhens are the other species of interest.

Go back to the centre of the island through the bus parking lot and head towards Chenal Petite-Rivière *(Site 3)*. From the bridge over the channel, you may see Great Blue Herons, American Black Ducks, Mallards or American Wigeons in the spring. Go to the Bois du Grand-duc on the other side of the bridge for forest birds in May, and, with a little luck, you may see the Great Horned Owl. On the other side of the wood, is

Iles-de-Boucherville Provincial Park

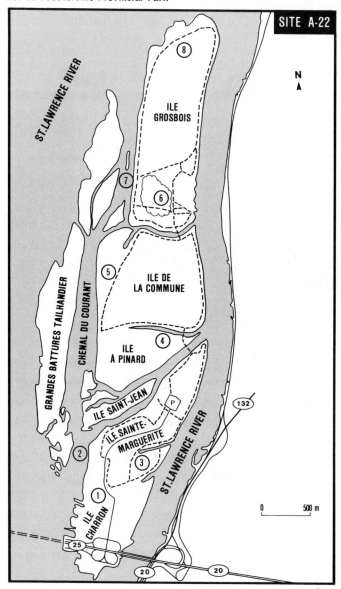

SITE A-22

ST. LAWRENCE RIVER

N

ILE GROSBOIS

GRANDES BATTURES TAILHANDIER

CHENAL DU COURANT

ILE DE LA COMMUNE

ILE À PINARD

ILE SAINT-JEAN

ILE SAINTE-MARGUERITE

ILE CHARRON

ST. LAWRENCE RIVER

132

0   500 m

25

20   20

an old road along Chenal Petite-Rivière that crosses marshy areas frequented by ducks and Northern Harriers.

Ile de la Commune : This island and Ile Grosbois are only accessible by cable ferry, which runs continuously on week-ends only. During the week it runs once every hour. The ferry only operates after the beginning of May and not before 10:00 a.m. The person who thought up this schedule obviously did not have birdwatchers in mind! On Ile de la Commune, take the trail to the left along Chenal à Pinard that goes along the west side of the island. Chenal à Pinard *(Site 4)* has a number of wetland species: Pied-billed Grebes, ducks, Common Moorhens, Swamp Sparrows. The west side of the island *(Site 5)*, is a shrubby area where Eastern Kingbirds, Yellow Warblers and Song Sparrows are common. Willow Flycatchers, which are expanding their range in southern Quebec, have been seen here recently.

Ile Grosbois : The most interesting sites here are the woods and the west shore. In the woods *(Site 6)* in summer are several nesting species common to the deciduous forests in southern Quebec. In spring and fall, migrating birds swell the bird population. On the other side of La Passe footbridge is a trail to the woods. The trail along the west shore of the island *(Site 7)* affords a view of an interesting section of the Chenal du Courant. In the summer, Black Terns are always very much in evidence, and Pied-billed Grebes and Common Moorhens are seen with their broods. Dabbling ducks are also common.

A shrubby area at the north end of the island *(Site 8)*, draws numbers of passerines in spring and fall. Diving ducks frequently rest off the point: Canvasbacks, Redheads and Surf Scoters are among the many species that have been sighted here over the years.

West of Montreal

SECTOR B

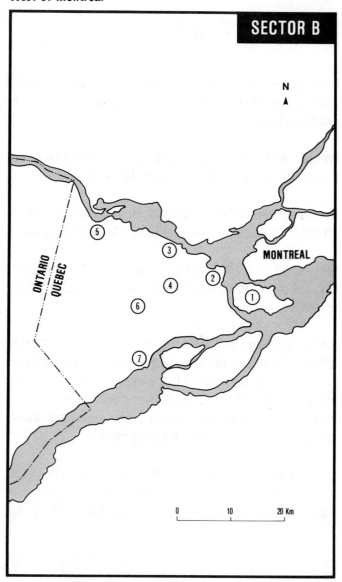

N

MONTREAL

ONTARIO
QUEBEC

⑤

③

②

④

①

⑥

⑦

0   10   20 Km

Ile Perrot

What to look for : Wildfowl, hawks, passerines. *Special species :* Horned Grebe, Red-necked Grebe, Canvasback, American Woodcock.

Where : Ile Perrot is located west of the Island of Montreal. It is within 30 minutes of downtown Montreal.

How to get there : From downtown Montreal, take Autoroute 20 west and cross the bridge at Sainte-Anne-de-Bellevue.

When to go : Ile Perrot is a popular birdwatching spot all year long but is best in spring and fall. It takes at least half a day to visit.

Site description : Ile Perrot consists of about 40 km² bordered to the south and east by Lake Saint-Louis, to the north by the Lake of Two Mountains and to the west by the Ottawa River. Many waterfowl flyways cross over these large bodies of water. They mostly bring diving ducks, which are always abundant around the island in spring and fall.

Ile Perrot also lies on the flight path of southward migrating hawks. Hawks prefer not to migrate over large bodies of water; hence they pass over Ile Perrot, thereby avoiding Lake

Saint-Louis and the Lake of Two Mountains, which lie on either side. This migration is often spectacular, as on September 12, 1981, when 1,500 hawks passed over the island in the space of three hours. The spring count is not as large.

There are also several square kilometres of wooded area, cultivated and fallow fields that attract passerines. But signs of urban sprawl are appearing on Ile Perrot, as in many of the areas on the outskirts of Montreal. Housing development is flourishing in the island's five municipalities, in many cases in woodland and in areas generally attractive to birds.

About 217 bird species have been recorded on Ile Perrot; about 100 of these nest every year.

Suggested route : Before visiting Ile Perrot, you might like to make a side trip to Ile Claude, just north of Ile Perrot *(Site 1)*. When arriving on Ile Perrot by Autoroute 20, take the first exit after the Sainte-Anne-de-Bellevue bridge. Ile Claude is covered by a magnificent stand of maple. In winter the Sainte-Anne rapids, which are ice-free, harbour Common Mergansers and sometimes Hooded Mergansers.

A little further west on Autoroute 20, to the left, is Don Quichotte Boulevard, one of the main roads that crosses through the island to Pointe du Moulin. Follow Don Quichotte past Le Grand Boulevard until you come to a wooded hill, which is a good site for passerines. The path through this area begins on the right, just at the top of the hill, 1 km south of Le Grand Boulevard *(Site 2)*. Less than 1 km further on is La Perdriolle primary school, which in winter has ski trails maintained by the Club Les Skieurs de l'Ile. These trails go through this same area.

Further on, Don Quichotte Boulevard passes through cultivated and fallow fields visited by Snow Buntings and Rough-legged Hawks in winter. These fields are mainly south of Saint Joseph Boulevard. About 1.3 km south of this same intersection, to the right of Don Quichotte Boulevard, is a low hill where surveys on migrating hawks are conducted *(Site 3)*.

At the end of Don Quichotte Boulevard is the Pointe du Moulin historical park *(Site 4)*, which has a splendid view over

Ring-necked Duck

Ile Perrot

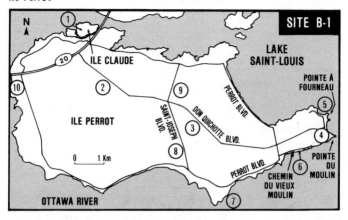

Lake Saint-Louis. To the left of the park, Chemin Cousineau leads to some cottages. Once you pass La Pointe à Fourneau, you will have a view over a small bay *(Site 5)*. You will have to make your way through the underbrush to reach the shore. There are several species of diving ducks, as well as Horned and Red-necked Grebes, to be seen here in spring and fall. Access to this site may eventually be restricted by housing development.

Come back along Don Quichotte Boulevard and turn left onto Caza Boulevard, left onto Rue Daoust and go to Chemin du Vieux-Moulin. Either end of this road is good for scanning Lake Saint-Louis *(Site 6)*. Drive back as far as Perrot Boulevard, which will take you along the shore in either direction. If you go left, you will find a number of good vantage points from where you can scan the lake. One of these is a small point behind Sainte-Jeanne-de-Chantal parish church *(Site 7)*. To get there, turn left onto Rue de l'Eglise. When you go back to Perrot Boulevard, you can continue on to Saint-Joseph Boulevard, which will take you to Don Quichotte Boulevard. On the left of Saint- Joseph Boulevard is a stand of coniferous trees with a trail that starts 0.7 km from Perrot Boulevard *(Site 8)*. Golden-crowned Kinglets are permanent residents in this dense stand of conifers. In the winter you may find Northern Goshawks and a few owls, including Long-eared. The site should be avoided in summer because it is used for archery.

If you go east on Perrot Boulevard, you can come back to Don Quichotte Boulevard by taking the other end of Saint-Joseph Boulevard. There is a wooded area south of Saint-Joseph Boulevard that you can reach by walking through the fields *(Site 9)*.

Another interesting place to visit, especially in winter, is the ice-free area on the Ottawa River, just south of the bridge between Ile Perrot and Dorion *(Site 10)*. This sector has often harboured such unusual wintering species as the Ring-necked Duck and Lesser Scaup observed in 1987, the Red-breasted Merganser in 1986 and the Canada Goose in 1981.

The Vaudreuil Area

What to look for : Diving ducks, hawks, shorebirds. *Special species :* Canvasback, Rough-legged Hawk, Snowy Owl, Short-eared Owl.

Where : This site is west of Montreal in Vaudreuil-Soulanges County. It can easily be reached in 30 minutes from downtown Montreal.

How to get there : This site is readily accessible from Montreal by the Metropolitan Autoroute, Autoroute 40 west (Trans-Canada Highway) and Exit 35.

When to go : Fall and winter are the most interesting seasons. The area can be visited in a few hours.

Site description : Vaudreuil is a fast-growing suburb where old agricultural land is gradually being taken over by residential parks. The fallow agricultural lands on the outskirts of Montreal are always excellent birdwatching sites and the Vaudreuil area is no exception. Small rodents are plentiful in these fields, and they attract many birds of prey during migration and in winter – Rough-legged Hawks, Red-tailed Hawks, Northern Harriers, Snowy Owls and Short-eared Owls. The latter species – spectacular in flight – has nested on several occasions in the Vaudreuil area.

The nearby Lake of Two Mountains is a good site for studying ducks, especially in the fall. Counts by the Canadian Wildlife Service show that the Lake of Two Mountains is visited by an average of 21,000 scaup, in autumn. As many as 8,000 scoters have also been counted here. Pointe Cavagnal in Vaudreuil and Ile Cadieux have good vantage points for scanning the lake. At the end of the summer, when the water level is lowest, the shores around L'Anse de Vaudreuil attract shorebirds.

Suggested route : Take Exit 35 from Autoroute 40 and turn right onto Chemin Roche. You will come to Chemin Les Rigollets which goes to Vaudreuil-sur-le-lac and Ile Cadieux. There are lookouts here over the Lake of Two Mountains. Chemin Roche will also take you to Montée Cadieux and Chemin de l'Anse, which goes along L'Anse de Vaudreuil to Pointe Cavagnal, where you will have another view of the Lake of Two Mountains. In August, the shores of the bay draw a number of shorebirds, while from October until early December, when the lake freezes over, the bay is visited by diving ducks, including Canvasbacks.

Montée Cadieux is a much different habitat. The fallow fields along this road are frequented by Rough-legged Hawks, Red-tailed Hawks, Northern Harriers, Snowy Owls and Short-eared Owls in autumn and winter. Nine Snowy Owls were seen in these fields at the same time in April 1981. Recent housing development in this area has caused significant habitat deterioration. At the far end of Montée Cadieux, you can continue your circuit by turning left onto Highway 342 (Harwood

The Vaudreuil Area

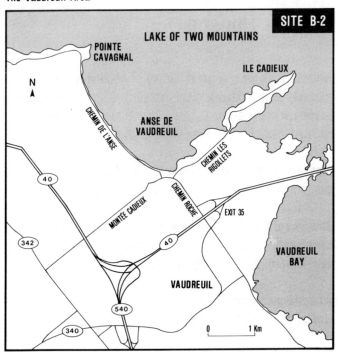

SITE B-2

LAKE OF TWO MOUNTAINS

POINTE CAVAGNAL

ILE CADIEUX

N

ANSE DE VAUDREUIL

CHEMIN DE L'ANSE

CHEMIN LES RIGOLETS

CHEMIN ROCHE

EXIT 35

MONTÉE CADIEUX

40

40

342

VAUDREUIL BAY

VAUDREUIL

540

340

0   1 Km

Boulevard) to take Highway 340 east (Cité-des-Jeunes Boulevard), which will bring you to Autoroute 40 in Vaudreuil. Both these highways pass through cultivated and fallow fields visited by birds of prey in autumn and winter.

What to look for : A great variety of nesting and migrating species; ducks, hawks, owls, passerines. *Special species :* Green-backed Heron, Canvasback, Red-shouldered Hawk, Pileated Woodpecker, Pine Warbler, Northern Cardinal.

Where : Hudson is located in Vaudreuil-Soulanges County on the south shore of the Lake of Two Mountains.

How to get there : From downtown Montreal, Autoroute 40 west (Trans-Canada Highway) will take you to Hudson in less than 45 minutes. Exits 26 and 22 both lead to the village.

When to go : Hudson is one of the few sites in the area that birdwatchers visit in every season.

Special information : Except for a few public parks, this area is essentially private land. Asking permission from the owners before entering private land is part of the birder's code of ethics. You will have to make more than one trip to explore the area fully.

Site description : Hudson, which has a population of about 7,000, has a number of large homes surrounded by many tall trees. Around the village are stands that link it to the vast woodland areas in nearby Saint-Lazare and Rigaud. This makes the area attractive to forest interior species which are relatively common here. The large stands of eastern white pine and eastern hemlock contribute to the diversity. Numerous feeding stations in the village attract birds in winter, so it is not surprising that over 50 species are recorded in Hudson each year during the Christmas Bird Count. Gray Jays, Boreal Chickadees, Bohemian Waxwings and Red Crossbills are among those seen. The number of nesting birds recorded during the Quebec Breeding Bird Atlas Project from 1984 to 1989 establishes Hudson as one of the most attractive summer birding sites in the area. Some 120 nesting birds can be found here every year, some of which are rare in the Montreal area.

The Province of Quebec Society for the Protection of Birds has been holding field trips in this area in winter, spring and fall for many years now. These trips are very worthwhile, particularly for beginners. Among other things, they help the members acquire an understanding of the seasonal movements of birds.

Suggested route : The seven main points of interest lie in an east-west direction. Any one of these would make for an interesting field trip; in fact, it would take several visits to complete all the suggested routes. Spring and summer are best, but in winter species that visit feeding stations can be seen by walking through the village.

Manson Road (Site 1) : This very picturesque and relatively uninhabited road crosses fields used for growing fodder crops. These fields are dotted with small wooded areas. A great variety of land birds can be found along this road. To get there, take Exit 26 from Autoroute 40 and Highway 342 west.

Drive 0.4 km, turn right onto Murphy Road and left onto Manson Road. This road will eventually take you to Main Road.

The Royal Oak Tennis Club trail (Site 2) *:* This trail goes from Main Road to Chemin Harwood (Highway 342). It is approached through the parking lot of the Royal Oak Tennis Club. Take Exit 26 from Autoroute 40, Highway 342 west and Bellevue street north. Turn left onto Main Road and drive the 0.9 km to the tennis club. The parking lot is for club members and can only accommodate a few outsiders. It is a good idea to visit early in the morning, before too many people arrive. The parking lot is not cleared in winter.

Go to the end of the parking lot, turn left and walk for 300 m to where the trail begins on the right. The path is not easy to find. It first goes through an area of dense shrubbery. If you cross a railway track and pass an old sugar shack, you will know you are on the right trail. South of the railway track, you will find yourself in a magnificent grove of old maple. The trail continues to Highway 342 through wet habitat dominated by mixed stands of deciduous and coniferous trees. Passerines are numerous here, particularly in spring and during the nesting period. In June you can see up to 50 species of birds in only a few hours of careful observation along this trail. You will no doubt find Pileated Woodpecker, Red-breasted Nuthatch, Winter Wren, Golden-crowned Kinglet, Northern Waterthrush, Mourning Warbler, Scarlet Tanager and Northern Cardinal. You might also hear Pine Warblers singing along the Como golf course close by. It will take one or two hours to complete the route.

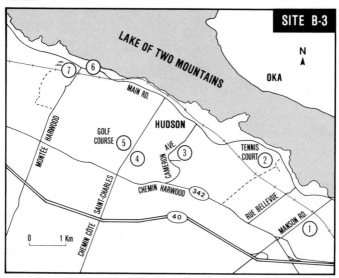

SITE B-3

LAKE OF TWO MOUNTAINS

OKA

N

MAIN RD.

HUDSON

MONTÉE HARWOOD

GOLF COURSE (5)

(4)

(3)

CAMERON AVE

TENNIS COURT (2)

SAINT-CHARLES

CHEMIN HARWOOD (342)

RUE BELLEVUE

MANSON RD.

(40)

(1)

CHEMIN CÔTE

0   1 Km

Olympic Park (Site 3) : Take Exit 26 from the Trans-Canada and Highway 342 west. Turn right onto Cameron Avenue and drive 0.8 km to Olympic Street. The park is 0.4 km along this road. On the left is a trail that leads to a swampy area. There are three forks in the trail. The one on the left and the one over the stream are less than 500 m long. In 1989, beavers built a dam along the left trail. The right trail is 2 km long and crosses a forest of eastern hemlock and yellow birch to a beaver pond. Pileated Woodpeckers visit this area year-round, and Black-backed and Three-toed Woodpeckers may be present in winter. Passerines are abundant at any time.

Dwyer Park (Site 4) : Take Exit 22 from the Trans-Canada and Côte-Saint-Charles north (on the right). Drive exactly 0.8 km from the intersection with Highway 342 (Harwood Road). The tall eastern white pines on the left are visited by Pine Warblers in the summer. On the right of the road is the entrance to a trail. It crosses open habitat bordered by a stream. Species characteristic of this habitat – Gray Catbird, Cedar Waxwing, Eastern Kingbird, Common Yellowthroat, Yellow Warbler, Red-winged Blackbird, Northern Oriole, Song Sparrow – are plentiful. Further on, the trail divides into several forks, one leading to a stand of eastern hemlock inhabited by Barred Owls for the past 50 years. Unfortunately, housing development will eventually cause this species to leave the area. Sharp-shinned Hawks, which are also very sensitive to habitat change, are still seen in the vicinity.

The Whitlock golf course (Site 5) *:* This site has a number of ski trails. It can only be visited in winter, when the most common species are Pine Grosbeak, Evening Grosbeak, Bohemian Waxwing and American Goldfinch. Pileated Woodpeckers are also seen from time to time. This site, like the previous one, is approached by Chemin Côte-Saint-Charles. The entrance to the golf course is on the left side of the road, not far from Dwyer Park.

Thompson Park (Site 6) *:* From the Trans-Canada Highway, take Exit 22 and Chemin Côte-Saint-Charles to Main Road, turn left and drive 2.3 km. Scan the Lake of Two Mountains in the fall for diving ducks. Lesser Scaup, Greater Scaup, Redhead, Canvasback, Common Goldeneye and Bufflehead are regular visitors here.

Aird's Pond (Site 7) *:* This small pond is located at the west end of the village. Take Main Road to Finnegan's flea market, 0.7 km west of Thompson Park *(Site 6)*. The flea market, which on weekends is very crowded, has a huge parking lot in a field north of Main Road. The owners are always happy to meet birdwatchers.

From Main Road, walk south of the flea market towards the pond. Should you arrive very early, it is best to take another route to the pond so as not to disturb the owners. Take Montée Harwood, just after Thompson Park, and drive to the railway tracks, where you can park. From here it is about a 15-minute walk west along the tracks to the pond. During the nesting period, the thick growth of cat-tails around the pond is inhabited by Pied-billed Grebes, Blue-winged Teals, Least Bitterns, American Bitterns, Virginia Rails and Soras.

South of the railway tracks is a trail leading through the forest toward a slope covered with tall eastern white pine. This trail joins Montée Harwood further on. If you have time, you can make a complete circle by taking this trail, Montée Harwood and the railway track back to the pond. By taking this route, you can see forest species such as Red-shouldered Hawk, Pileated Woodpecker, Hermit Thrush, Pine Warbler and Scarlet Tanager. It will take one or two hours to complete the route.

About 300 m west of Aird's Pond, you will find a wet meadow that was visited by a small population of Sedge Wrens in 1989. Green-backed Herons also visit the area

157

Barred Owl

surrounding the meadow. Further west, the railway tracks cross fallow and cultivated fields bordered on the south by woodland in various stages of maturity. This edge habitat is favoured by Mourning Warblers, Northern Cardinals and Indigo Buntings.

This is a very popular site among birdwatchers. On a spring evening, you can hear Great Horned Owls, Eastern Screech-Owls and Northern Saw-whet Owls. Several unusual species have been noted here over the years: Snowy Egret, Tricolored Heron, Yellow-billed Cuckoo, Red-headed Woodpecker, Loggerhead Shrike, any of which will gladden the heart of a birdwatcher.

Saint-Lazare Area

What to look for : Hawks, owls, nesting passerines, wintering species. *Special species :* Northern Goshawk, Whip-poor-will, Pileated Woodpecker, Gray Jay, Boreal Chickadee, White-winged Crossbill.

Where : This site is west of Montreal in Vaudreuil-Soulanges County. Allow about 45 minutes to reach it by car.

How to get there : From Montreal, take the Metropolitan Autoroute and the Trans-Canada Highway west (Autoroute 40). Then take Autoroute 540 (Exit 32 to Toronto) and Highway 340 west (Exit 3 Cité des Jeunes Boulevard).

When to go : The site is interesting all year round, particularly in winter and during the breeding period, at which time woodland birding is best just after dawn. You will need at least half a day to explore this site.

Site description : Of all the sites in this guide, the Saint-Lazare area has the most forest cover and, with the exception of the Laurentian sites, probably has the most softwood trees. This characteristic is, of course, reflected in the composition of the bird life.

It is one of the few sites near Montreal with nesting Golden-crowned Kinglets, Hermit Thrushes, Solitary Vireos and Dark-

The Saint-Lazare Area

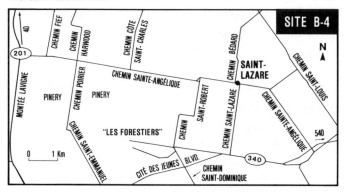

eyed Juncos. White-winged Crossbills, Gray Jays and Boreal Chickadees are not unusual in winter, and Northern Goshawks have nested on several occasions in the summer. Great Horned, Barred and Northern Saw-whet Owls also nest.

Suggested route : When coming from Montreal on Highway 340 (Cité des Jeunes Boulevard), you will notice fallow fields north of the highway after the intersection with Chemin Sainte-Angélique. Check the fields around the small airport, especially along Chemin Saint-Lazare. Rough-legged Hawks and Snowy Owls are found here in winter.

Further west is a huge plantation of 50-year-old pine and spruce that extends north of Highway 340 between Chemin Saint-Robert and Highway 201 (Montée Lavigne). The woods are crossed by many trails, all covered with pine needles. The trails can be approached from two places. You can go to the Centre de plein air les Forestiers, at the north end of Chemin

161

Saint-Dominique, where numerous ski trails are maintained throughout the winter. There is an admission charge. Near the Centre is a huge sand pit with ponds at the bottom visited by shorebirds in late summer.

Other trails in the pine grove can be taken from Chemin Poirier, which is approached by turning north onto Chemin Saint-Emmanuel. The trails cross Chemin Poirier at many points. They are frequented in winter by White-winged Crossbills and occasionally Gray Jays and Boreal Chickadees. It is not unusual to see Pileated Woodpeckers or even Three-toed and Black-backed Woodpeckers. Among the numerous nesting species are Whip-poor-wills, which only reveal their presence at dusk or during the night. A pair of Northern Goshawks and a pair of Great Horned Owls once used the same nest to rear their young at different times in one year. This nest is only a few hundred metres from Chemin Poirier.

Chemin Poirier north joins Chemin Sainte-Angélique which in turn leads to some very picturesque roads such as Chemin Fief, Chemin Harwood and Chemin Côte Saint-Charles. All are worth visiting, particularly Chemin Fief, which goes through a deciduous forest crossed by numerous trails. Northern Goshawks have nested in this forest too, as have Red-shouldered Hawks. You can come back toward Montreal on Chemin Sainte-Angélique east to Highway 340.

Great Horned Owl

Rigaud Area

What to look for : Large flights of hawks in autumn, ducks, passerines. *Special species :* Green-backed Heron, Turkey Vulture, Golden Eagle, Upland Sandpiper, Pileated Woodpecker, Common Raven, Blue-gray Gnatcatcher, Eastern Bluebird, Yellow-throated Vireo.

Where : The Rigaud area is 70 km west of Montreal, near the Ontario border. It takes between 45 and 60 minutes to get there.

How to get there : Autoroute 40 (Trans-Canada Highway) is the main access to this region.

When to go : Birdwatching here is interesting at any time of the year, but exceptional species are most often seen in spring and autumn. You can easily spend a whole day visiting the various sectors in the region.

Special information : The whole area is privately owned, which is a major constraint as permission must be sought before venturing onto any property. Road conditions are another factor to consider, especially in spring.

Site description : The Rigaud landscape is characterized by its forest-covered mountain that rises 230 m from the surrounding agricultural lowlands. The lowlands are comprised of cultivated fields, pastures and fallow lands. The extensive marshes and their dense growth of emerging vegetation along the Ottawa River contribute to the area's diversity of habitat. More than 235 bird species have been recorded in the area in the last 15 years.

More than 180 species have been recorded in spring, the most rewarding season by far. Summer brings about 120 nesting species and about 30 others that are sighted occasionally. Approximately 170 species have been listed for the fall, a spectacular season because of the raptors that stop to feed in the fields surrounding the mountain. Many ducks and other water birds also arrive then, in the many bays along the Ottawa River and the Lake of Two Mountains. More than 70 species have been recorded in the winter in Rigaud; their presence is encouraged by the 150 or so feeding stations maintained by local residents. An impressive number of irregular species has also been noted during the last few years, the most unusual of all being the Fieldfare, a Eurasian species sighted in 1976, and the Harris' Sparrow, a western species sighted in 1987.

Suggested route : There are six routes, each less than 20 km long. They all leave from Autoroute 40 (Trans-Canada Highway).

Route #1, northwest(Exit 1, about 10 km) : From the Ontario-Quebec border, take Exit 1 from Autoroute 40 to the road called Grande-Montée (on the Ontario side) or Interprovincial (on the Quebec side). Go north towards the village of Pointe-

Fortune and the Carillon hydroelectric dam, about 2.5 km from the Trans-Canada Highway.

In spring and fall, there are large numbers of water birds on the Ottawa River near the dam. The road up to the dam gives a good view of the reservoir upstream. Continue east along Boulevard des Outaouais, stopping from time to time to scan the river. About 4.5 km from the dam, after a wide turn in the road, there is a small bridge across from a sand pit. A stop here for a look at the ponds and the fields that are flooded in spring could prove to be most rewarding.

At the intersection with Highway 342, turn left and go to Chemin de la Montée Wilson, which will take you to the Trans-Canada Highway (Exit 2).

Route #2, west (Exit 2, about 20 km) : From Exit 2, take Chemin de la Montée Wilson south to Chemin du Rang Saint-Thomas. This sector is visited by birds of prey in the autumn. The Golden Eagle stops over here, mostly in October or early November, in the fields near a small wood.

Turn left onto Chemin Saint-Thomas and drive about 6 km toward the mountain to the intersection with Chemin du Haut-de-la-Chute, watching for hawks in the lone trees in the fields. Watch the summit as well, as you may see Turkey Vultures or Common Ravens. At Chemin du Haut-de-la-Chute, turn right and go westward to Ontario, checking the river on the left and the farmlands on the right.

The Rigaud Area (routes 1, 2, 3)

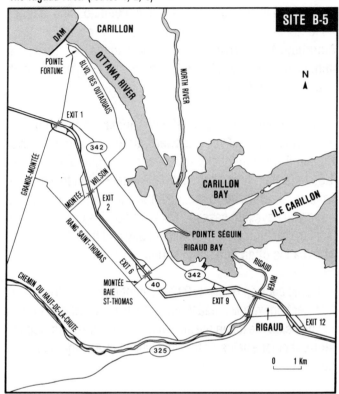

At Chemin de la Grande-Montée, turn right, or north, to come back to Exit 1 at Autoroute 40. Watch both sides of the road for hawks in autumn and Snowy Owls in winter.

Route #3, north-centre (Exit 6, 10 or 20 km) : From Exit 6, take the service road along the north side of Autoroute 40. The road is not very good, but this is the best place to get close-range views of hawks in the autumn. In winter the road is closed, and in spring it is in very poor condition and at times flooded. At the end of the road, you can go to Exit 2 on Autoroute 40 by crossing the overpass to the left. Turn right immediately to return to the Autoroute and the starting point, at Exit 6. This route is about 10 km long.

At Exit 6, take Montée Baie-Saint-Thomas north to Highway 342. This will take you westward, or left, to a lookout over Rigaud Bay where ducks stop over during migration. About 1.5 km farther, take Chemin de la Pointe-Séguin to a marina, where you can leave your car. Come back on foot to scan the pond you have just passed. At the end of this dead-end road is a far-reaching view over Rigaud Bay and the Ottawa River. The road is often flooded in spring.

Come back on Highway 342 and continue west; drive to the intersection with Montée Wilson, 3 km away. Hawks hunt in the fields on the left in the autumn, and ducks and shorebirds stop over in the fields on the right when there is flooding in the spring.

From Montée Wilson, go to Autoroute 40 (Exit 2). The second part of Route #3 is also about 10 km long.

Route #4, northeast (Exit 17, about 15 km) : From Exit 17, turn left and take Montée Lavigne north to the river. This is a good place for hawks. The small wood on the right of the road, just before the railway tracks, attracts woodland birds in the spring.

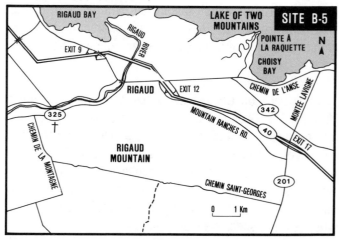

At 2.5 km from the starting point, turn left, or west, onto Chemin de l'Anse. Here you will be driving along Choisy Bay where ducks and shorebirds stop over in spring and autumn. You will need a spotting scope to scan the Lake of Two Mountains.

At 3 km from where Montée Lavigne intersects with Chemin de l'Anse, just before the railway tracks, is Chemin de la Pointe-à-la-Raquette, a stop that should not be missed. This road is virtually impassable, particularly in the spring, because of flooding. Unless you have the proper vehicle, it is best to walk to the end. Drive about 1.5 km to the end of the passable section, near the last houses. There is not much space to park, and you must watch out for soft ground, the ditch and private property. These inconveniences are well worth the trouble because Pointe à la Raquette is an extraordinary birdwatching site. The main habitats are a silver maple grove and a huge marsh dominated by a dense growth of emergent vegetation. Herons, ducks, shorebirds and gulls abound, and warblers and sparrows are found in the wooded portion.

Once back on Chemin de l'Anse, turn right and go to Highway 342 (Chemin des Prairies), a little farther along. Turn left to go east. Not far from here is a place along the road where you can park and look over a marshy area. The sandpit on the south side of the road is inhabited by a colony of Bank Swallows in the summer, and the pools of water are visited by shorebirds. Further on, near Autoroute 40, is a drained marsh where several species are still found.

Complete the circuit by coming back to Exit 17.

Route #5, southeast (Exit 17, about 10 km) : From this exit, go southward on Highway 201. Just after the bridge spanning Rivière à la Raquette, turn right onto Mountain Ranches Road. This sector is thickly wooded and is an excellent place for owls, woodpeckers and several passerines. At 3.5 km from Highway 201, go up Chemin de la Sucrerie to Look-out Street. Go to the end of the street to Clear Creek Lane which in turn leads to Chemin Pointe-Coupée. Leave your car here and hike through the forest to the fallow fields, provided they have not been swallowed up by housing development. Many unusual sightings have been made here: Golden-winged Warbler, Yellow-breasted Chat, Clay-colored and Field Sparrow. Thrushes and warblers are numerous in the spring.

Once back on Mountain Ranches Road, go west toward Rigaud Village, where you can return to Autoroute 40 (Exit 12).

Route #6, south (Exit 17, about 20 km) : From this exit, take Highway 201 south for about 2 km to Chemin Saint-Georges, on the right. This road winds around the top of the mountain to the heart of an almost continuous stretch of forest. You can be sure of seeing Red-shouldered Hawks along the way, as this is where they breed in the spring. After driving about 1 km along Chemin Saint-Georges, look for Blue-gray Gnatcatchers near a small bridge. They have nested in the area on many occasions. This is also a Whip-poor-will haven.

Drive 2.5 km and, after a series of broad curves, park your car well off the road and come back on foot towards the summit. This is a spot where you could easily spend 30 to 60 minutes. This area may soon be spoiled by intensive housing development. In early morning and late evening, the woods ring with the songs of the different thrushes. Vireos, hidden in the foliage, are more difficult to find. Warblers abound and Pileated Woodpeckers visit the area regularly. You may see White-winged Crossbills in the clumps of coniferous trees.

Ganivet Street, about 3 km away, leads to the south slope of the mountain where you can have a pleasant hike through the cedar groves. Return to Chemin Saint-Georges and stop after 1 km across from a sandpit. This type of habitat is usually worth exploring.

Half a kilometre further on, to the right, is Chemin de la Croix, a dirt road that goes to the most noticeable peak in the

Northern Hawk-Owl

region. This is an excellent hawk watching site in spring. A walk through this area will turn up several woodland species.

Once back on Chemin Saint-Georges, turn right onto Chemin de la Montagne. At the bottom of the slope, turn right towards Rigaud. If you have time, stop at the Mont Rigaud ski centre to admire the view.

To get back to Autoroute 40, go to the traffic lights in Rigaud Village. Turn left and you will be heading towards Autoroute 40 (Exit 9).

Sainte-Marthe and Saint-Clet

What to look for : Hawks, sparrows. *Special species :* Turkey Vulture, Rough-legged Hawk, Snowy Owl, Whip-poor-will, Eastern Bluebird, Grasshopper Sparrow, Field Sparrow, Rufous-sided Towhee.

Where : These two agricultural villages are located in Vaudreuil-Soulanges County, south of Rigaud Mountain. You can get there in less than one hour from Montreal.

How to get there : From Montreal, take Autoroute 40 (Trans-Canada Highway) and Highway 201 south (Montée Lavigne, Exit 17).

When to go : Spring and winter are the most active periods of the year here. A half-day is usually sufficient to cover the area.

Site description : The area is mostly pasture land and cultivated fields. North of Sainte-Marthe, however, the Rigaud Mountain foothills are covered with beautiful forest in various stages of growth. These are interspersed with pasture. The fields in this region are particularly interesting in winter and even late fall and early spring. This is when you find Rough-legged Hawks, Red-tailed Hawks, Snowy Owls, Gray Partridge, Horned Larks, Snow Buntings and Lapland Longspurs. The wooded parts of the area are more interesting from May

173

to August. These are good sites for learning the woodland species and those that favour regenerating habitat. There are Red-shouldered Hawks, Turkey Vultures, American Woodcocks, Whip-poor-wills, Eastern Bluebirds, Rufous-sided Towhees, Vesper Sparrows and Field Sparrows. Grasshopper Sparrows are found in the fields where the grass is short.

Suggested route :

Chemin Saint-Henri : When coming from Montreal on Autoroute 40, take Highway 201 south (Montée Lavigne) and turn right onto Chemin Saint-Henri. If you stop near Rivière à la Raquette (0.3 km), you will probably see the Northern Rough-winged Swallows that nest under the bridge. Continue on through the fields and look for Eastern Bluebirds, which are most likely to be in the vicinity of the nest boxes put up by the Province of Quebec Society for the Protection of Birds. About 1.0 km from the bridge, the road goes through a wooded section where Red-shouldered Hawks and other woodland species nest. The fields on the south side of the road are visited by American Woodcocks, Eastern Bluebirds, Vesper Sparrows, Field Sparrows, Grasshopper Sparrows and Indigo Buntings. Turkey Vultures are often sighted here. At the Chemin Saint-Henri and Montée Saint-Henri intersection (4.6 km) is a good lookout for watching migrating hawks in April. A woodland road about 500 m west of Montée Saint-Henri links Chemin Saint-Henri to Chemin Saint-Georges in Rigaud. The colourful Mourning Warbler, Scarlet Tanager and Indigo Bunting are common all along here in summer.

The Sainte-Marthe Area

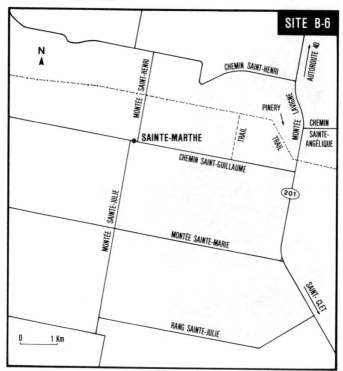

SITE B-6

N

AUTOROUTE 40

CHEMIN SAINT-HENRI

MONTÉE SAINT-HENRI

PINERY

MONTÉE LAVIGNE

CHEMIN SAINTE-ANGÉLIQUE

SAINTE-MARTHE

TRAIL

TRAIL

CHEMIN SAINT-GUILLAUME

201

MONTÉE SAINTE-JULIE

MONTÉE SAINTE-MARIE

SAINT-CLET

0   1 Km

RANG SAINTE-JULIE

The Sainte-Marthe pinery : This site is approached from the intersection of Highway 201 (Montée Lavigne) and Chemin Sainte-Angélique (1.2 km south of Chemin Saint-Henri). You can leave your car on the side of the road and walk along the many trails in the pine grove. Whip-poor-wills are usually present but are difficult to spot. Listen for them at dusk, especially in May and June.

Red-shouldered Hawk

The Saint-Clet Area

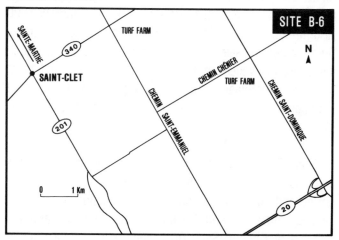

West of the pine grove, a trail runs northwest below the Hydro-Québec power line. It then veers off and joins Chemin Saint-Guillaume, going south. The hike along this path and back along Chemin Saint-Guillaume and the highway takes about two hours. Along with the Whip-poor-wills, the most characteristic species during the summer are Red-breasted Nuthatch, Hermit Thrush, Gray Catbird, Brown Thrasher, Nashville Warbler, Yellow-rumped Warbler, Blackburnian Warbler, Rufous-sided Towhee, Field and Vesper Sparrows. Clay-colored Sparrows have also been seen here.

The agricultural land : There are many roads through the fields south of Sainte-Marthe and around the Saint-Clet area. The main roads are Highway 201 and Highway 340 (Cité-des-Jeunes Boulevard) which lead to Chemin Saint-Emmanuel, Chemin Saint-Dominique, Rang Sainte-Julie and Montée

Sainte-Julie. In winter, Snowy Owls and Rough-egged Hawks are sometimes seen in great numbers. For instance, 20 Rough-legged Hawks and 5 Snowy Owls were seen within a 5-km radius of Saint-Clet on December 31, 1980. Such invasions are cyclical, and one cannot hope to see such great numbers every year. This is also a good area for Lapland Longspurs, especially Montée Sainte-Julie near Montée Sainte-Marie.

Along Chemin Saint-Dominique and Chemin Chénier are colonies of reed grass visited by Short-eared Owls, mostly in spring and fall. The turf farms at the junction of Cité-des-Jeunes Boulevard and Chemin Saint-Emmanuel and the junction of Chemin Saint-Dominique and Chemin Chénier sometimes attract large gatherings of Lesser Golden-Plovers in August and early September (see Site B7).

The Coteau-Station Turf Farms

What to look for : Shorebirds. *Special species :* Lesser Golden-Plover, Buff-breasted Sandpiper.

Where : This site is west of Montreal in Vaudreuil-Soulanges County. It takes about one hour to get there from Montreal.

How to get there : Take Autoroute 20 west, Exit 12 and Rue Sauvé toward the village of Coteau-Station on the left.

When to go : Shorebirds are seen only in late August and early September. It takes about an hour to explore this site.

Site description : In Coteau-Station vast areas of turf are cultivated to be sold. Lesser Golden-Plovers and Buff-breasted Sandpipers, two species that breed in the Arctic, are particularly drawn to this habitat of fields of short grass. Their nesting habitat is the relatively dry tundra of grass and moss. Lesser Golden-Plovers are sighted every year at Coteau-Station, sometimes even in flocks of hundreds. Buff-breasted Sandpipers are much rarer and are not seen every year; usually one bird is seen; once there were three. Black-bellied Plovers and Baird's Sandpipers have also been seen here, and there are great numbers of Killdeers and Horned Larks at this time as well.

Song Sparrow

The Coteau-Station Turf Farms

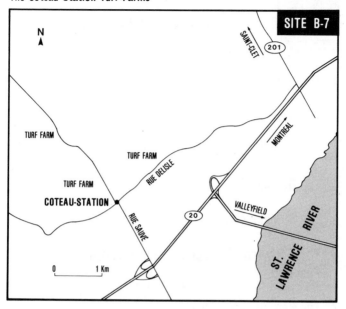

Suggested route : From the village, drive along Rue Delisle in both directions (east and west). Another road, which is unpaved, goes north through the turf farms to other, smaller farms beyond a small wood. From Coteau-Station, you can go to the turf farms in Saint-Clet, at the corner of Chemin Saint-Dominique and Chemin Chénier. To get there, take Rue Delisle east, turn left onto Highway 201 north and right onto Cité des Jeunes Boulevard (Highway 340). A spotting scope is essential here.

Southwest of Montreal

1. The Beauharnois Dam

2. The Saint-Etienne-de-Beauharnois Area

3. The Valleyfield-Saint-Barbe Area

4. The Dundee Area

5. The Huntingdon Area

6. The Pitch Pine Ecological Reserve and the Saint-Pierre Peat Bog

7. The Hemmingford Area

Southwest of Montreal

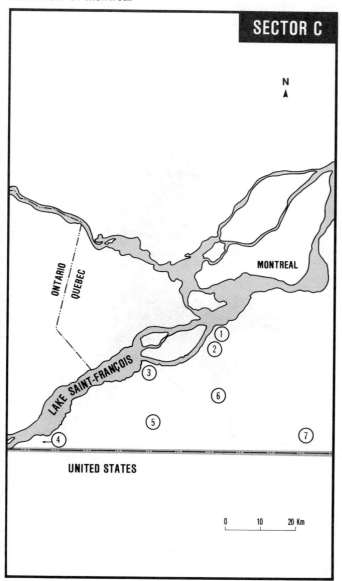

SECTOR C

N

MONTREAL

ONTARIO
QUEBEC

LAKE SAINT-FRANÇOIS

① ②
③
⑥
⑤
④
⑦

UNITED STATES

0   10   20 Km

Black Tern

Beauharnois Dam

What to look for : An excellent site in the fall for gulls, terns, diving ducks and shorebirds; 23 species of laridae have been observed here. *Special species :* Little Gull, Common Black-headed Gull, Thayer's Gull, Lesser Black-backed Gull, Black-legged Kittiwake, Sabine's Gull.

Where : The Beauharnois dam is about 30 km southwest of Montreal on Lake Saint-Louis, a 30-minute drive from down-town Montreal.

How to get there : From Montreal, take the Mercier, Champlain or Jacques Cartier bridge to Highway 132 west. The dam is just west of Beauharnois on Highway 132.

When to go : Late summer (August to mid-September) and late autumn (late October to mid-January) are the two periods when the gulls gather in greatest numbers. It takes at least one hour to explore the site, longer when there are large numbers of birds.

Special information : This site affords little protection from rough weather, especially from the strong winds off Lake Saint-Louis. Be sure to wear warm clothing in late fall and winter. A spotting scope is practically indispensable here.

Site description : The small industrial town of Beauharnois does not strike one as being productive birdwatching territory. Nothing indicates that in the fall this town, which is plagued by industrial pollution, turns into the setting of an ornithological panorama unique in Quebec. Yet every year the hydroelectric dam at the east end of the Beauharnois canal becomes a backdrop for the thousands of gulls that gather there to rest and feed before leaving for warmer areas. Their main food is fish of all kinds, including alewives, the small, silver-sided fish of the herring family that come to reproduce in fresh water in the spring and return to salt water in the fall.

A two-act play is staged here, with the first act beginning in August and continuing until mid-September. Terns are the featured attraction at this time – hundreds of Common and Black Terns. There are also a few Bonaparte's Gulls, Little Gulls and, on occasion, much rarer species such as Sabine's Gull (now seen almost every year in September), Common Black-headed Gull, Black-legged Kittiwake, Franklin's Gull, Forster's Tern and even Parasitic Jaeger.

Then comes a long intermission. Towards the end of October, the second act begins, bringing a second migratory wave of a few Bonaparte's Gulls and, above all, ever-increasing numbers of Ring-billed Gulls, which by mid-November number about 10,000. The Ring-billed Gulls are gradually replaced by Herring Gulls until mid-December, when there are about 10,000 Herring Gulls and almost no Ring-billed Gulls. As the weather grows colder, the number of Herring Gulls gradually decreases. Other species arrive on the scene, but in much smaller numbers – Great Black-backed Gull, Iceland Gull and

The Beauharnois Dam

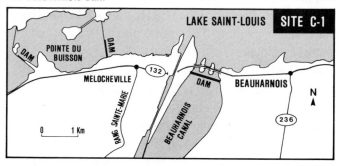

Glaucous Gull. By the end of January almost all the players have left. The second act occasionally brings rarer species such as the Mew Gull, Thayer's Gull, Lesser Black-backed Gull, Black-legged Kittiwake (seen every year in November), Ivory Gull (seen only twice, in January), and California Gull (seen once, in October 1989).

By spring the stage is almost empty. The only actors are Bonaparte's Gulls, now in breeding plumage, Common Terns and a few Ring-billed Gulls that nest near the dam.

The autumn display at the Beauharnois dam is not entirely taken up by gulls and terns, although they definitely have centre stage. Lake Saint-Louis also attracts several thousand diving ducks, including Canvasbacks, Redheads and some-times rarer species. Shorebirds are also seen on the lawns near the dam. Beauharnois definitely offers the birdwatcher a full programme.

Suggested route : The water flows through three canals in the rock in front of the dam. These are separated by strips of lawn. The bridge on Highway 132 crosses the canals a few hundred metres in front of the dam. You can either park your car on the east side of the bridge or on the west side along the third canal. In cold weather you can use a spotting scope to scan the canals and Lake Saint-Louis from the comfort of your car. You can walk across the bridge on the sidewalk to the lawns for a closer look at the birds feeding in the canals. This makes for easy viewing of the gulls resting there, provided you move unobtrusively so as not to disturb them. Sometimes there are other birds resting quite far out on Lake Saint-Louis or, in early winter, on the ice floes. Do take the time to study each group of birds carefully; an unusual species wandering amongst several thousand gulls might easily be overlooked and found only after several hours of scrutinizing. You should also explore the west side of the third canal up to the mouth of the Beauharnois canal; this spot affords the best light conditions for studying Lake Saint-Louis, especially in the afternoon. This is where rafts of scaup can be seen in November.

A visit to the Beauharnois dam in the fall can be combined with a short stop at the Pointe-du-Buisson archeological park. Drive about 4 km west on Highway 132 and turn right on Rue Emond. At this time of year there are many gulls resting in the rapids across from the point. At the end of October and beginning of November shorebirds can be seen on the rocks in the rapids. These include Dunlin, Pectoral Sandpiper, White-rumped Sandpiper and at times Purple Sandpiper, a rare visitant in southwestern Quebec.

The Saint-Etienne-de-Beauharnois Area

What to look for : Marsh birds, hawks, owls, blackbirds. *Special species :* Least Bittern, Common Moorhen, American Coot, Black Tern, Willow Flycatcher, Yellow-headed Blackbird.

Where : South of Beauharnois, at least 45 minutes by car from downtown Montreal.

How to get there : After taking the Mercier, Champlain, Victoria or Jacques Cartier Bridge or the Lafontaine Tunnel from Montreal, follow Highway 132 to Beauharnois. At Beauharnois, turn left onto Highway 236 (Chemin Saint-Louis) to Saint-Etienne.

When to go : The ponds along the Beauharnois canal are particularly active in spring and summer. The farm fields in this area are especially interesting in the fall, winter and early spring. It may take several hours to cover the site completely.

Site description : The village of Saint-Etienne is surrounded by farmland used primarily for growing corn. A large uncultivated stretch of land, owned by Hydro-Québec and bordering the Beauharnois canal, is the main point of interest in this area. Dominated by reed grass and clumps of willow, the site is invaded by hundreds of thousands of blackbirds during migration : Red-winged Blackbirds, Common Grackles, Brown-

189

headed Cowbirds and European Starlings. These birds spend the night here and during the day move out to feed in the nearby cornfields.

Ducks Unlimited has created a few ponds in this area to encourage wildfowl reproduction. One of these ponds is the best site in this area for American Coot. In 1988, a brood of Ruddy Ducks, a rare species in the Montreal area, was sighted on this pond. The Canadian Wildlife Service recently designated the land along both sides of the Beauharnois canal – 36 km^2 in all – as a resting area, which means that duck hunting is now prohibited. Along with the water birds are raptors that prefer moist habitat, such as Northern Harrier and Short-eared Owl.

Because this area attracts blackbirds, some are inclined to overwinter. In late fall and winter they can be found scattered amongst the corn driers and bird feeding stations in nearby towns such as Beauharnois and Léry. At dusk, all the birds converge on the reed grass to spend the night. For the past few years, a few Yellow-headed Blackbirds, a western species, have occurred in this area in winter, joining up with flocks of Brown-headed Cowbirds.

Several hawk species visit the farmland around Saint-Etienne during migration and in winter : Northern Harrier, Red-tailed Hawk, Rough-legged Hawk, Snowy Owl, Short-eared Owl. The woodlots harbour Great Horned Owls. Horned Larks, Snow Buntings and Lapland Longspurs can be seen on the roadside when the fields are covered with snow.

The Saint-Étienne-de-Beauharnois Area

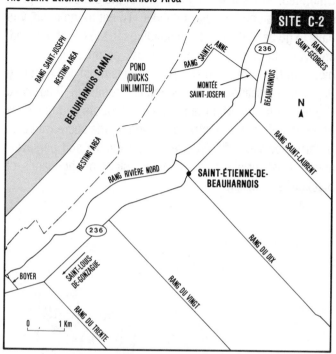

Suggested route : Take Highway 236 (Chemin Saint-Louis) from Beauharnois to Montée Saint-Joseph (5.2 km). Cross the Saint-Louis River and Rang Rivière Nord and take Rang Sainte-Anne. A pair of Great Horned Owls has been living in the small woods along this road for several years, and they can often be heard hooting at the end of the day, especially in February and March. It is not unusual to see Short-eared and Snowy Owls in the neighbouring fields in winter. Rang Sainte-Anne comes to a dead-end near a pond dug by Ducks

Unlimited. You can get a good view of the birds on the pond by walking along the adjacent dyke. To get to the pond, you have to go behind some farm buildings to the left of the road, and you should, out of courtesy, ask permission from the owner of the farm to do so. This pond is most active during the nesting season, with its many broods of Pied-billed Grebes, Common Moorhens, American Coots and the Black Terns that dive-bomb intruders. Finding the secretive Least Bittern, however, will require more patience and perseverance. Dusk brings the fascinating sight of thousands of blackbirds returning to roost.

Savannah Sparrow

Once back on Rang Rivière Nord, you could head west, checking the fields and areas around the corncribs for blackbirds, which can be sighted even in winter. This is where Yellow-headed Blackbirds, though few and far between, are most often spotted. You could continue on to Montée Boyer and come back towards Saint-Etienne on Highway 236 east. Many of the roads that intersect Highway 236 are worth visiting in the winter, especially early and late in the season. These are Rang du Trente, Rang du Vingt, Rang du Dix, Rang Saint-Laurent and Rang Saint-Georges. Here you might see flocks of Snow Buntings and Horned Larks, a few hawks and, with luck, a Yellow-headed Blackbird.

You can come back to Beauharnois by Highway 236 east or by the north side of the Beauharnois canal. If you decide on the second alternative (not shown on the map), then you should go west on Highway 236 to Saint-Louis-de-Gonzague, turn right on Avenue du Pont and take the bridge that crosses the Beauharnois canal. On the north side of the canal there is a small private road that crosses this land, which belongs to Hydro-Québec. If the gate is open, you can explore this area, which has several ponds dug by Ducks Unlimited. To get back to Beauharnois, you will have to come back through the gate, drive north on Pie XII Boulevard and turn onto Rang Saint-Joseph, which will take you to Highway 132 by Rang Sainte-Marie. The last part of Rang Saint-Joseph and Rang Sainte-Marie follow the wildfowl resting area north of the Beauharnois canal. Willow Flycatchers are common in summer in the clumps of willows in this area.

In winter the Saint-Etienne area and the Beauharnois dam *(Site C1)* can be visited in one trip.

The Valleyfield - Sainte-Barbe Area

What to look for : Wildfowl, hawks. *Special species :* Horned Grebe, Red-necked Grebe, Greater White-fronted Goose, Golden Eagle, Willow Flycatcher.

Where : South of Valleyfield, at the eastern tip of Lake Saint-François – a 60-minute drive from Montreal.

How to get there : From Montreal take the Mercier, Champlain, Victoria or Jacques Cartier Bridge or the Lafontaine Tunnel. Then follow Highway 132 to Saint-Timothée where you take Autoroute 30 west. Cross the Larocque Bridge over the Beauharnois canal south of Valleyfield. When leaving from the west end of the Island of Montreal, take Autoroute 20 west and Highway 201 south to where it joins Autoroute 30.

When to go : This site is only worth visiting in spring, especially from late March through late May. It may take a full day to visit the entire area.

Site description : The land between the Beauharnois canal and the village of Sainte-Barbe is predominantly agricultural, with corn as the main crop. The shore along Lake Saint-François is completely lined with cottages.

For a short period in spring, from late March through mid-April, the fields directly north of Sainte-Barbe attract large gatherings of Canada Geese, Snow Geese, and dabbling ducks. Recent soil drainage, however, has reduced this period considerably, sometimes to only a few days around the end of March. The Canada Geese also sojourn on Lake Saint-François at this time, and flocks are continually moving between the lake and the flooded fields. Rafts of diving ducks begin appearing on the lake as early as March. These are mainly scaups, goldeneyes and mergansers. Often they will delight the birder by venturing onto the Beauharnois canal and allowing themselves to be viewed at close range.

Along with the waterfowl are the hawks that migrate north around the eastern tip of Lake Saint-François. This is where they funnel around the lake, taking advantage of the warm updrafts from the land. Each year, all the hawk species that nest in Quebec are sighted as they fly over this site, most of them in April. With patience you might even turn up a Bald or Golden Eagle. Mid-April is the best time for Golden Eagles. Broad-winged Hawks are the most abundant, with flights of over 500 occasionally observed in the space of one day; this usually occurs between April 24 and May 9. Large numbers of Red-tailed Hawks and Ospreys also pass over in April. Turkey Vultures are being increasingly observed between mid-April and early May.

Suggested route : Take Highway 132 from Valleyfield and cross the Beauharnois canal by the Larocque Bridge. Turn right just after the bridge. Hawk watchers refer to this site as "Eagle Crossing" *(Site 1).* The best way to spot the hawks is to ensconce yourself near the bridge and scan the southern horizon with binoculars or a spotting scope. This requires a lot of patience and perseverance. Weather is an important factor too, as hawks only migrate under favourable conditions, namely in light southerly or easterly winds. The birder should be familiar with flight patterns and silhouettes, as this is often the only means of identifying these birds.

West of the Larocque Bridge is a road that follows the Beauharnois canal on Hydro-Québec land *(Site 2)*. If the gate is open, you can explore the road by car. Often you will be rewarded by close-range views of several species of diving ducks and sometimes Horned and Red-necked Grebes. Follow the road until you come to Chemin du Petit-Canal, which goes along Lake Saint-François *(Site 3)*. Here too are many species of diving ducks, including Canvasbacks.

If you prefer to hawk watch away from the traffic noise at the Larocque Bridge, you can find a quieter site a bit further south. Continue west on Highway 132 and turn right onto Chemin de la Baie, about 1 km south of the bridge. Migrating hawks are often seen along this little-travelled route *(Site 4)*, and in summer Willow Flycatchers live in the shrubby areas.

If you continue west on Chemin de la Baie, you will come to Chemin du Petit-Canal, mentioned above. After Chemin de la Baie crosses Chemin Seigneurial, it goes through fields – flooded in spring – until it joins Highway 132. Note that the last part of Chemin de la Baie is usually in very bad condition during the spring thaw. Every spring up to 5,000 Canada Geese gather on either side of the road and in the fields west of Highway 132 *(Site 5)*. Snow Geese are being sighted in increasing numbers each year, along with the occasional

The Valleyfield - Sainte-Barbe Area

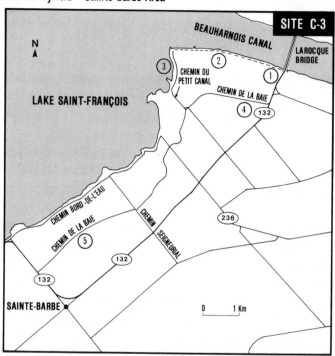

Greater White-fronted Goose. Northern Pintails are the most common of the dabbling ducks you will see foraging in the fields. Snowy Owls also occur in spring. When you get to the end of Chemin de la Baie, you can go back to Valleyfield by Highway 132 east (on the left) or by Highway 132 west (on the right) and Chemin Bord-de-l'eau along Lake Saint-François.

The Dundee Area

What to look for : Herons, ducks, rails. *Special species :* Great Egret, Redhead, Red-headed Woodpecker, Willow Flycatcher, Sedge Wren.

Where : Dundee is located in the southwestern corner of the province in Huntingdon County, about 90 km from Montreal. The trip should take 75 to 90 minutes from Montreal.

How to get there : From downtown Montreal or from the east end of the Island of Montreal, take the Mercier, Champlain, or Jacques Cartier bridge or the Lafontaine Tunnel, and follow Highway 132 west on the south shore of the St. Lawrence River. From the west end of Montreal Island, take Autoroute 20 west and cross the river at Valleyfield by the Monseigneur-Langlois bridge; from Valleyfield follow the signs to Highway 132 west. A third way to get there is by Autoroute 20 west to Autoroute 401, crossing the river at Cornwall, Ontario. From there, take U.S. Highway 37 east and watch for signs to Saint-Régis.

When to go : Birding is interesting year-round in the Dundee area, but spring and summer are the most productive seasons. Winter can be rewarding, especially during the years of northern owl invasions. The best time of the day is, of course, early morning, particularly during the breeding season. A minimum of 3 hours is needed to visit all the sites, but 4 to 6 hours would certainly be a good investment.

Special information : The unpaved roads may be in very bad condition in early spring, and you will need rubber boots in the marshes. A spotting scope is definitely an asset in this open habitat. Be sure to take any papers you may need to cross the border, as some sites are only accessible via the U.S.

Site description : With its vast expanse of freshwater marshes, the Dundee area is without doubt one of the most remarkable birding sites in southern Quebec. About two-thirds of the area shown on the accompanying map is in fact marshland, the remainder being covered with a variety of forest habitats. The western portion of nearby Lake Saint-François, which encompasses about 60 low-lying islands, also provides excellent habitat for marsh birds. In 1971, the Canadian Wildlife Service of Environment Canada, recognizing the value of this area, created the Lake Saint-François National Wildlife Area, a representative territory of 12 km^2 along the south shore of Lake Saint-François. The other areas shown on the map include the Akwesasne Indian Reserve and some private properties at the tip of Hopkins and Fraser points.

A study published by the Canadian Wildlife Service in 1982 reports that 265 species of birds have been found within the 300 km^2 that surround the reserve; 200 have been seen inside the reserve and 110 have nested. Recent estimates indicate that about 130 species nest in the territory shown on the map.

The Dundee area is a well-known waterfowl breeding site. Canada Goose and 13 species of ducks, including Redhead and Lesser Scaup, have nested there. Lake Saint-François is also an important staging area for ducks and geese, where an estimated 70,000 birds, mainly diving ducks, stop over during migration.

The area is also a productive site for herons: American Bittern, Least Bittern, Great Blue Heron, Great Egret, Green-backed Heron, and Black-crowned Night-Heron all nest there. The last four species have been found nesting in a mixed colony on Dickerson Island. This island is the only site in Quebec where the Great Egret is known to nest, the first nests having been discovered in 1984. The population appears to be small, yet 14 birds were counted in a single day in August 1983, and six nests were found in 1985.

Dundee is not particularly good for raptors, although the Northern Harrier is common in the area. Ospreys are common only during spring migration, and Bald and Golden Eagles have been sighted sporadically. In the last few years, Turkey Vultures have been reported with increasing frequency, particularly during spring.

Since 1970, the Dundee area has attracted Great Gray Owls in invasion years, as indicated by the sighting of nine birds there in the winter of 1978-79 and 15 birds on January 15, 1984.

Dundee is also a haven for rails, the Virginia Rail and Sora being the most abundant. It may be that the Yellow Rail nests here, as it has been sighted on a few occasions in the area in May and June. Nesting, however, has not yet been confirmed.

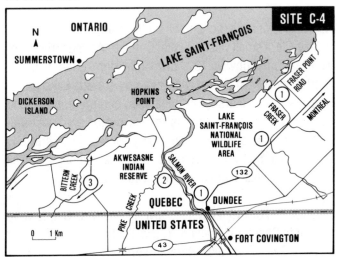

Passerines having an affinity for moist habitat are very common around Dundee. The most abundant of these during the nesting season are Swamp Sparrow, Common Yellowthroat, Yellow Warbler, Veery and Red-winged Blackbird. Two special species for the Dundee area are Willow Flycatcher and Sedge Wren, which are very uncommon in Quebec. A study made during the summer of 1983 revealed an unsuspected abundance of these two species: 25 territorial males of the former and 28 males of the latter were counted in the National Wildlife Area. This is probably the highest density for these two species in southern Quebec.

Other species that rarely nest in southern Quebec but can occasionally be found in the Dundee area include Red-headed Woodpecker, Yellow-billed Cuckoo, and Loggerhead Shrike.

Suggested route :

The Cazaville area (not shown on the map): Begin your trip in Cazaville, a small village east of Dundee. As you arrive from Montreal on Highway 132, turn right onto Chemin Saint-Charles west. This road will take you toward Lake Saint-François and the marshes dominated by emergent vegetation. The many canals and streets in this sector are lined with summer cottages. Look for Willow Flycatchers in the shrubby marshes along 142nd Avenue and a small colony of Black Terns in the shallow marsh along 148th Avenue.

At the end of 148th Avenue, turn left onto Rue Gagnon and right onto Chemin Trépanier. You will come to a public wharf on Lake Saint-François. Here, in spring, you can study the rafts of diving ducks with a spotting scope. Follow Chemin Trépanier south to come back to Highway 132.

A little further west, north of Highway 132, are two parallel roads 400 m apart. These roads, Chemin de la Pointe-Leblanc and Montée Gordon, cross a shallow marsh. Between the roads are Green-backed Heron, Wood Duck, Virginia Rail, Common Snipe, and, in the shrubbier areas, Willow Flycatcher and Sedge Wren. Come back to Highway 132 west and continue on to Fraser Point Road.

The Lake Saint-François National Wildlife Area (Site 1): This area is bordered to the east by Fraser Point Road and to the south by Highway 132. Turn right onto Fraser Point Road and stop alongside the adjacent marsh for Virginia Rail and

Sora. Sedge Wrens have also been heard here. At the end, turn round and come back to Highway 132.

When heading towards Dundee, watch the large dead trees on the right for Red-headed Woodpeckers. In winter, the fields to the south of the road are hunting grounds for Rough-legged Hawk, Red-tailed Hawk, Snowy Owl and Northern Shrike. In spring, thousands of ducks gather in the flooded fields. During invasion years, as in 1979 and 1984, several very tame Great Gray Owls were seen on both sides of the road.

At the present time, Dundee has no interpretation programme or observation facilities, except for a boardwalk built just outside the town in 1983. It has since deteriorated and must be used with caution. There are several duck species nesting along the boardwalk, and Red-headed Woodpeckers and Sedge Wrens have been seen close by.

Hopkins Point (Site 2) : This site and the next *(Site 3)* are accessible only after crossing the international border, as there is no bridge across the Salmon River on the Quebec side. Drive for 1.3 km from the border at Dundee to Fort Covington. Cross the river on a steel deck bridge, drive to the end of the street and then turn right. The road crosses a railroad track and then a second bridge over a branch of the river. At 0.2 km after the second bridge, a right turn will take you to Hopkins Point Road. This narrow road goes through a wooded section where passerines abound. It then crosses a huge marsh where Willow Flycatcher, Sedge Wren, ducks and rails are found in large numbers.

Just before Pike Creek is a worthwhile stop where Sedge Wren and Yellow Rail have been observed on the left side of the road. Beyond the bridge the road is private property. Cars are not allowed here, but there seems to be no objection if anyone enters on foot.

The Akwesasne Indian Reserve and Bittern Creek (Site 3):

When you come back to Fort Covington, take Highway 43 west towards the Akwesasne Reserve. Drive for 4.3 km and turn right onto a gravel road. After 1.5 km, you will be back in Quebec. Here the road crosses about 1 km of swampy woodland. At the end of the road, turn left and cross the marshes along Bittern Creek. Great Egrets feed regularly here. (If you want to see Great Egrets on their nests, take a boat from Summerstown, Ontario.) There are various species of herons, rails and ducks in this marsh and a colony of Black Terns. At the end of the road, turn right and follow the Lake Saint-François shoreline. There is a little bridge at the mouth of Bittern Creek that offers an excellent view of the lake and the possibility of spotting Redheads. Willow Flycatchers and Sedge Wrens are other possible sightings.

Red-headed Woodpecker

Huntingdon Area

What to look for : Exceptionally large numbers of nesting species, especially warblers and sparrows. *Special species :* Cooper's Hawk, Yellow-throated Vireo, Golden-winged Warbler, Cerulean Warbler, Field Sparrow, Henslow's Sparrow.

Where : This site is about 60 km southwest of Montreal and can usually be reached by car in 60 minutes.

How to get there : Take Highway 138 west by crossing the Mercier Bridge. Drive through Châteauguay, Mercier, Sainte-Martine and Ormstown to Huntingdon. When coming from the west end of Montreal, take Autoroute 20 west and Highway 201 south to Highway 138 in Ormstown.

When to go : The most productive seasons are spring and summer, especially between May 15 and July 15. It is best to arrive very early and bird all morning. Allow four to five hours to explore the whole area.

Special information : You should seek permission before venturing onto much of this land as it is mostly private property. There are few cars here. Nonetheless, if you leave your car, make sure it is parked well out of the way of traffic.

Site description : Most of this site is in the municipality of Hinchinbrook, and includes two picturesque little villages,

Herdman and Rockburn. Two-thirds of the area is covered by forest in various stages of regrowth. This includes mature stands, particularly of maple, and a few stands of pine and hemlock. The rest of the territory is ploughed and fallow land, pasture and a few orchards, all of which contribute to the diversity of habitat. There is little moist habitat here. There are no sizable marshes, only a few streams and beaver ponds, so there are few water birds. Despite this, the area is exceptionally rich: about 130 species nest here every summer. Also of interest are the large mammals – White-tailed Deer, Coyote and Black Bear.

Cooper's Hawk, Broad-winged Hawk, Red-shouldered Hawk and American Kestrel all nest here and, in all likelihood, Red-tailed Hawk and Northern Goshawk. Large numbers of Red-tailed Hawks and Rough-legged Hawks visit the cultivated fields during fall migration and in winter. Turkey Vultures are seen mainly during spring migration. Barred Owl, Great Horned Owl and Northern Saw-whet Owl nest, and Snowy Owls often visit the cultivated fields in winter.

The five vireo species that nest in Quebec are all found here, and this is one of the few sites where the Solitary Vireo nests in the Montreal area. But the area is especially interesting for its impressive numbers of nesting warblers – 19 species in all, including Golden-winged, Cerulean, Magnolia and Pine. Thirty or so Golden-winged Warblers were counted here in 1984, the largest concentration in the Montreal area.

Eleven species of sparrows have been observed in this area during the nesting season. These include Clay-colored, Field,

Grasshopper, Henslow's and Lincoln's. Henslow's Sparrow is a particularly interesting species for this area. This bird, which has only been sighted three times in Quebec in the past 20 years, was seen twice in Hinchinbrook, in July 1985 and June 1989.

Other species of note are Wild Turkey, which is being reported more often, and Red-headed Woodpecker, which has nested at least once.

Suggested route :

The municipality of Huntingdon (not shown on the map): When you arrive from Montreal on Highway 138, stop at the Rest-O-Route restaurant, just before the bridge. Use the parking lot beside the Châteauguay River. A few Northern Rough-winged Swallows nest along the river just opposite and are easily spotted in spring and early summer. There are House Finches year-round on Prince Street, between Bouchette and Lake Streets. To get there, turn right on Prince Street, across from the bridge.

Gowan Road : When you come from Montreal on Highway 138, turn left onto Highway 202 east. Gowan Road is 8.2 km from the bridge over the Châteauguay River in Huntingdon. Be on the lookout as there is no sign. You will find a little dirt road that goes through approximately 8 km of dense woods. Few such idyllic spots remain in southwestern Quebec today. There is little traffic; you can park your car at an entrance to a wood road and walk at will, for birding is productive all along

The Huntingdon Area

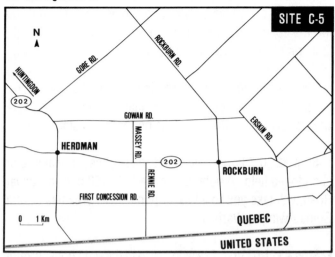

The Huntingdon Area (Gowan Road)

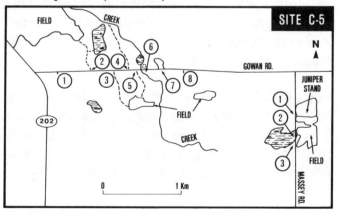

209

this road. The wood roads are not marked and some are heavily overgrown, so be careful not to get lost. The mileage for the following suggested stops is measured from the junction of Gowan Road and Highway 202.

• **Stop #1** (0.3 km) : During nesting season, there are Barred Owls, Pileated Woodpeckers, Solitary Vireos and several warbler species in the hemlocks on the south side.

• **Stop #2** (0.7 km) : The wood road to the left leads to an abandoned field. A right turn at the fork, 350 m from Gowan Road, will take you to a beaver pond. This area has several Golden-winged Warblers.

• **Stop #3** (1.0 km) : The wood road to the right goes through mature maple woods where Barred Owls probably nest. Walk for 550 m to a fork where you turn left. The damp woods on the left of this path harbour Cerulean Warbler, Yellow-throated Vireo and Northern Waterthrush. The path ends a little further on in an abandoned field. Check the edge for Golden-winged Warblers and Indigo Buntings.

• **Stop #4** (1.2 km): The path to the left goes through sapling woods and then more mature forest, ending on the east side of the beaver pond mentioned above for Stop #2. It is heavily overgrown. Golden-winged Warblers and Yellow-throated Vireos are found all along, the vireo in the more mature habitat.

• **Stop #5** (1.3 km) : Just before the creek is a path leading to a field mentioned for Stop #3.

- **Stop #6** (1.4 km) : The road to the left leads to a beaver pond near an incinerator. There are several Golden-winged Warblers around this pond.

- **Stop #7** (1.6 km) : On the left of the road is an old overgrown dump. Here you will find Indigo Buntings and Golden-winged Warblers.

- **Stop #8** (1.9 km) : In the forest regrowth to the left of the road are several warbler species, including Mourning and Golden-winged. "Brewster's" Warbler, a hybrid of the Golden-winged and Blue-winged Warblers, nested here in 1984. The more mature woods to the right of the road are nesting habitat for Cerulean Warbler and Yellow-throated Vireo. A Cerulean Warbler carrying food was observed 300 m from the road in 1986.

- **Stop #9** (4.1 km) : In the pine woods to the right of the road are Pine Warbler, Solitary Vireo and Hermit Thrush. These species can be seen from the road.

Massey Road : This road goes to Highway 202; it is 3.3 km from the western end of Gowan Road.

- **Stop #1** (0.5 km) : The path to the left goes through a juniper stand where Magnolia Warblers nest. During the nesting season, Northern Saw-whet Owls and Barred Owls have been heard at night, just before this stop.

- **Stop #2** (0.8 km) : The swamp to the right is Wood Duck nesting habitat. Red-headed Woodpeckers nested here in

Golden-winged Warbler

1984, and Great Horned Owls, Northern Saw-whet Owls and Pileated Woodpeckers probably nest here as well.

• **Stop #3** (0.9 km) : On the right of the road is a field with some juniper and young pine. This is a spot for Field Sparrows and Rufous-sided Towhees.

Erskin Road :

• **Stop #1** : Whip-poor-wills nest at the corner of Erskin and Gowan roads. Barred Owls and Great Horned Owls live in the majestic stand of maples that lines the right side of the road to the next stop.

• **Stop #2** (0.9 km) : On the left is a path through a stand of young pines. Indigo Buntings are much in evidence around the edge of this sector.

Rockburn Road : Approach this road from Highway 138 in the village of Dewittville (not shown on the map). In the cultivated fields and pastures before Gore Road are Rough-legged Hawk, Red-tailed Hawk and Snowy Owl, mainly during migration and in winter.

South of Gore Road, Rockburn Road goes through a mixed stand of forest regrowth. In this moist habitat are Yellow-throated Vireo, Solitary Vireo, Broad-winged Hawk, Barred Owl, Great Horned Owl and several species of warblers. Unfortunately there are not many safe parking spots here.

First Concession Road : This road goes in an east-west direction through habitat consisting mainly of cultivated fields and orchards. This is a good place to see Upland Sandpiper, Horned Lark and Eastern Bluebird. Bluebirds are particularly abundant in the fall in an area about 1.5 km west of Rennie Road. Clay-colored Sparrow and Henslow's Sparrow have been sighted along this road. As you head west to the Châteauguay River, you will see one of the oldest covered bridges in the region, the Powerscourt Bridge, built in 1861 (not shown on the map).

The Pitch Pine Ecological Reserve and the Saint-Pierre Peat Bog

What to look for : Nesting passerines. *Special species :* Black-billed Cuckoo, Whip-poor-will, Rufous-sided Towhee, Field Sparrow, Lincoln's Sparrow.

Where : The area is found southwest of Montreal in Saint-Antoine-Abbé and Saint-Jean-Chrysostome, a 45-minute drive from downtown Montreal.

How to get there : Take the Mercier Bridge from Montreal and Highway 138 west through Châteauguay, Mercier and Sainte-Martine. Drive 1.2 km past the road to Allan's Corner, cross the railway tracks and turn left onto Bryson Road.

When to go : This site is worthwhile only in spring and summer. Allow two or more hours to explore the area.

Site description : The site encompasses a series of peat bogs, known as the "tourbière de Saint-Pierre", and one of the only two known stands of pitch pine in the province. In 1978, a 66-hectare section of the stand was set aside as an ecological reserve. The pitch pine is at its extreme northern limit in this area.

Sparrows have the best representation here – eight nesting species, including Rufous-sided Towhee, Field Sparrow and

Lincoln's Sparrow. Lincoln's Sparrows are mostly found around the edges of the bogs. Savannah Sparrow, Swamp Sparrow and White-throated Sparrow are very common to abundant. Nashville Warbler and Common Yellowthroat are the most frequently sighted warblers.

Hermit Thrushes, uncommon elsewhere around Montreal, abound here. Black-billed Cuckoos may be very common some years and almost absent others. The several waterbird species include Mallard, Black Duck, Green-winged Teal, American Bittern, Pied-billed Grebe and Common Snipe. Northern Harriers nest and Whip-poor-wills abound.

Suggested route : Make several stops along Bryson Road, especially south of where it crosses Fertile Creek Road. From late May through early summer, Field Sparrows and Rufous-sided Towhees are common between Fertile Creek Road and Rang 5.

Watch for the Lincoln's Sparrows that nest in the peat bog to the right of Chemin du Rocher, south of Rang 5. As you continue south, you will see the Pitch Pine Reserve that extends on the right to Rang 8. Ecological reserves are areas set aside to protect endangered plant and animal species, and it is illegal to enter a reserve without special permission from the Environnement Québec. Such permission is granted only for research or educational purposes.

Across from the reserve on the left is another bog where Lincoln's Sparrows and a few duck species can be found. A path follows the south side of the bog for about 1 km.

You will find Rang 8 to be an excellent spot for Field Sparrows and Rufous-sided Towhees. At twilight, especially in May and June, the whole area resounds with the calls of Whip-poor-wills.

If you have time, continue on to Gowan Road (see Site C5). Go to the end of Chemin du Rocher, turn right onto Chemin Savary, right onto Route 201 and left onto Rang 8 (1.3 km). This will take you to Erskin Road and eventually Gowan Road. Rang 8 is prime territory for woodland birds.

Rufous-sided Towhee

The Pitch Pine Ecological Reserve and the Saint-Pierre Bog

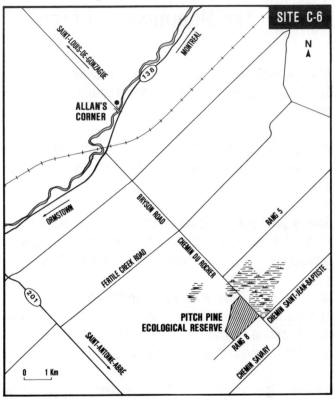

The Hemmingford Area

What to look for : Accipiters, owls, nesting passerines. *Special species :* Wild Turkey, Northern Cardinal, Field Sparrow.

Where : This area lies directly south of Montreal near the Canada-U.S. border, about 45 minutes from downtown Montreal by car.

How to get there : Take the Champlain Bridge and Highway 15 south towards New York State. Just before the border crossing, take Exit 1 and head west on Montée Glass.

When to go : Birding here is best in spring and summer. Wild Turkeys are present throughout the year but are mostly seen in early spring. Arrive very early during the nesting season and plan on spending a full morning.

Special information : Most of the sites described here are on private property, so it is preferable to bird by car rather than on foot. Since there is not much space to park along the roads, there should not be too many cars at one time. This site is not suitable for group outings.

Site description : The site overlaps Hemmingford and Saint-Bernard-de-Lacolle. Large stands of mixed forest subsist here. White-tailed deer are abundant, and there have been recent sightings of black bears, which are very rare in the Montreal lowlands. There are many apple orchards, cultivated fields and cedar stands.

Woodland birds abound, but waterbirds are scarce. Nonetheless, more than 100 species nest here. The Wild Turkey is much sought-after by local birders, having only become established here in 1982. It was first seen when a program for reintroducing the species was launched in northern New York State. In February 1982, 18 birds were released near Champlain in the County of Clinton. A few others were released in February 1983. The first birds, bearing wing tags, were seen in the fall of 1982 in Saint-Bernard-de-Lacolle. The species seems to have spread rapidly in this area, judging by reports of several birds (as many as 40 seen together) by residents in subsequent years. At least three nests with eggs have been discovered to date.

Great Horned Owls and Barred Owls are often sighted here, along with a number of hawks. Broad-winged, Red-shouldered and Red-tailed Hawks nest and Turkey Vultures are often seen during migration, especially in April. All three accipiters have been sighted in winter, Sharp-shinned Hawk and Northern Goshawk more frequently than Cooper's Hawk, which is rare anywhere in the Montreal area.

Fifteen species of warblers nest in the wooded sections. These include Magnolia Warbler, which is not often found in the Montreal area during the nesting season. Solitary Vireos also appear to be nesting in the stands of mixed forest. Field Sparrows can be considered common here, while the Clay-colored Sparrow has been sighted once. This species, which is extending its range, will no doubt be sighted again. The profusion of young coniferous stands, its preferred habitat, increases the likelihood.

Suggested route : From Highway 15, take Montée Glass west to Alberton Road (2.4 km). The roadsides along Alberton Road and Montée Glass, between Alberton Road and Roxham Road, are well worth exploring. There is much edge habitat here, and this is where Wild Turkeys are most likely to be seen. They have nested here, and the male turkeys can be heard gobbling very early in the morning in April and May. Observing them, however, is a matter of luck and persistence, as these birds are more often heard than seen. The forest south of Montée Glass extends to the border. There are nesting warblers here and Barred and Great Horned Owls. Further west on Montée Glass, Magnolia Warblers and Yellow-rumped Warblers flit through the stands of young pine and cedar along the road.

A left turn onto Roxham Road at the end of Montée Glass will take you to the border. This is a spot for edge and garden species such as Black-billed Cuckoo, Northern Cardinal and Indigo Bunting. Turn back and go west on Fisher Street. Field Sparrows are common at the corner of Fisher and Brownlee, and a Clay-colored Sparrow visited here in 1987. Drive 6.0 km north on Brownlee Road and stop beside the pine woods at the corner of Williams and Shields roads. Red-shouldered Hawks have nested here. Magnolia Warblers can be seen a bit further north in the young pines along the road.

The Hemmingford Area

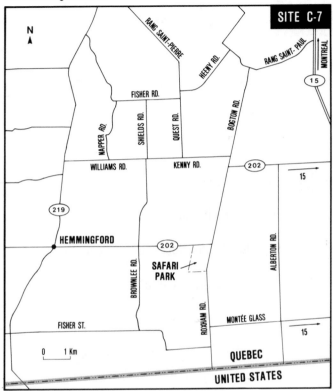

You can then proceed to explore the fields along Fisher and Quest roads. Wild Turkeys have been seen at the edge of the woods, most often at the intersection of Quest Road and Rang Saint-Pierre. Complete your tour of the Hemmingford area with a leisurely drive along Heeny Road to a stand of young pine, a good spot for Field Sparrows. At the end of Heeny Road, turn right onto Rang Saint-Paul south. This will take you to Highway 15.

The Richelieu Valley

1. Mount Saint-Bruno

2. Mount Saint-Hilaire

3. Rougemont

4. Mount Saint-Grégoire

5. Saint-Jean-sur-Richelieu

6. Saint-Paul-de-l'Ile-aux-Noix and Rivière du Sud

7. The Philipsburg Migratory Bird Sanctuary

The Richelieu Valley

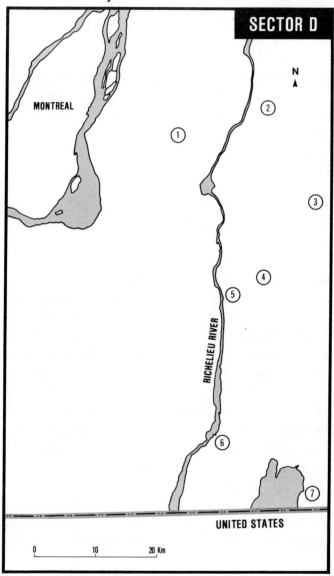

SECTOR D

MONTREAL

RICHELIEU RIVER

UNITED STATES

0   10   20 Km

Mount Saint-Bruno

What to look for : Raptors and land birds. *Special Species :* Turkey Vulture, Northern Goshawk, Red-shouldered Hawk, Barred Owl, Northern Saw-whet Owl, Pileated Woodpecker, Common Raven, Winter Wren, Blue-gray Gnatcatcher, Yellow-throated Vireo, Cerulean Warbler, Northern Cardinal, Red Crossbill.

Where : Mount Saint-Bruno is in southwestern Quebec, east of Montreal in Chambly County. It is a 25- to 35-minute drive from Montreal.

How to get there : The main access to this site is through Mount Saint-Bruno provincial park, which has three parking lots and a visitors' centre. From Montreal, it can be approached by three different routes. When leaving from the downtown area, take the Jacques Cartier Bridge and continue along Taschereau Boulevard. Take Highway 116, Autoroute 30 and exit by Chemin des 25. From the west end of the city, take the Eastern Townships Autoroute (10) and Autoroute 30. The easiest route from Montreal north and outlying regions is Autoroute 20 west and the Boulevard Montarville exit. Boulevard Montarville goes to Chemin des 25, where a left turn will take you to the site.

When to go : Mount Saint-Bruno offers good birding throughout the year. The best times, however, are spring, from early April through late May, June, mid-August to late November, and February and March in winter. The best time of the day is early morning, although late morning is good for hawk watching. It takes at least half a day to visit the main sites, especially in spring.

Special information : Wear a pair of sturdy hiking boots as there are loose rocks on the paths and in the surrounding woods. Maps showing most of the paths are available at the visitors' centre. Even the lakes offer little open habitat, so you will not need a spotting scope.

Site description : Mount Saint-Bruno, barely 200 m high, is the lowest of the ten Monteregian Hills. It has five lakes and several hollows. There are a few escarpments but no sizable cliffs. Most of the area is forested, the largest sections dominated by sugar maple, red oak and American beech. Also found are Yellow Birch, shagbark hickory and bitternut hickory. Although they only cover a small area, there are some coniferous trees: a few small stands dominated by eastern hemlock, one jack pine plantation south of Lac des Bouleaux, a mixed stand with eastern white pines east of Lac du Moulin.

Because of the area's biological value, the Department of recreation, fish and game created Mount Saint-Bruno park in 1977. The park covers about 7 km^2, mostly on the mountain itself. It was inaugurated in October 1985 and officially designated a conservation park.

Mount Saint-Bruno is one of the most fascinating birding sites in southern Quebec. Since 1972, 230 species have been sighted on and around the mountain, a total area of 20 km². During this period, about 112 species have nested, the latest confirmed nesting being Turkey Vulture in the spring of 1990.

The site is nesting habitat for a great variety of woodland birds, some of which are quite rare: Yellow-throated Vireo, Blue-gray Gnatcatcher and Cerulean Warbler. The most recent of the few Quebec breeding records for Red Crossbills was in Mount Saint-Bruno in 1977. Northern Cardinals are fairly abundant in Saint-Bruno and around the park. Among the several nesting warblers are Northern Waterthrush, Blackburnian Warbler, Black-and-white Warbler and Black-throated Blue Warbler. Pine Warblers are sighted almost every year and may have nested here for a few years. Other nesting species are Black-billed Cuckoo, Pileated Woodpecker, Eastern Wood-Pewee, Red-breasted Nuthatch, Winter Wren, Hermit Thrush, Northern Mockingbird and Indigo Bunting.

Mount Saint-Bruno is also known for its nesting birds of prey. The most abundant of these are Red-shouldered Hawk and Barred Owl (five pairs in 1987). Others include Northern Goshawk, Broad-winged Hawk, Great Horned Owl and Red-tailed Hawk. Raptor species also occur during migration – with Golden and Bald Eagles seen almost every year. The spring of 1987 was particularly fruitful, with three Golden Eagles and two Bald Eagles seen during only two outings. Turkey Vultures are being reported with increasing frequency, especially from late March through early June. Northern Saw-whet Owls are seen throughout the year but are easiest to find in fall and winter. Six were once observed within a few hours in November, and four once wintered together. Migrating hawks can be viewed from the open areas on the mountain. On a few good days, mostly around mid-September, several hundred migrating hawks were seen in only a few hours. The most abundant species are Broad-winged Hawk and Sharp-shinned Hawk.

Although water birds and shorebirds are never abundant at any one time, a wide variety has been recorded over the years. Seen almost every year are Common Loon, Pied-billed Grebe, Red-necked Grebe, Great Blue Heron, Green-backed Heron, Canada Goose, Ring-necked Duck and Hooded Merganser. Solitary Sandpipers are regularly seen in spring and fall.

Suggested route :

The artificial ponds and the parking area (Site 1) : The two small artificial ponds are north of the first parking lot. These are frequented by several ducks and herons, Great Blue Herons in particular. In spring and summer there are Indigo Buntings, Northern Mockingbirds and several other edge species. The Blue-gray Gnatcatcher has been seen west of the visitors' centre. In fall and winter, there are Rough-legged and other hawks, Northern Shrike and Pine Grosbeak.

The hollow (Site 2) : This site is about 1 km or a 15-minute walk along one of the trails or roads leaving from the visitors' centre. Near Lac Seigneurial, the road crosses a swampy hollow. Barred Owls are year-round residents here. Northern Saw-whet Owls are found in fall and winter, and Winter Wrens are present from the end of March to November. Numerous other woodland species have been observed here.

Lac Seigneurial and surrounding area (Site 3) : To get to this site, take the road that goes around the lake. It is a 20-minute walk from the visitors' centre and 5 minutes from the hollow. Lac Seigneurial is the best place on the mountain for watching water birds. Most species of ducks have been seen here, including Ruddy Duck and the scoters. The best periods are in the spring, between late April and mid-May, and in the fall, between mid-August and late November. Canada Goose is the most common species. Woodland birds abound in the forest around the lake, with Cerulean Warblers, Yellow-throated Vireos and Blue-gray Gnatcatchers occurring in spring and summer. In May, the spring migration brings hundreds of warblers, among which are Scarlet Tanagers and vireos. Barred Owls and Red-shouldered Hawks are frequently observed along the road around the lake, where two pairs of Barred Owls nest every year. The west side of the lake is one of the best spots for watching Pileated Woodpeckers.

Lac des Bouleaux (Site 4) : A 10-minute walk along a path from Lac Seigneurial will bring you to this site. Or you could take a road from the visitors' centre via the hollow, which would take about 25 minutes. Lac des Bouleaux is a good birding site at any time of the year but is best in fall, winter and spring. A stand of jack pine of about 0.3 hectares to the west of the lake is one of the best sites in the area for Northern Saw-whet Owls. As many as four have been seen here in one day, and a Boreal Owl was seen in February 1980. Unfortunately, an ice storm in the fall of 1983 spoiled much of the habitat for these species. It remains nonetheless a good site for Ruffed Grouse and a number of other species, especially in winter. Common Ravens regularly visit the lake side. The Cerulean

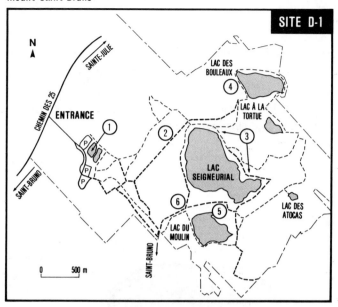

SITE D-1

Warbler has been observed to the north of the lake. A path goes around most of the lake.

Lac du Moulin and surrounding area (Site 5) : There are many departure points for this site, which is only a short walk from Site 3. It is located between Lac Seigneurial and Lac du Moulin. You will find a grassy area, an old orchard, a small abandoned field, two lakes, gardens and the forest nearby – a rewarding spot at any time. The variety of habitat brings a variety of species, the most interesting being Pileated Woodpecker, Pine Warbler, Red-shouldered Hawk, Northern Rough-winged Swallow and Red Crossbill. The large number of coniferous trees, apple trees and feeders nearby attract finches and other species in winter.

***The end of Rabastalière and du Moulin streets (Site 6)* :** This site is a 10-minute walk from the visitors' centre, or about 0.5 km from Lac du Moulin. You will find Northern Cardinal and several edge species. Winter brings Pine and Evening Grosbeaks and Northern Shrikes.

Barred Owl

Mount Saint-Hilaire

What to look for : Raptors, numerous woodland species.
Special Species : Turkey Vulture, Red-shouldered Hawk,
Peregrine Falcon, Pileated Woodpecker, Common Raven.

Where : Mount Saint-Hilaire is situated east of Montreal,
about 35 km or a 30- to 40-minute drive from the downtown
area.

How to get there : There are three ways of getting to this
Monteregian Hill. When leaving from the east end of Montreal,
take the Lafontaine tunnel, Autoroute 20 and Highway 133,
which goes south towards Mount Saint-Hilaire. From the
downtown area, take the Jacques Cartier Bridge and Taschereau
Boulevard to Highway 116, which goes towards the mountain.
When coming by the Champlain Bridge, continue on Autoroute
10 east (the Eastern Townships Autoroute) to Exit 29, where
you follow Highway 133 north to Mount Saint-Hilaire.

At Mount Saint-Hilaire village there are road signs indicat-
ing the exact route to the nature conservation centre. From
Highway 116, follow Rue Fortier, then Chemin Ozias-Leduc to
Chemin de la Montagne, where you turn left. At Chemin des
Moulins, turn left to the Gault Estate, 200 m further on.

When to go : The best birding times are spring and summer,
when the number of birds and variety of species are at their

peak. In fall, many water birds stop on Lac Hertel, and woodpeckers and other species visit the feeders in winter. Plan to spend at least half a day.

Special information : You will have to pay a small admission fee to get into the nature centre. Hiking boots are not an absolute necessity on these trails, nor are snowshoes essential in winter, as some of the trails are cleared of snow. You might want a spotting scope to view the wildfowl on Lac Hertel, especially in fall. During bad weather, you can seek shelter at the visitors' centre.

Site description : Rising 400 m above the Richelieu River, Mount Saint-Hilaire is the most imposing of the Monteregian Hills. The Gault Estate, which belongs to McGill University, covers most of the mountain, about 11 km^2.

The estate is divided into two sectors. The Nature Centre, which covers about 6 km^2, is open to the public, while the other sector is used for research. The nature centre is run by the Centre de la conservation de la nature. Its purpose is to preserve and manage the mountain and offer nature interpretation programs.

Mount Saint-Hilaire has two special statuses. In 1960, it was established as a migratory bird sanctuary, which means that firearms are prohibited. In 1978, UNESCO declared it a biosphere reserve for educational, scientific and cultural purposes because of its unique geological and biological characteristics.

The mountain is covered by mature forest which has remained almost intact over the centuries. A lake of 0.3 km^2 fills a depression formed by the surrounding summits.

The steep slopes of Mount Saint-Hilaire are covered by pine, oak and maple. Around the lake, the trees are mainly deciduous: sugar maple, American beech, red oak, basswood and white ash. This is the habitat of the Red-shouldered Hawk and the striking Pileated Woodpecker.

The pronounced topography of this Monteregian Hill makes it an excellent hawk-watching site during migration. It is also one of the few natural sites in southern Quebec where one can watch a pair of nesting Peregrine Falcons. When they return from their long migration, they can be seen circling above the rocky cliffs overlooking Highway 116. In summer, it is not unusual to see large numbers of Turkey Vultures. Although no nest has been discovered yet, the area is typical of their breeding habitat. The Turkey Vulture will probably soon be added to Mount Saint-Hilaire's list of breeding birds – 80 species, out of a total of 187 sighted.

Suggested route : The Nature Centre has a 24-km network of trails. There are five main trails, each leading to one of the five summits. The trails are all well marked: the red trail goes to Rocky Summit, the blue to Sunrise Summit, the green to Dieppe, the yellow to Pain de Sucre and the orange to Burned Hill.

The visitors' centre : Soon after arriving, you will come to the visitors' centre. The feeders here afford close-range views of birds in fall and winter. During the winter of 1988-89, a Red-bellied Woodpecker visited these feeders – a most unusual record for this area.

Lac Hertel : A 15-minute walk from the centre will bring you to Lac Hertel. If you go in the fall, you can watch the hundreds of water birds that visit the lake. From mid-September to mid-November, Canada Geese, scaups, scoters and loons rest and feed here before departing southward.

Many species nest around the lake in summer, including the Yellow-throated Vireo and Cerulean Warbler. A few of the

Dark-eyed Junco

Mount Saint-Hilaire

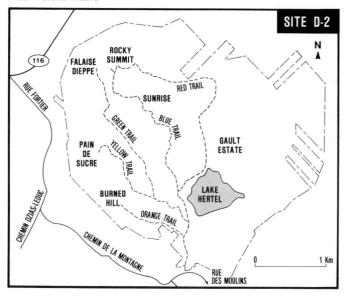

SITE D-2

latter species, which is almost nonexistent in the rest of Quebec, used to be sighted here regularly, i.e. 1961-1980. In the early '80s, however, a severe ice storm damaged the habitat of this small nesting population. Occasional reports indicate that the warblers have probably managed to establish themselves elsewhere on the mountain.

Dieppe and Pain de Sucre : These summits, 75 and 60 minutes respectively from the lake, serve as lookouts for Common Ravens and many hawks, accipiters and falcons. Vultures are frequently sighted here, and sometimes a Bald or Golden Eagle is seen hovering in mid-air.

Rougemont

What to look for : Nesting land birds. *Special species :* Turkey Vulture, Yellow-throated Vireo, Cerulean Warbler, Rufous-sided Towhee.

Where : As the crow flies, Rougemont is 40 km east of Mount Royal. Both these mountains are part of the Monteregian Hills. Rougemont lies between the Richelieu and Yamaska rivers in the agricultural lowlands of the St. Lawrence River. It can easily be reached from Montreal in less than one hour.

How to get there : You can take either of two Autoroutes to Rougemont – the Eastern Townships Autoroute (10) or the Trans-Canada (20)

If arriving by the 10, you will have a spectacular view of the Monteregian Hills, 3 km before taking Exit 37 to Marieville. In Marieville, take Highway 112 east. The first of the four exits to Rougemont goes to the tourist centre for the local apple industry. This centre is a reference point on the map and is about 35 minutes, or 44 km, from the Champlain Bridge.

If arriving by the 20, take Exit 115 and Highway 229 south towards Saint-Jean-Baptiste. Then drive towards Rougemont until you get to the tourist centre. There is a nice view of Mount Saint-Hilaire along this highway (about 40 minutes or 48 km from the Lafontaine tunnel).

When to go : The mountain is an interesting place to visit at any time. There are birds to be seen during the spring migration, the summer nesting season, amid the changing colours of fall or on a winter ski outing. This mountain has fewer visitors than the others and is a more peaceful site to visit. It takes more than one visit to truly discover it.

Special information : Three municipalities, Rougemont, Saint-Jean-Baptiste and Saint-Damase, are all found on the mountain, and they all have their own cross-country ski trails. The whole mountain is subdivided into about 100 lots of private property. The two highest peaks are launching sites for a deltaplane club, and the paths that lead to them are rutted from all-terrain vehicles. The going is rough on this uneven ground, which is often muddy as well.

The trails cover a wide area, and you can walk for great distances. It may be best to stay on the cross-country ski trails if you do not have a good sense of direction. The accompanying map will serve as a guide, but it is best to be cautious.

Rougemont is known for its apple orchards and makes for a scenic outing, especially in fall. The apple centre offers apple products for sale and is an interesting place to visit.

Site description : Surrounded by the vast agricultural lowlands and bordered by apple orchards, Rougemont harbours a variety of woodland birds. Although the original forest has been mostly cut down, there is regenerating forest in various stages, and sugar bushes take up a large part of the area. The most common coniferous tree is eastern hemlock.

Five woodpecker species (including Pileated Woodpecker) nest in these woodlands, along with five flycatchers, the three mimic thrushes, three vireos and at least thirteen warblers. The Cerulean Warbler has been seen in the past and remains to be rediscovered. You might come across a Great Horned Owl, Barred Owl or Broad-winged Hawk discreetly hunting about the area or a family of Ruffed Grouse in the woods. Ruby-throated Hummingbirds, Brown Creepers and both nuthatches are all around, and the woods ring with the songs of Winter Wrens. Blue Jays, Northern Cardinals, orioles, grosbeaks, Scarlet Tanagers, American Goldfinches and Purple Finches enliven an outing with their colour and music. In spring, migrating birds join the throng.

In the orchards are Mourning Doves, Eastern Kingbirds, European Starlings, Song Sparrows and Chipping Sparrows.

Killdeers, Horned Larks, Savannah Sparrows, Bobolinks, Eastern Meadowlarks, Northern Harriers and Vesper Sparrows inhabit the fields.

Suggested route : There are four departure points to the mountain:

Chemin du Moulin (Site 1) : Located 2.8 km from the tourist centre on Route 229 north. When you see the sign "Erablière Mont-Rouge, F. Goyette, prop.", turn right. After 1.0 km, you will see a sign prohibiting access to cars other than those of the deltaplane club members. You can, however, continue up to the cross on foot. Once at the top, you will have a spectacular view. You will also find paths leading to Lake Saint-Damase.

The Au Pied du Mont campground (Site 2) : Located 6.1 km from the tourist centre. To get there, take Route 229 north and turn right onto Rang du Cordon. There are some 42 km of cross-country ski trails that you can follow to explore the west

Rougemont

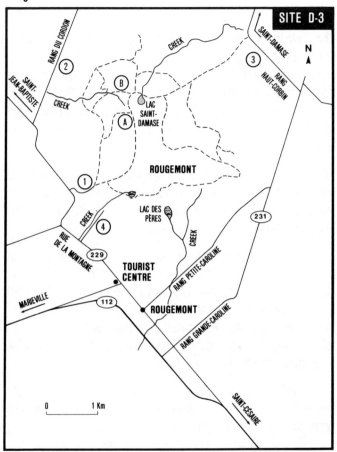

side of the mountain. This centre is linked to the next by an intermediate trail. In summer, a $2.00 admission fee will give you access to the trails and the pool (!). In winter there is a $3.00 charge for skiing or snowshoeing (3225 rang du

Cordon, Saint-Jean-Baptiste, tel: (514) 467-6318, M. Weber, proprietor.)

The Relais de l'Écureuil (Site 3) : Located 9.0 km from the tourist centre on Highway 231 north. Some 40 km of trails crisscross the northwest side of the mountain, some of them leading to the Au Pied du Mont campground. $3.00 in winter, no charge in summer (314 Rang Haut Corbin, Saint-Damase, tel: (514) 797-3958, Gilles and Raymond St-Pierre, proprietor).

The Rougemont cross-country ski club (Site 4) : Situated 1.3 km from the tourist centre on Rue de la Montagne. About 55 km of trails on part of the south side. Trails leave from the McArthur farm, tel: (514) 469-2521.

A woodland outing can be nicely complemented by a tour around the mountain to bird in more open habitat. Begin at Rang Petite-Caroline, which offers a splendid view. Turn left towards Saint-Damase at the intersection with Highway 231 north. Drive 7.0 km and turn left onto Rang Saint-Louis. Turn left on Rang du Cordon, which will bring you to Highway 229. The complete tour is 28 km long.

The following observations were made during an outing to the mountain in 1988. These interesting records may well be reconfirmed in the future.

- Rufous sided Towhee nesting in a clearing at *Site A*;
- Yellow-throated Vireo singing along a rocky road at *Site B*;
- Turkey Vultures seen at mid-day during hot weather, over any part of the mountain (up to five at one time);
- Northern Cardinal visiting feeders at houses near tourist centre;

Upland Sandpiper

- Northern Mockingbird nesting on Rang Petite-Caroline;
- Upland Sandpiper nesting along the road to the Rougemont cross-country ski centre.
- Indigo Bunting near the Mont-Rouge sugar bush.

Mount Saint-Grégoire

What to look for : Insect-eating passerines. *Special species :* Turkey Vulture.

Where : Southeast of Montreal, at least 45 minutes by car from the downtown area.

How to get there : Take the Eastern Townships Autoroute (Autoroute 10), Autoroute 35 (Exit 22) and Highway 104 east. At Saint-Grégoire (6.0 km), continue straight to the flashing light and turn left (1.6 km) onto Chemin Sous-Bois. You can also take Exit 37 from Autoroute 10. In this case, take Highway 227 south and turn right onto Chemin Sous-Bois (3.0 km).

When to go : This site is most interesting between May and July. A few hours in the early morning will bring the best results.

Site description : Mount Saint-Grégoire is the smallest of the ten Monteregian Hills. A forested area surrounded by farmland, Mount Saint-Grégoire is known for its sugar bush industry. The species that live here are typical of the deciduous forests of southwestern Quebec: Wood Thrush, Eastern Wood-Pewee, Red-eyed Vireo, etc. For the past few years, Turkey Vultures have been visiting the cliff on the east side during the nesting season.

Suggested route : The main point of interest is the Centre d'interprétation du milieu écologique, located on Chemin Sous-Bois. The Centre was established to develop public

Mount Saint-Grégoire

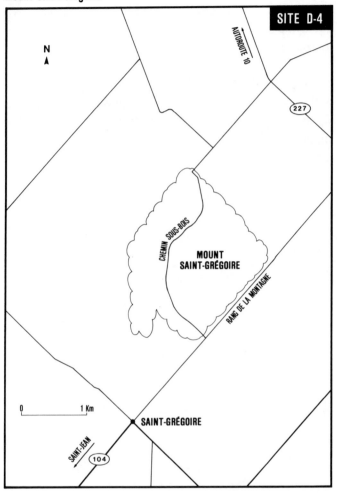

awareness concerning the conservation of Mount Saint-Grégoire. There are several hiking trails with explanatory signs, and guided tours are available on reservation. This is an excellent site for beginners.

If you park across from the Mount Saint-Grégoire cemetery at the intersection of Chemin Sous-Bois and Rang de la Montagne, you will have a view of the east side of the mountain. Turkey Vultures are seen here in spring and summer.

Saint-Jean-sur-Richelieu

What to look for : Diving ducks. *Special species :* Barrow's Goldeneye.

Where : Saint-Jean-sur-Richelieu lies southeast of Montreal on the west side of the Richelieu River. It can easily be reached in 30 minutes.

How to get there : From downtown Montreal, take the Champlain Bridge, Autoroute 10 east (Eastern Townships Autoroute) and Autoroute 35 south.

When to go : Fall, especially November, is the most interesting time. The site can be covered in less than one hour.

Site description : The Richelieu River pursues its leisurely course from Lake Champlain to Sorel, where it empties into the St. Lawrence. The Richelieu Valley is a major flyway for ducks and geese, especially in spring. In the past few years, however, far fewer birds have been observed. Pleasure boating on the river, housing development along its shores and drainage of the surrounding farmland have all taken their toll. Still, there are certain areas where wildfowl gather in spring (see Site D6) and fall. One of these sites, located in the heart of downtown Saint-Jean, attracts several species of diving ducks in the fall. Since the river is not very wide here, the ducks can be easily viewed with binoculars or, better still, a spotting scope. The following diving ducks have been seen here in the past few years: Canvasback, Redhead, Ring-necked Duck, Greater Scaup, Lesser Scaup, Oldsquaw, Black Scoter, White-winged Scoter, Common Goldeneye, Barrow's Goldeneye, Bufflehead, Hooded Merganser, Common Merganser, Red-breasted Merganser, Ruddy Duck.

Suggested route : From Autoroute 35, take Exit 7 onto Du Séminaire Boulevard. Turn left onto Rue Loyola and drive to Champlain Boulevard, which follows the river. There are two strategic points from where the river can be viewed. The first is a parking space across the street from the Harris Motel. You will find it 500 m to your left along Champlain Boulevard. The second site is to the right. Drive south on Champlain Boulevard to the corner of Rue Saint-Paul (1.5 km). Leave your car here and walk across lock no.9 of the Chambly Canal. The path here will give you another view of the river. The light is best in the afternoon when the sun is west of the river.

Other observation points along the river have better light conditions in the morning. If you go back to Autoroute 35, cross the river and take Exit 6, you will find yourself on the east side of the Richelieu. You can park your car beside the road under the bridge and view the river from there. Or you can drive another 1 km upstream and park across from the Frères Maristes college.

Saint-Jean-sur-Richelieu

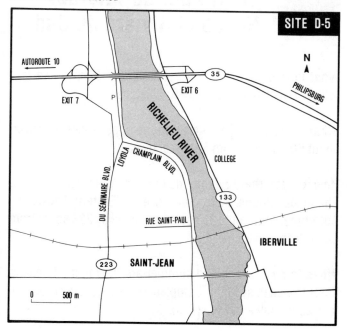

Saint-Paul-de-l'Ile-aux-Noix and Rivière du Sud

What to look for : Wildfowl, shorebirds. *Special species :* Willow Flycatcher, Blue-gray Gnatcatcher.

Where : South of Saint-Jean on the upper Richelieu River, about 60 minutes from Montreal by car.

How to get there : From downtown Montreal, take the Champlain Bridge, Autoroute 10 east (Eastern Townships Autoroute), Autoroute 35 south and Highway 223 south from Saint-Jean-sur-Richelieu.

When to go : Spring and summer are the most interesting times to visit this region. Completing the suggested route will take about half a day in spring.

Site description : Saint-Paul-de-l'Ile-aux-Noix is located on the west side of the Richelieu River, about halfway between Saint-Jean and the U.S. border. The area is primarily agricultural. The Richelieu Valley has always been a major flyway for wildfowl, but the region has been considerably altered in recent years by housing development and drainage of the farmland along the river. Fewer birds are being observed, and observation points are less accessible.

This is also true of the Rivière du Sud. In 1983, dredging and landfill operations considerably reduced the extent of the basin and its marshes.

The most frequently sighted species here in the spring are Snow Goose, Canada Goose, various species of diving ducks (including Canvasback) and dabbling ducks, a few herons, bitterns and shorebirds. The Great Blue is the most common heron, and Great Egrets and Glossy Ibises have been sighted on a few occasions. Over 20 species of shorebirds have been recorded, including such unusual species as Ruff and Curlew Sandpiper.

In spring, the upper Richelieu River is also a good place for hawks, such as Osprey.

There are still some good places to find breeding ducks and other wetland species.

Suggested route : Begin your trip on the west side of the Richelieu River south of Saint-Blaise, on Highway 223. The

Eastern Meadowlark

fields along the river between Saint-Blaise and Saint-Paul-de-l'Ile-aux-Noix are often flooded in the spring. This flooding attracts wildfowl, sometimes as early as the end of March. The extent of this flooding varies, however, from year to year. Late flooding, say at the end of May, brings shorebirds. The flooded fields can be studied by driving slowly along the many dead-end streets leading from Highway 223 to the Richelieu. The best site seems to be between 81st Avenue and 93rd Avenue *(Site 1)*. It is crossed by a small stream just north of 81st Avenue. The stream empties into the Richelieu at Point Bleury. Many ducks breed and raise their young along this stream. Wood Ducks are found here, and Green-winged Teal, Mallard, Blue-winged Teal, Northern Shoveler and American Wigeon. Other species that nest at Point Bleury are Pied-billed Grebe, Common Moorhen, Common Snipe, Black Tern, Willow Flycatcher (abundant here) and Marsh Wren. In spring, there are gatherings of wildfowl south of Saint-Paul-de-l'Ile-aux-Noix, but the river is not very accessible.

Continue for 8 km south of Saint-Paul-de-l'Ile-aux-Noix and turn left onto Highway 202. This will bring you to the other side of the Richelieu. You can turn right onto Chemin Bord-de-l'Eau south and follow the shore to the border *(Site 2)*. Rafts of scaups are sighted here in April. Come back towards Highway 202 and take Chemin Bord-de-l'Eau north and Highway 225 north. The flooded fields along this road attract wildfowl. Chemin Melaven about 7 km north of Route 202, goes to the end of a point between the Richelieu and the mouth of Rivière du Sud. This is known as Pointe du Gouvernement *(Site 3)*. Environnement Québec recently established an ecological reserve on part of this point – the Marcel-Raymond

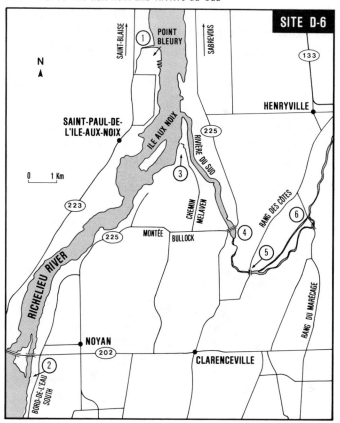

SITE D-6

reserve – to protect a stand of swamp white oak. Blue-gray Gnatcatchers and Yellow-throated Vireos have recently nested here.

Come back to Route 225 (Montée Bullock) and cross Rivière du Sud *(Site 4)*. The shallow marsh on either side of the bridge is nesting habitat for dabbling ducks, Common Moorhens, Black Terns, Marsh Wrens and others. In the fall, shorebirds gather here. Rang des Côtes and Rang du Marécage both cross Rivière du Sud further east *(Sites 5 & 6)*.

Highway 225 north goes to Sainte-Anne-de-Sabrevois. From there, Highway 133 north will bring you back towards Saint-Jean. A few marshes remain along the Richelieu north of Sabrevois. Take one of the avenues leading to these marshy areas – 16th avenue, for example – for possible sightings of Virginia Rails and Soras.

Green-backed Heron

The Philipsburg Migratory Bird Sanctuary

What to look for : Marsh birds, hawks, land birds. *Special species :* Green-backed Heron, Wood Duck, Turkey Vulture, Cooper's Hawk, Yellow-throated Vireo, Cerulean Warbler, House Finch.

Where : Located in the extreme southern part of the province, the Sanctuary extends from the village of Philipsburg to the Vermont border. It includes the entire shore of Missisquoi Bay between these points.

How to get there : Take the Champlain Bridge from Montreal and continue on Autoroute 10 east (Eastern Townships Autoroute). Then take Autoroute 35 south and Highway 133 south.

When to go : Birding in Philipsburg is worthwhile at any time of the year, but spring and summer are the most productive seasons. The most rewarding time, of course, is just after sunrise. You should plan on spending half a day to visit the area.

Special information : All this area is private property and visitors should keep this in mind when using the Sanctuary. The parking lot northeast of Streit's Pond and the adjacent picnic area are also on private property. A voluntary contribution of $2.00 goes towards maintenance. The Sanctuary's network of trails is maintained by the Province of Quebec Society for the Protection of Birds (PQSPB). The trail numbers on the map correspond to the numbers on the triangular signs marked PQSPB. There are also square signs in the

Sanctuary that are numbered but not marked PQSPB. These numbers should not be confused with those used in this text.

Site description : The Philipsburg Migratory Bird Sanctuary was established in March, 1955. It covers 480 hectares of land along the Missisquoi Bay, some of which is owned by the PQSPB, the rest being in private hands. Included are part of the village of Philipsburg, a small body of water surrounded by marsh and swamp (Streit's Pond) and a large section of forest. North of Streit's Pond are fields and abandoned land. The Sanctuary is crossed by two roads, Highway 133 and Saint-Armand Road.

The Sanctuary's diversity of habitat attracts a corresponding diversity of bird life. Over 180 species have been recorded, some of which are rare in Quebec. About 115 of these nest. During the field trips organized by the PQSPB, in May and September, more than 100 species are normally recorded.

About two dozen Wood Duck nest boxes have been put up by the PQSPB in the swamp around Streit's Pond. Nest box use averages around 50 per cent. Other birds have used these nest boxes as well: Hooded Merganser, Common Goldeneye, Eastern Screech-Owl, American Kestrel. In June and July, it is not unusual to see a mother duck being followed by her brood. Several other species nest around the pond: American Bittern, Least Bittern, Green-backed Heron, Green-winged Teal, Black Duck, Mallard, Northern Pintail, Northern Harrier, Virginia Rail, Sora, Killdeer, Spotted Sandpiper, Common Snipe, Marsh Wren and Swamp Sparrow.

Hawks can be observed around the pond, especially during migration. Almost all the raptor species have been seen here, including Bald Eagle and Golden Eagle. The most common raptor, especially in spring and fall, is probably the Turkey Vulture, and it is possible that it nests here. In September, as many as 40 Turkey Vultures have been seen at one time over the ridge south of the pond. Two spectacular birds of prey, Cooper's Hawk and Red-shouldered Hawk, nest in the Sanctuary. Common Ravens have been sighted for the past few years and have nested nearby.

Yellow-throated Vireo, Golden-winged Warbler and Cerulean Warbler are three of the many passerine species that nest or have nested in the Sanctuary. These birds are at the northernmost limit of their range here. The first Golden-winged Warbler nest ever found in Quebec was discovered in the Sanctuary in 1971; the first Cerulean Warbler nest was found here in 1989. Just a few of the more tantalizing sight records for the Sanctuary are Sandhill Crane, Tufted Tit-mouse, Yellow-throated Warbler, Summer Tanager and Clay-colored Sparrow.

Suggested route : The Philipsburg Sanctuary is divided into three sectors. The most interesting sector lies east of Highway 133 and south of Chemin Saint-Armand. It includes Streit's Pond, which is owned by the PQSPB, and a large wooded area. The other two sectors, one between Missisquoi Bay and Highway 133 and the other north of Chemin Saint-Armand, are somewhat less productive.

The main access point to the Sanctuary is northeast of Streit's Pond. From Highway 133, drive 0.8 km on Chemin Saint-Armand and turn right onto a gravel road that leads to a parking lot.

From here you can set out to explore the pond, which you will find close by. Follow the north side of the pond, and you will come to an observation hut and a feeding station near a dense patch of cat-tails – a good place for Least Bittern, Wood Duck or rails. If you take the opposite direction and follow trail No. 6 along the cliffs southeast of the pond, you will have an excellent vantage point over the whole area. Continue along this trail and trail No. 19 (take this to avoid a hazardous section along trail No. 6) and you will come to the southern tip of the pond. An observation tower here offers an unobstructed view of the marsh. A quicker way to get to this tower is to start from the other end of trail No. 6, leaving from Highway 133 near the junction with Route 7. To do so, however, you will have to leave your car along Route 7 near the cemetery, as there is no parking area nearby.

The forest between the pond and the border can be explored by the network of trails that covers the whole area. Yellow-throated Vireos and a dozen warbler species nest here. Every spring for the last few years, a small group of Cerulean Warblers has been returning to the maple stand that extends north and east from the sugar house near the border. At the present time, it appears that this is the only place in Quebec where the species can be sighted with any certainty. To get to the sugar house, take trail No. 9 or trail No. 10 followed by trail No. 13. The departure point for these trails is a little field 300 m south of the parking lot. (Check the nest boxes around the edge of this field because they often house Eastern Bluebirds.) Trail No. 10, which follows the ridge, is rather strenuous. If you prefer a faster route, you might take trail No. 9. The hike along this trail is about 5 km, from the parking lot to the sugar house and back.

The Philipsburg Migratory Bird Sanctuary

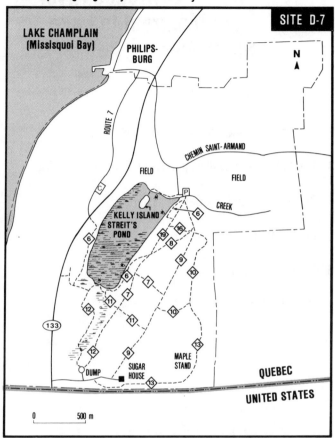

If you want to look for Cerulean Warblers, go in the early morning in June. Finding them is no easy task, as they live almost exclusively in the topmost branches of the highest trees. Knowing their song will increase your chances of spotting them.

The St. Lawrence River from Montreal to Lake Saint-Pierre

The St. Lawrence River from Montreal to Lake Saint-Pierre

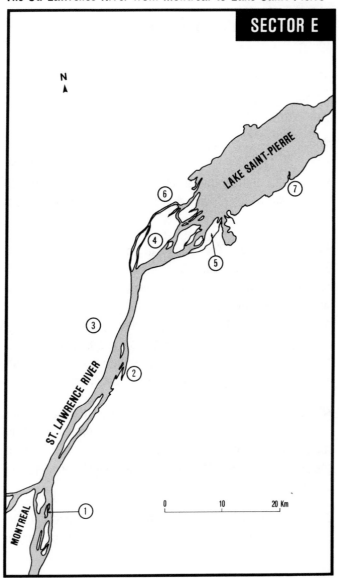

SECTOR E

N

LAKE SAINT-PIERRE

ST. LAWRENCE RIVER

MONTREAL

0   10   20 Km

Ile aux Fermiers

What to look for : Herons, ducks and shorebirds. *Special species :* Least Bittern, Redhead, Wilson's Phalarope, Black Tern, Short-eared Owl, Sharp-tailed Sparrow.

Where : Ile aux Fermiers is situated near the eastern tip of the Island of Montreal, on the St. Lawrence River between Boucherville and Varennes. The island is 28 km or about 25 minutes from downtown Montreal and can be seen from Varennes.

How to get there : The island can only be reached by boat, either from Boucherville or Varennes. As you leave Montreal, head towards these towns on Highway 132 east on the South Shore. In Boucherville, the wharf closest to Ile aux Fermiers is at the corner of Marie-Victorin Boulevard and Rue de Mézy. If you go to Varennes, follow Highway 132 east and turn left onto Rue Sainte-Anne as you enter Varennes. Turn left again onto Rue Sainte-Thérèse and drive to the wharf.

When to go : Birding is good from mid-May to the beginning of September, before the hunting season opens. It takes about four to five hours to cover the island, including the shores and marshes. The area is productive at any time of the day but less so in high wind.

Special information : You may need boots, especially after periods of wet weather. The area is very flat and can only be birded properly with a spotting scope; otherwise you risk flushing the ducks, shorebirds and gulls.

Mr. Hugues Durocher provides transportation to the island from Varennes. Phone ahead at (514) 652-0543. He is not available in July and August. The charge is $5.00 per person, $20.00 minimum.

The shortest route for people using their own boats is underneath the power lines between Boucherville and Varennes.

If you leave your boat on the east side, make sure it is well out of the range of the heavy wake from vessels using the Seaway.

Site description : This flat, low-lying island, 3.0 km long and 0.6 km wide, was once a group of four islands which were linked together several years ago by deposits from dredging operations in the Seaway. A large bay and three ponds were also formed.

Today the island appears as one large field interspersed with marsh. Clay beaches have formed on the west side, which is slightly higher, as a result of erosion by the wake of passing freighters.

Transport Canada owns the island, except for a thin strip belonging to Hydro-Québec, for its pylons. The fields are used in summer to pasture a hundred head of cattle. This has affected the original shoreline and taken its toll on the ground nesting birds and the diversity of plant life. In the fall, some

150 hunters arrive on the island for the opening of the hunting season.

For a unique view of the whole island, you can climb up the 12-m-high lighthouse.

At least 32 species have nested on the island and 82 others have been observed over the last ten years. Many of these are exceptional. The Long-billed Curlew, sighted in July 1987, Smith's Longspur in September 1989 and American Avocet in May 1980 and 1985 are three examples.

Flooding in May will often affect the whole character of the island, and it becomes attractive to shorebirds. These never appear in any great numbers, but the variety of species is impressive. Twenty-eight shorebird species have been observed, some of which are very unusual. The spring migration brings a few scaups, goldeneyes and mergansers.

All the surface-feeding ducks nest here in June: Gadwall, American Wigeon, Northern Pintail, Mallard, Northern Shoveler, American Black Duck, Blue-winged and Green-winged Teal. Wood Ducks have been sighted here but cannot nest because there are no trees, only five small elms near the large bay. A dozen or so pairs of Redheads share the three ponds with Pied-billed Grebes and Common Moorhens. American Coots nested here in 1985. Marsh Wrens and Red-winged Blackbirds live in the reeds around the ponds. American Bitterns, Northern Harriers and Short-eared Owls nest in the fields along with Bobolinks and Savannah Sparrows. Other interesting nesting birds are Least Bittern, Black Tern and Wilson's Phalarope.

Ile aux Fermiers

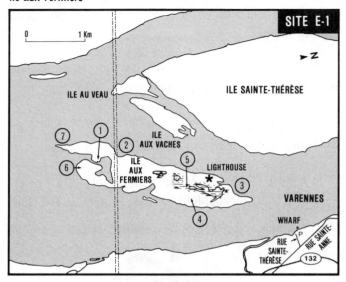

In July there are a few Herring Gulls among the hundred or so Ring-billed and Great Black-backed Gulls. Caspian Terns have been seen here for the last few years. At the end of July, shorebirds return to the island and linger until September.

August brings large numbers of Great Blue Herons and Black-crowned Night-Herons, as many as 40 of each species. Ducks are seen in the hundreds, until the opening of the hunting season in mid-September.

Suggested route : Three spots are particularly good for shorebird watching: the entrance to the large inner bay *(Site 1)*, the beach near the pylon *(Site 2)* and the beach at the northern tip *(Site 3)*.

Wilson's Phalarope and Sharp-tailed Sparrow are mostly found in the field between the ponds and the east shore of the island *(Site 4)*.

At *Site 5* a colony of 20 or so Black Terns noisily defend their territory. With luck you might spot a Least Bittern here.

Gulls are found mainly at *Sites 2, 3 and 7,* and Bank Swallows nest on the steep banks of *Sites 2 and 6.*

In August a Peregrine Falcon often perches on the pylon, keeping a sharp lookout for swallows, shorebirds and teals.

Sora

Contrecoeur and the Contrecoeur Islands

What to look for : Dabbling ducks and other wetland species. *Special species :* Pied-billed Grebe, Common Moorhen, Black Tern, Willow Flycatcher, Pine Warbler.

Where : Contrecoeur is about 75 km northeast of Montreal on the south shore of the St. Lawrence. It takes about one hour to get there.

How to get there : From Montreal, take one of the several routes to the South Shore. Then take Highway 132 east to Contrecoeur. You can also take Autoroute 30 east, via Autoroutes 10 or 20, to Exits 158 or 160 to Contrecoeur. The Contrecoeur marina is located in front of the church.

When to go : The best time to visit the islands is between May 15 and September 15. As summer progresses, the aquatic vegetation grows so tall that it obstructs the view. Mosquitoes are a major hindrance at the beginning of summer, especially on Ile Bouchard.

Special information : You need a boat to visit these islands. In 1989, two local youths used their motorboat to provide ferry service on weekends. Phone Francis Saint-Pierre (tel: (514) 743-0620) or Stephane Caisse (tel: (514) 587-2625). For a reasonable rate, you can visit several islands, including the northeast tip of Ile Bouchard. Mr. Denis Lamothe, a member of the Club d'ornithologie Sorel-Tracy, who lives in

Contrecoeur, is sometimes available to accompany visitors (tel: (514) 742-9792).

Site description : The St. Lawrence River between Montreal and Lake Saint-Pierre is dotted with islands. Most of these are only accessible by boat. If you have your own boat, you can easily reach the most productive of these, the Contrecoeur and Verchères islands, from the Contrecoeur marina.

The Contrecoeur Islands lie a little over 11 km along the river across from Contrecoeur. There are a dozen or so larger islands and about 15 smaller ones separated by channels overgrown with emergent vegetation. Because there is so little elevation, the islands look like one huge wetland. Most of them belong to Public Works Canada and are a National Wildlife Area. The highest parts are fields, and the more than 500 hectares of channels between them are filled with aquatic vegetation.

Dabbling ducks are the most obvious species here. In 1975, biologists from the Canadian Wildlife Service counted 322 duck nests, almost half of which were Gadwall nests. Other nesting ducks are Northern Pintail, American Wigeon, Northern Shoveler, Mallard and American Black Duck. There are also Great Blue Herons, Black Terns, Pied-billed Grebes, Common Moorhens, Common Snipes and American Bitterns. A few shorebirds visit here at the beginning of June. Red-winged Blackbirds, Bank Swallows, Song Sparrows, Swamp Sparrows, Common Yellowthroats and Yellow Warblers abound. Huge breeding colonies of Ring-billed Gulls have established themselves on Ile Saint-Ours and the other dredging heaps.

The eight Verchères islands, over 18 km in length, are situated somewhat upstream from Contrecoeur. Marie and Bouchard are the two main islands, and they are much larger than the Contrecoeur Islands. They are also slightly higher. A considerable portion is used by farmers, but the northeast end of Bouchard Island, which is the closest to Contrecoeur, has remained unspoiled and still has a few wooded sectors along

Common Moorhen

the edge of its swamps and marshes. The silver maple stand here is about the only woodland to be found on any of these groups of islands.

Bouchard Island has dabbling ducks (including Wood Duck), Common Moorhens, Black Terns and other species such as the Marsh Wren and Willow Flycatcher. There are also several woodland birds. In 1979, a heronry was located on the island. Great Horned Owls, Short-eared Owls and Northern Harriers have nested. Although this island has never been extensively birded in winter, sightings of three Great Gray Owls, a Boreal Owl, Barred Owl and Snowy Owl towards the end of winter in 1974 suggest this may be an interesting winter birding site.

Suggested route :   You can easily visit the Contrecoeur Islands and the northeast part of Bouchard Island in four or five hours if you have a motor boat. If you only have a canoe or rowboat, it is best to limit your visit to the Contrecoeur Islands. The Club d'ornithologie Sorel-Tracy plans to run field trips here. You can contact the club for information on these trips.

If you want to see land birds, the Contrecoeur and Tracy areas have several productive woodland sectors. In one of them, you can even see Pine Warblers, a much sought-after species with a very localized distribution in Quebec. The following is a suggested route (not shown on the map): Drive east from Contrecoeur on Highway 132 for about 15 km to Rue Annie in Tracy. Every year, Pine Warblers visit the white pines still remaining in a residential district here. Return to Highway 132 and continue a little further east to Chemin du

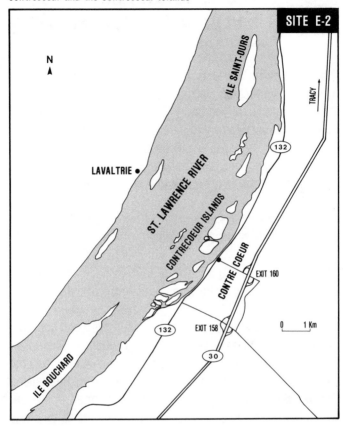

Golf, where you turn right to the railway tracks. A sandy road goes west along the tracks through a wooded area. There are Pine Warblers in the small clumps of white pine here. The road is a few kilometres long and is not really passable by car. It is best explored on foot in the early morning, at which time you will surely encounter other woodland species to brighten your walk.

269

The Lanoraie, Lavaltrie and Saint-Thomas Peat Bog

What to look for : Hawks and land birds. *Special Species :* American Woodcock, Northern Saw-whet Owl, Whip-poor-will, Olive-sided Flycatcher, Sedge Wren, Rufous-sided Towhee, Vesper Sparrow, Lincoln's Sparrow, Red Crossbill.

Where : The peat bog is located north of Lanoraie, 50 km east of Montreal. It takes less than one hour to get there.

How to get there : Take Autoroute 40 east from Montreal and Exit 130 onto Chemin Joliette north.

When to go : Late April to mid-June is definitely the best period. Arrive early and plan on spending half a day.

Site description : To understand how this peat bog was formed, one must go back 10,000 years, when the Champlain Sea covered a large part of southern Quebec. At that time the land heaved up, preventing the sea from entering the east end of Lake Saint-Pierre. A huge lake was formed upstream, which has been named Lake Lampsilis from the name of the molluscs that were the most abundant at that time. A delta of islands, like those found today at Sorel, was formed where the river flowed into this lake. Between 6500 and 8500 B.C., these islands were next to Lanoraie. The Rivière Assomption once flowed into the sea at Sainte-Mélanie, but its course was changed by these islands. Unlike the other tributaries of the St. Lawrence, this river flows westward. Pointe du Coteau-Jaune was formed from an ancient bend in this river. Periods

The Lanoraie, Lavaltrie and Saint-Thomas Peat Bog

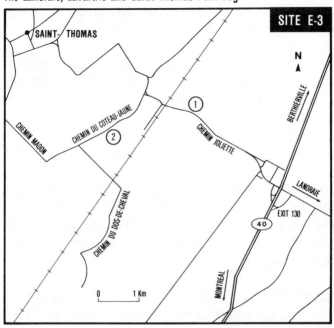

of warming and cooling changed the forests considerably. The peat bogs were formed 3,500 years ago, when mosses appeared on the ancient channels. This is when the leatherleaf, rhododendron and bog rosemary that are found today first appeared. Detritus had accumulated to a depth of 3 m, and the sphagnum developed above the ground water. Being watered only by rain, its growth was minimal: barely 3 mm per year. Its height, therefore, was uniform throughout the area; it formed a stable, balanced eco-system that ceased to evolve.

Indians occupied this territory as the climate allowed. Berries were abundant and game flourished. Before the

Europeans arrived, however, the climate cooled, and the Indians left the region. Spruce and fir sprang up, and this was how Lanoraie appeared to the first settlers.

Today, the peat bogs are threatened by development projects involving extraction, power lines, frog marshes and horticulture. But even the tilled land and irrigation ponds are not without a certain charm.

A total of nearly 100 species, mainly land birds, inhabit this sector. The most interesting of these are American Woodcock, Whip-poor-will, Vesper Sparrow, and Lincoln's Sparrow. Until the 1940s, Palm Warblers nested in the peat bogs, and this is the only known nesting site for this species in the Montreal area. Today Palm Warblers are seen only rarely during migration.

Suggested route : There are two sites of interest. The first of these has the greater expanse of peat. To get to it, leave Autoroute 40 by Exit 130 onto Chemin Joliette north. Just outside Saint-Thomas and Lanoraie, about 2.7 km north of Exit 130, you will come to an observation post. Walk along Chemin Joliette early in the morning, before the onset of traffic, to discover the bog's ornithological delights. You might also take the road under the power lines near the railway tracks, 0.7 km further north.

The second site is the Coteau-Jaune peat bog. Continue north on Chemin Joliette. After the railway tracks (0.6 km), turn left onto Chemin du Coteau-Jaune. Drive 2 km and turn left onto Chemin Dos-de-cheval. This road is about 4 km long and passes mainly through cultivated land.

Berthierville and the Berthier Islands

What to look for : Ducks and geese, shorebirds and other wetland species. *Special species :* American Bittern, Great Blue Heron, Great Egret, Green-backed Heron, Canada Goose, Osprey, Common Moorhen, Upland Sandpiper, Snowy Owl, Willow Flycatcher, Marsh Wren, Pine Warbler.

Where : At the extreme western tip of Lake Saint-Pierre, on the north shore of the St. Lawrence, at least an hour's drive from Montreal.

How to get there : From Montreal, take Autoroute 40 east and Exit 144 onto Highway 158. You can also go by the South Shore, by taking the ferry from Sorel to Saint-Ignace-de-Loyola. From Highway 132 take Fiset Boulevard in Sorel. Turn left onto Avenue de l'Hôtel-Dieu, right onto Rue Elizabeth and drive to the ferry. When you get off the ferry, take Highway 158 west to Berthierville.

When to go : This is a good birding site at any time. Spring, of course, is the peak period, but there are good days in summer and fall as well. Allow at least half a day to visit the islands.

Special information : Keep a weather eye out in early spring because the islands are often heavily flooded. You will need rubber boots and warm clothing, as the onshore winds are always more bracing than anticipated. A spotting scope is definitely an asset. A birder's site guide to Lake Saint-Pierre is available for purchase.

Site description : The Berthierville area and islands have always been a mecca for fishermen and hunters. Lately, it has been attracting birdwatchers as well. Despite the considerable human activity, the bird life is diversified and abundant. The whole area is a well-known staging ground for migrating waterfowl.

The habitat is extremely varied: deep and shallow marshes, shrubby and treed swamps, wet fields, cultivated land. Some islands are accessible by car, but others can only be reached by canoe or motor boat.

Data from the Quebec Breeding Bird Atlas Project show a total of 115 species. The nesting ducks are mainly Mallard, Northern Pintail, Northern Shoveler, American Wigeon and Blue-winged Teal. Projects by Ducks Unlimited ensure an increase in the potential of these habitats.

Great Blue Herons are common on every expanse of water, but they nest on a more distant, undisturbed island. American Bitterns also nest, and every year an occasional Great Egret is sighted by a fortunate few. Common Moorhens, Virginia Rails and Soras are found in the dense vegetation of the shallow marshes.

Birds of prey are also plentiful. These include the Northern Harrier, Broad-winged Hawk, Red-shouldered Hawk, Peregrine Falcon, American Kestrel and the occasional Bald Eagle. Late autumn and early winter bring other raptors, such as Rough-legged and Red-tailed Hawks, that tend to linger when the snow cover is light.

Great Horned Owls and Short-eared Owls are breeders, and many Snowy Owls arrive with the winter.

The variety of habitat attracts a variety of passerines. The Common Yellowthroat, Swamp Sparrow, Red-winged Blackbird, Marsh Wren and Willow Flycatcher live in the moist habitat. The Berthierville nursery, with its large natural forests dominated by white pine, is another productive spot. Pine Warblers are seen here every year.

American Black Duck

Suggested route : There are six main points of interest in the area, each one as attractive as the other.

The Berthierville rest area (Site 1) : This site is on Highway 138, 6.0 km west of where it crosses Highway 158. It affords a vista of a vast expanse of the St. Lawrence. To the east is Ile aux Foins, where the main habitat is wet grassland. In spring, Canada Geese gather on the marshy shores, along with all the species of dabbling ducks, Northern Pintail in particular. Several of these duck species remain for the breeding season.

In spring and fall, diving ducks are found near the aquatic vegetation. These are the Hooded Merganser, Common Merganser, Red-breasted Merganser, Common Goldeneye and Greater and Lesser Scaup.

In the spring of 1985, a Great Egret was seen from this spot. A colony of Purple Martins lives in a martin house nearby.

The Berthierville provincial nursery (Site 2) : The nursery is across from the rest area. Before visiting, telephone for permission or ask the caretaker.

After you walk through the plantations bordered by cedar hedges, you will come to a beautiful grove of maples. White pines grow here as well, because of the sandy soil. You will find a variety of passerine species: Pine Warbler, Bay-breasted Warbler, Ovenbird, Brown Creeper, Yellow-rumped Warbler, White-breasted Nuthatch, Wood Thrush, Rose-breasted Grosbeak, Red-eyed Vireo, Least Flycatcher, Eastern Wood-

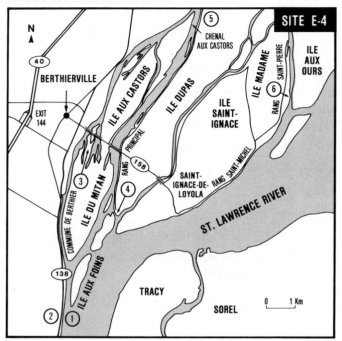

Pewee, Great Crested Flycatcher and Scarlet Tanager. Often there are Broad-winged Hawks and even Great Horned Owls.

***The Commune de Berthier (Site 3)* :** From Berthierville, head towards the islands on Highway 158 east. The Commune is situated to the west, just after the first bridge or, if you are coming from Sorel, just before the third bridge.

This area covers just over 6 km² and is still used for pasture. The Société de conservation, d'interprétation et de recherche de Berthierville et ses Iles (SCIRBI) has made a nature interpretation trail with observation towers and blinds. Hunting is now prohibited on this trail.

The habitat consists of grazed pasture land and cultivated fields with relatively large ponds throughout the area. There is excellent birding around the huge marsh filled with broad-leaved vegetation and wild rice. The shrubby and treed swamps also contribute to the richness of the habitat.

By the end of April you can start enjoying the wide variety of bird life here. Ducks, already present as of early April, are joined by Osprey, Great Blue Heron, Northern Harrier, Belted Kingfisher and a few shorebirds. As the breeding season begins in May, all the wetland species converge on the area: Common Moorhen, Pied-billed Grebe, Virginia Rail, Sora, Black Tern, Swamp Sparrow, Marsh Wren, Green-backed Heron, etc.

The Ile Dupas lighthouse (Site 4) : As you leave the above site, continue on Highway 158 east. Cross the second bridge and go west (right) on Rang Principal, keeping an eye on Chenal aux Castors. There is a municipal picnic area just before the end of the road near the lighthouse. If you are coming from the Sorel ferry, take Highway 158 west to Rang Principal on Ile Dupas and turn left.

If you follow Chenal aux Castors in spring, you will have close views of diving ducks, and you may very well see an Osprey plummeting after its prey. Snowy Owls are frequent in winter, as they are at most of the points of interest here. If you are lucky, you might see a Horned Grebe, Barrow's Goldeneye or even a Peregrine Falcon. A Tundra Swan was seen here by a few fortunate birdwatchers in May 1985. Another extraordinary sighting was a Bald Eagle being chased by Northern Pintails in May 1989.

The Ile Dupas Commune (Site 5): When coming from Berthierville, take Route 158 east. After the second bridge, turn east (left) onto Rang Principal on Ile Dupas and continue for about 7 km. There are roads from here to the gate, but they are not maintained. If you take the ferry from Sorel, continue on Highway 158 west and turn east (right) just before the second bridge onto Rang Principal. The habitat here is mostly grazing land around a stand of silver maple. Projects realized by Ducks Unlimited in 1987-88 ensure the future of this waterfowl nesting site.

Hawks migrate through here in spring, and shorebirds visit the muddy strip north of the commune in fall. Stilt Sandpipers and Hudsonian Godwits have been sighted here. In early summer, Willow Flycatchers, a rather uncommon nesting species in Quebec, inhabit all the shrubby areas. Later in summer, gulls gather on the north shore, where the occasional Great Egret may also be found.

It takes a full day to cover this site completely.

Ile Saint-Ignace and Ile Madame (Site 6): From Berthierville, follow Highway 158 east to the Ile Saint-Ignace wharf. Then head east (left) on Rang Saint-Michel. Turn right onto Rang

Saint-Pierre. If you take the Sorel ferry, turn right onto Rang Saint-Michel, near the ferry wharf.

In April, rafts of diving ducks occupy the river to the right of Rang Saint-Michel. These are mostly Greater and Lesser Scaups and Common Goldeneyes.

Follow Rang Saint-Pierre to see dabbling ducks in the flooded fields. This is also the preferred habitat of the Upland Sandpiper. In spring, shorebirds linger on the little islands in Chenal aux Ours to the right of the highway. In May 1989, a Ruff in spectacular breeding plumage was seen on one of these islands.

Ile du Moine

What to look for : Herons, dabbling ducks, rails, shorebirds, gulls and terns. *Special species :* Peregrine Falcon, Wilson's Phalarope, Sedge Wren, Sharp-tailed Sparrow.

Where : Approximately 75 km from Montreal, on the South Shore of the St. Lawrence, in Saint-Anne de Sorel – about 75 minutes by car and 10 minutes by boat from Montreal.

How to get there : From Montreal, take Autoroute 30 on the South Shore via Autoroute 10 east (Champlain Bridge) or Autoroute 20 east (Lafontaine Tunnel). This will take you to Sorel, 60 km away. In Sorel, Autoroute 30 ends after three sets of traffic lights on Highway 132 or Fiset Boulevard. Here you take Fiset to the left for 100 m and turn right onto Rue Monseigneur-Desranleau. Continue on this road, which becomes Chenal-du-Moine, for 14 km. Just before the bridge over Chenal d'Embarras, you will come to "Chez Bedette" restaurant, 3703 Chenal-du-Moine, where you can park.

If you come by the North Shore, take the ferry to Sorel at Saint-Ignace-de-Loyola (near Berthierville). When you get off the ferry, take one of the streets to the left to Fiset Boulevard. Here you turn right and drive 2 km to Rue Monseigneur-Desranleau.

Ile du Moine can only be reached by boat. Transportation is available through Mr. Jean Rousseau, 3706 Chenal-du-

Moine, but it is best to reserve ahead of time (tel: (514) 743-3025). If you have your own boat, you can launch it from the slip beside "La Grange du Survenant" restaurant, 1665 Chenal-du-Moine.

When to go : The best time to visit is when the shorebirds arrive, around May 15. Before that the island is often flooded. Go in July to see Sharp-tailed Sparrows and the other nesting birds and in August for dabbling ducks, shorebirds, and gulls. After mid-September, hunters arrive and the island becomes less interesting.

Birding is good at any time of the day, but it is best to spend a full day and make a complete tour of the island.

Special information : You will need waterproof footwear as the fields are often flooded. A spotting scope is useful for finding birds on Ile des Barques, a place where many interesting species have been discovered.

Site description : Ile du Moine was once shared pasture land and is still used for sheep, cattle and horses from May to November. It was purchased in 1987 with funds made available by Wildlife Habitat Canada and Ducks Unlimited. This was to discourage speculation and to promote wildlife management projects with Ducks Unlimited.

The island is a vast expanse of wet fields covered by reed phalaris and meadowgrass. A beach runs along the north shore and shallow marshes cover the southeast part, some of which are bordered by willow shrubs.

The northeast end is a low, wet field. It is washed over by the wake from every passing ship and resembles a tideflat.

The silty beaches on Ile du Moine are among the very few to be found around Lake Saint-Pierre. These are very attractive to shorebirds. In mid-May, there are sandpipers (Short-billed Dowitcher, Pectoral Sandpiper, Dunlin, Red Knot, Least Sandpiper, White-rumped Sandpiper), plovers (Killdeer, Black-bellied Plover, Semipalmated Plover), waders (Greater Yellowlegs, Lesser Yellowlegs, Solitary Sandpiper and Spotted Sandpiper) and Wilson's Phalarope. Ruddy Turnstones arrive at the beginning of June. These shorebirds are sometimes accompanied by rarities such as Marbled Godwit and Ruff.

The shorebirds return to Ile du Moine between late July and late September in increasing number and variety (Baird's Sandpiper, Stilt Sandpiper, Sanderling). Rarities seen during this period are Western Sandpiper, Buff-breasted Sandpiper and Long-billed Dowitcher. Check the phalaropes from the end of August to mid-September, because all three species have been seen during this period: Wilson's Phalarope (nesting), Red-necked Phalarope and Red Phalarope.

The best places for watching shorebirds are the northeast point of Ile du Moine and the southeast end of Ile des Barques, which can be seen from the centre-north area of Ile du Moine.

There are many species of ducks and geese occurring in large numbers. At the end of May, there is often a flock of Brant feeding on the northeast point. All the species of dabbling ducks nest on the island. After July they gather in large numbers in the marshes on the northeast point and in the bay opposite Ile des Barques.

Ducks and shorebirds taking off in alarm often indicate the presence of a Peregrine Falcon. Northern Harriers are very common and Red-tailed Hawks occasional.

Great Horned Owls nest in a little silver maple grove in the centre of the island. Short-eared Owls nest in the wet field that in winter is patrolled by Snowy Owls.

The beaches on the north end of the island and the southeast point of Ile des Barques are staging grounds for gulls and terns. The most common are Ring-billed Gull, Herring Gull, Great Black-backed Gull, Common Tern and Black Tern, and the more unusual are Caspian Tern, Bonaparte's Gull, Little Gull, Sabine's Gull and Franklin's Gull. The best period is between mid-August to mid-September, although gulls are abundant from May to November.

During the summer, Great Blue Heron, American Bittern and Black-crowned Night-Heron are common in the marshes on the northeast and southeast points of the island. Every year rare birds are seen at these spots: Great Egret, Snowy Egret, Little Blue Heron and Tricolored Heron.

Rails are fairly abundant, although the Yellow Rail has not been sighted recently. The Marsh Wrens in the marshes on the east end of the island are hard to miss. Sedge Wrens are seen every year, in the wet field or the willow shrubs across from Ile des Barques. Perched on reeds in July, Sharp-tailed

Ile du Moine

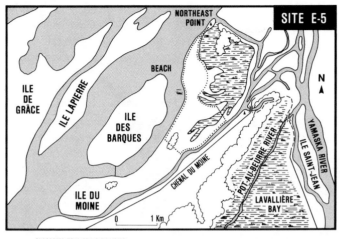

.... SUGGESTED TOUR OF ILE DU MOINE
---- TRAIL TO LAVALLIÈRE BAY

Sparrows are easy to spot, especially if you know their song. Every shrub in the centre of the island harbours a Swamp Sparrow, while Savannah Sparrows favour the sandy border. A Northern Wheatear was once seen at the beginning of September.

Suggested Route : It takes time to visit Ile du Moine; the tour around the island is a good day's walk (13 km). Start at the northeast end and follow the north shore to Ile des Barques. Cross the wet field to the south shore, which you follow to the marsh. You then work your way north, ending where you began, at the northeast point (7-8 km). This route gives complete coverage of all the main points of interest :

American Bittern

1) the northeast point and marshes;
2) the north beaches;
3) the beach on the southeast end of Ile des Barques;
4) the wet field;
5) the southeast marsh.

Lavallière Bay :

The path to Lavallière Bay makes a nice early morning walk before a trip to Ile du Moine. It is not easy to find. From the parking lot in front of "Chez Bedette" Restaurant, follow the south side of Chenal d'Embarras to the silver maple grove. Here you must cross private property, so it is best to ask permission. Nesting in the maple grove are Great Horned Owls, Warbling Vireos, Least Flycatchers, Rose-breasted Grosbeaks, Veeries, White-breasted Nuthatches,Eastern Wood-Pewees, Great Crested Flycatchers, Northern Orioles, and Yellow-bellied Sapsuckers.

The path goes through the woods to a dyke built by Ducks Unlimited. Even if the water level is high, the dyke is rarely flooded and you can walk along the top. It will take you across the marsh along a canal. In summer there are many Common Moorhens, Pied-billed Grebes, Marsh Wrens, Swamp Sparrows, Eastern Kingbirds, dabbling ducks, and Great Blue Herons. The dyke ends 1.0 km further on, at the mouth of the Pot-au-beurre River. Another path here will take you along the Yamaska River. Dabbling ducks are plentiful here in spring. Retrace your steps to come back.

Saint-Barthélemy

What to look for : Dabbling ducks, diving ducks, hawks, shorebirds. *Special species :* Greater White-fronted Goose, Eurasian Wigeon, Peregrine Falcon.

Where : On the north shore of Lake Saint-Pierre, about 75 km or a one-hour drive from Montreal.

How to get there : Leave Montreal by the Metropolitan Autoroute east or Autoroute 25 north (Lafontaine Tunnel). Drive about 75 km on Autoroute 40 east towards Trois-Rivières along the north shore of the St. Lawrence. Take the 155 or Saint-Barthélemy exit. This leads to two service roads on the north and south sides of the autoroute. Drive to the end of each of these roads; there are birds along both. Then go south towards the river to Route du Fleuve, where you turn east (left) and continue to the Maskinongé River.

To come back on the Autoroute in the opposite direction, after you get to the Maskinongé River, take the overpass above the Autoroute. Turn right immediately and cross the little bridge over the Maskinongé River and come back towards Autoroute 40.

When to go : The ideal time to visit is around mid-April. A few hours will prove to be a worthwhile investment.

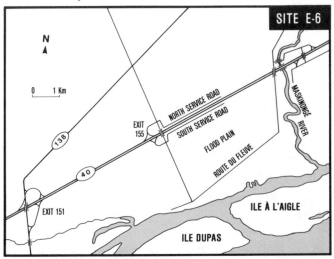

Site description : Lake Saint-Pierre and its shoreline appear as one vast, flat stretch with scarcely any rise in the land. During the spring thaw, the lake swells and floods the surrounding cultivated area. The water warms quickly and, being the ideal depth for surface-feeding (15-45 cm), it becomes the preferred habitat of dabbling ducks.

The Saint-Barthélemy flood plain is one of the largest spring migration staging grounds for dabbling ducks in Quebec (up to 3000 ducks). Every species in Quebec is found here, the most abundant being Northern Pintail. The other species are seen in varying numbers, depending on the period. The best time is from early April to early May, with numbers peaking in mid-April. The best observation point is the service road south of the Autoroute. The Eurasian Wigeon is seen here almost every year.

The Canada Goose is the dominant species along the service road north of the Autoroute. As many as 5000 may be seen at one time. Check all the geese foraging in these fields because one or two Greater White-fronted Geese are found here every year, mostly in the ditches between mid- and late April. There is less flooding on the north side of the Autoroute, but dabbling ducks come here as well. Peregrine Falcons are sighted regularly, searching the fields for ducks. Rough-legged Hawks are abundant until late April and often roost in the lone trees.

Shorebirds, mainly Greater and Lesser Yellowlegs, feed regularly around the edge of the flooded fields, and occasionally a Ruff is spotted amongst them.

The Mute Swan and Sandhill Crane are two rare species that have been sighted here.

By mid-May the birds have left and the farmers are working the fields, so the site is no longer of interest.

Suggested route : The service roads on either side of the Autoroute are the best observation points. Make a round trip by heading south and taking Route du Fleuve east to the Maskinongé River. This road goes along flooded fields that attract dabbling ducks. Take Autoroute 40 west to come back to your departure point.

Baie-du-Febvre

What to look for : Geese, dabbling and diving ducks, hawks, shorebirds, owls. *Special species :* Canada Goose, Snow Goose, Ross' Goose, Eurasian Wigeon, Redhead, Ruddy Duck, Wilson's Phalarope, Short-eared Owl, Snowy Owl.

Where : Baie-du-Febvre is on the south shore of Lake Saint-Pierre in the county of Nicolet-Yamaska, about 90 km from Montreal. It can be reached in about 90 minutes.

How to get there : The main access road is Highway 132 east. From Montreal, take either Autoroute 10 east (Champlain Bridge) or Autoroute 20 east (Lafontaine Tunnel) to get onto Autoroute 30 east to Sorel. Once in Sorel, continue on Highway 132 east to Baie-du-Febvre.

If you come by the North Shore, take the Sorel ferry at Saint-Ignace-de-Loyola near Berthierville or cross the lake at the west end by the bridge at Trois-Rivières. Both will bring you to Highway 132.

When coming by Autoroute 20, you can get onto Highway 132 by taking Highways 122, 143 or 226 north, near Drummondville.

When to go : Spring and summer are the best times. Winter brings numerous Snowy Owls, but fall field trips are hazardous because of hunters. The best times are between 7:00-9:00 a.m. and 5:00-7:00 p.m. Two hours are sufficient to visit the site, but you can easily spend a full day, especially in the spring.

Special information : In spring, the number of birds depends on the extent of flooding. When the lake is high, the fields are flooded, and the birds are plentiful and easy to see.

Site description : In summer, the south shore of Lake Saint-Pierre is one vast wetland, bordered to the south by wet fields and to either side by stands of silver maple. To the east is a huge cannon range belonging to the Department of National Defence. This area is fenced off and access is prohibited. In fall, it serves as a migratory bird sanctuary for dabbling ducks.

From late March through early May, the cultivated fields are flooded, creating a vast flood plain that attracts up to 15,000 Canada Geese, 56,000 Snow Geese and 4,000 dabbling ducks. This is the largest staging ground on the St. Lawrence for Canada Geese and the second largest for dabbling ducks and Snow Geese.

The Quebec Breeding Bird Atlas project has established approximately 130 possible nesting species for this site. The most interesting of these are Wilson's Phalarope, Ruddy Duck, Redhead, Wood Duck and Short-eared Owl.

Marsh birds abound in summer: rails, Common Moorhen, Pied-billed Grebe, Common Snipe, Marsh Wren, Swamp Sparrow and Black Tern.

Spring brings an influx of hawks; often Rough-legged Hawks perch on the lone trees in April. Northern Harriers quarter the marsh, vying for the Meadow Voles with Short-eared Owls, which in turn compete with Snowy Owls. Peregrine Falcons prey on the ducks, and Bald Eagles are on the lookout for beached carp. Sunny days bring Turkey Vultures and all the hawk species kettling overhead in their northward migration.

Several heron species inhabit the area. Great Blue Herons breed in the National Defence area, in a small heronry of 15 nests. American Bitterns frequent the partially flooded fields.

Keep an eye out in spring for Greater White-fronted Geese. One or two may be foraging with the Canada Geese on the west side of the flooded fields. Other possible rarities are the Ross' Goose, Great Egret, Ruff, Cattle Egret, Glossy Ibis, Long-billed Dowitcher, Forster's Tern and Tundra Swan.

Suggested route :

The Baie-du-Febvre settling pond (Site 1) : Take Highway 132 on the south shore of Lake Saint-Pierre to Baie-du-Febvre. From the village centre, take the gravel road that goes north (Route Janelle) for 1.0 km. The pond and an observation station are on the right side of the road.

The pond is used to purify waste water from the village. Its abundance of invertebrates makes it an attractive breeding ground for dabbling ducks.

The spring thaw begins around April 20, bringing diving ducks until early May: Greater Scaup, Lesser Scaup, Ring-necked Duck, Bufflehead, Common Goldeneye, Hooded Merganser and Redhead. Two or three dozen Wilson's Phalaropes stop here regularly during the first weeks of May. This is the only place in Quebec where they can be seen so readily and in such great numbers.

Ruddy Ducks may appear in June. This species nested here successfully in 1981 and 1989.

In July and August, young dabbling ducks of all species congregate here, often several hundred per hectare. Redheads nest around the pond.

The Baie-du-Febvre commune (Site 2) : This site is just after the settling pond. Simply continue north along Route Janelle to the shore of Lake Saint-Pierre.

The land here was once used for collective pasturing. Part of it has been turned into market gardens, and the rest will be managed by Ducks Unlimited to promote the breeding of dabbling ducks.

Southeast of the cottages belonging to the Club de la Landeroche is an observation tower with a view of the river and the National Defence marsh. There is a slip nearby for launching canoes or rowboats.

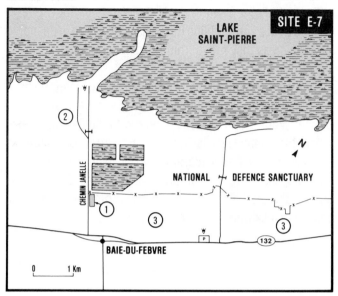

Snowy Owls are regular winter visitors. In spring, Short-eared Owls arrive to nest in the wet fields. Wilson's Phalaropes nest here as well.

The plowed fields south of the cottages attract a variety of shorebirds in spring: Pectoral Sandpiper, White-rumped Sandpiper, Least Sandpiper and Short-billed Dowitcher.

The Nicolet-Baie-du-Febvre flood plain (Site 3) : This site is on Highway 132, between Nicolet and Baie-du-Febvre. The low-lying farmland here is flooded from late March to early May, the amount of flooding affecting the number and variety of species. This is one of the most spectacular birding sites in Quebec. From dawn to dusk, thousands of Snow Geese, Canada Geese and dabbling ducks pass overhead in unending succession as they move from one site to another.

Two observation stations have been set up along Highway 132 and others will no doubt be added. Every year, one or two Greater White-fronted Geese mingle with the Canada Geese. When the water level is high in early April, Canvasbacks regularly join the Redheads, and one or two Eurasian Wigeons often appear in April. Peregrine Falcons and Snowy Owls quarter the area in search of ducks. Sometimes they will engage in a skirmish over their quarry.

Wilson's Phalarope

North of Montreal

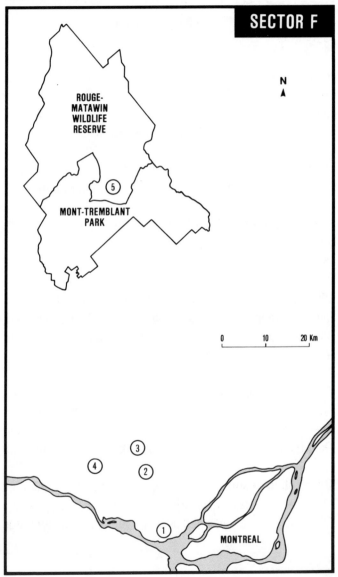

SECTOR F

N

ROUGE-
MATAWIN
WILDLIFE
RESERVE

⑤

MONT-TREMBLANT
PARK

0   10   20 Km

③

④   ②

①   MONTREAL

Oka and Paul Sauvé Provincial Park

What to look for : Wetland species, shorebirds, passerines. *Special species :* Red-throated Loon, Horned Grebe, Red-necked Grebe, Canvasback, Yellow-throated Vireo, Pine Warbler, Red Crossbill, White-winged Crossbill.

Where : The Oka region is on the north shore of the Lake of Two Mountains, about a 45-minute drive from Montreal.

How to get there : From Montreal, take Autoroute 13 north and Autoroute 640 west, which you follow to the end. A right turn onto Highway 344 west will take you to Oka village.

When to go : The site is especially interesting in spring and fall. The many cross-country ski trails in Paul Sauvé Park allow skiing and birdwatching to be combined in the winter. At least half a day is necessary to visit the site.

Special information : Paul Sauvé Park only opens at 7 a.m., so the only way to bird in the park before then is to camp overnight. Information on the park is available by writing to Parc Paul-Sauvé, Case postale 447, Oka (Québec) J0N 1E0.

Description of site : The Oka region is much hillier than the surrounding area, and these hills are known collectively as the Oka Hills. They are covered by large wooded areas, orchards and cultivated fields. The forest cover is dominated mainly by sugar maple, silver maple, white pine and red oak.

Paul Sauvé Park lies along the Lake of Two Mountains. It is a recreational park of 1,800 hectares, encompassing mixed habitat that includes wetland. La Grande Baie, a large swampy area in the eastern part of the park, is inhabited by a good number of water birds.

Camping, picnicking, swimming and hiking are popular here and, in winter, cross-country skiing and snowshoeing. The park has an interpretation program on its history and ecology and guided field trips for visitors. Canoe trips are held on La Grande Baie in summer.

According to information available at the park interpretation centre, 210 species of birds have been sighted within the park limits. Over 100 of these probably nest in the Oka region. Wetland species, including ducks and geese, are numerous, many of them nesting in the huge marsh along La Grande Baie. In autumn, diving ducks congregate in large rafts on the Lake of Two Mountains. There is a Great Blue heronry along La Grande Baie which unfortunately is threatened by the intense human activity in the area. The sandy beaches along the Lake of Two Mountains are a stopover for shorebirds during the fall migration.

Hawks and owls are also plentiful. Seen during the nesting period are Red-shouldered Hawk, Great Horned Owl, Barred Owl and Eastern Screech-Owl. Northern Saw-whet Owls have nested on occasion, and Turkey Vultures, a new species in the area, may be nesting on one of the Oka Hills.

Yellow-throated Vireo and Pine Warbler, two species with a very localized distribution in Quebec, are found here during nesting season. Blue-gray Gnatcatchers and Red-headed Woodpeckers have nested at least once within the park limits.

Suggested route :

La Grande Baie (Site 1) : At the traffic lights at the end of Highway 640, take Chemin des Collines to the Paul Sauvé Park interpretation centre. La Grande Baie trail leaves across from the centre. It goes through fallow fields, an old stand of maple and then follows La Grande Baie. This habitat mix attracts a wide variety of bird life. Yellow-throated Vireos are especially common in the maples from May to July, and Black Terns, Wood Ducks and both species of teal can be seen from the boardwalk and observation tower beside the bay. The route takes about two hours to complete. During the summer, there are organized canoe trips on La Grande Baie. Information on these is available at the interpretation centre.

The Lake of Two Mountains shoreline (Site 2) : The Paul Sauvé Park beach, especially the western section which attracts fewer bathers, is a popular shorebird-watching site in the fall. Twenty plover and sandpiper species have been observed here, including such rarities as Hudsonian Godwit, Stilt Sandpiper and Long-billed Dowitcher. Caspian Terns (as many as four in 1989) have spent the last few summers here.

Oka and Paul Sauvé Provincial Park

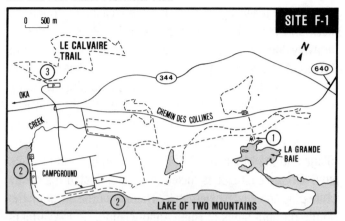

April and October bring Red-throated Loons, Horned Grebes, Red-necked Grebes and several diving ducks, including Canvasbacks. Among the many species breeding in the wet woodland along the beach are Blue-gray Gnatcatcher and Red-headed Woodpecker, which have successfully raised young here. Pine Warblers have been seen regularly in the small stands of white pine. If you want to reach this site more quickly, go by car and park at the parking lot next to the beach. There is an admission charge for this.

Le Calvaire (Site 3) : Located in the park north of Highway 344 across from the west visitors' centre. The trail leaves from a parking lot where you can park free of charge. Indigo Buntings are usually very much in evidence here, and many woodland birds nest in the mature hardwood forest along the trail.

La pinède (not shown on the map): This pine grove is located just north of the village of Oka. It can be reached through the Oka Municipal Park, which has a parking lot. When coming by Highway 344, turn right onto Rue Saint-Paul. Turn right onto Rue Saint-Denis and right again onto Rue des Pins. You can also go by Rue l'Annonciation. When coming west on Highway 344, take Rue Saint-Paul and turn right onto Rue Saint-Jacques, which leads to Rue l'Annonciation. Leave your car along this road. West of Rue l'Annonciation, between the village and the Municipal Golf Club, is a pure stand of white pine. On the east side is mixed forest dominated mainly by white pine and eastern hemlock. There are trails through the woods on both sides of Rue l'Annonciation. Pine Warblers nest here during the summer. Both crossbill species visit the area, mostly in winter. This superb pine forest is unfortunately threatened by development projects.

Marsh Wren

Sylvain Tanguay 1990

The Centre éducatif forestier Le Bois de Belle-Rivière

What to look for : Hawks, owls, warblers. *Special species :* Northern Goshawk, Great Horned Owl, Barred Owl, Pileated Woodpecker, Eastern Bluebird.

Where : About 65 km northwest of downtown Montreal in Argenteuil County.

How to get there : The Centre is located on Highway 148, halfway between Saint-Eustache and Lachute. Take Autoroute 640 and leave by Exit 11, heading towards Lachute. You can also go by Mirabel Boulevard, by taking Exit 35 from Autoroute 15. Mirabel Boulevard will take you to Highway 148, which is near the entrance to the site.

When to go : The Centre is open year-round, except between Christmas and New Year's Day. It offers interesting birding possibilities in all seasons. Winter is the best time for sighting Great Horned and Barred Owls or finding Pileated Woodpeckers. The two feeders that are maintained throughout the winter attract a variety of species, both common and rare.

Migrating birds abound in spring. The orchard is in bloom and is filled with warblers and other passerines. Spring is also the best time to see Eastern Bluebirds.

At the beginning of summer, the nesting season is at its peak. This is the time to study the bird life characteristic of the maple forest.

During the second and third weekends in May, the Centre opens at 6:00 a.m. to accommodate birdwatchers. Early-morning birding is possible at other times, if you walk the 1.0 km from the gate to the trails. With 8 km of paths through varying habitat, you can hike and birdwatch to your heart's content.

Ruffed Grouse

Special information : The Centre was officially opened to the public in September 1981. On April 15, 1987, the facilities were turned over to the Ministry of Energy, Mines and Resources, and it became the ninth of the Quebec provincial nature centres. Situated in the heart of one of Quebec's finest forests, the sugar-maple hickory stand, the Centre is used for study and appreciation of the forest and its components. It is open throughout the year from 8:30 a.m. to 4:30 p.m. from Monday to Friday (closed between 12:00 p.m. and 1:00 p.m.) and from 9:00 a.m. to 4:00 p.m. on Saturdays, Sundays and statutory holidays. In November and December, it is only open during the week, and in January and February it is closed on Saturdays.

The trails leave from the interpretation centre. There are three picnic shelters. Be sure to bring your lunch, as there are no facilities for buying food.

The Centre's vocation is one of educating the public and preserving habitat. It is not a recreational park, so no sports or games are allowed nor can you bring pets or drive any kind of vehicle. Plants and flowers are not to be picked. There is no admission fee, and all the services are free.

In winter, a 1.8-km hiking trail is kept open. The snowshoe trail through the maples takes about two hours to complete. There is no cross-country skiing.

Site description : The site encompasses 182 hectares, most of it forested with sugar maple. There are stands of eastern hemlock and cedar, an orchard, thickets and hedges of trees and shrubs. Some fields have been made into forest gardens and ornamental gardens. The Centre is in the heart of a farming area and is bordered by sections of woodland, pasture and cultivated and abandoned fields. The forest is part of the sugar-maple hickory stand typical of southern Quebec. The deciduous tree species are bitternut hickory, butternut, American beech and, of course, the dominant species, sugar maple. The forest types range from regenerating forest to full-grown timber, a habitat mix that attracts a variety of species of birds.

In 1976, a research program was conducted on the bird life around the Montreal International Airport. The Centre was part of the area studied. Of the 185 bird species counted, 97 can be considered as nesting.

Small rodents thrive in the farmland and abandoned fields enclosed by stone fences and hedges. These attract hawks, some of the commonly sighted ones being Broad-winged Hawk, Northern Harrier and American Kestrel. Red-tailed Hawks have been found nesting at the edge of the site, and Northern Goshawks and Sharp-shinned Hawks are sporadically sighted in the forest cover.

The forest habitat and the abundance of rodents also attract owls. Great Horned and Barred Owls are frequently sighted, especially in winter. Long-eared and Northern Saw-whet Owls are mostly seen during migration.

Pileated Woodpeckers live in the sections of mature forest, and their numerous excavations are much in evidence in the maple stand. The bird is most easily seen here in winter. Ruffed Grouse are common in the younger stands of forest.

In the open habitat are such common species as Eastern Kingbird, swallows, the mimic thrushes, Yellow Warbler, Common Yellowthroat, Indigo Bunting, sparrows, Bobolink and other blackbirds, and American Goldfinch.

The greatest variety of species is found among the woodland birds. Most frequently observed are flycatchers, jays, chickadees, nuthatches, creepers, thrushes, vireos and warblers. Also found are numbers of Rose-breasted Grosbeaks and Scarlet Tanagers.

Despite its name, the Bois de Belle-Rivière has no sizable body of water that might attract shorebirds or water birds. A few species such as Great Blue Heron and Black Duck are sporadically sighted in spring when low-lying areas are flooded by melting snow.

Suggested route : The strategically placed feeders and nest boxes draw certain species. Thirty bluebird houses have been erected in likely areas, and nesting records have already been established. Feeders bring the familiar Evening Grosbeaks, Blue Jays, Mourning Doves and other less frequently sighted birds such as Gray Jays, Northern Cardinals and Northern Shrikes. Hummingbird feeders attract some very tame individuals that obligingly pose for photographers.

The bird life in the Centre and the surrounding area has not been subject to much research or record-keeping to date, so

The Centre éducatif forestier Le Bois de Belle-Rivière

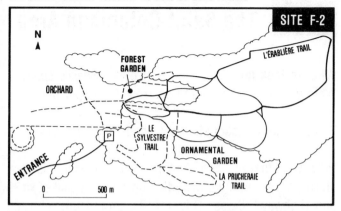

there is still much to be learned. The reports mentioned above list, for example, the Clay-colored Sparrow, a very rare species in the Montreal area. It is hoped that in the future substantiated sightings will provide a clearer picture of the bird life at this site.

The Saint-Colomban Area

What to look for : warblers, sparrows. *Special species :* Whip-poor-will, Clay-colored Sparrow, Field Sparrow.

Where : Northwest of Montreal, about an hour's drive.

How to get there : There are three main routes to this area. The first is by Autoroute 15 north, from which you take Exit 39 onto Highway 158 west. Drive for 13.8 km and turn right onto Montée Saint-Rémi. Cross the North River and turn left onto Chemin Rivière-du-Nord. The second route is also by Autoroute 15, but take instead Exit 35 onto Mirabel Boulevard. Drive about 15 km, turn right onto Rang Saint-Rémi and drive 4 km until you come to Highway 158. The third route is by Autoroute 13, Highway 640 west and Highway 148 west at Saint-Eustache (Exit 11). About 2.6 km after the Centre éducatif forestier Bois de Belle-Rivière, turn right onto Chemin Mirabel, left onto Rang Saint-Rémi and drive to Chemin Rivière-du-Nord.

When to go : May to July is the most interesting period. Allow two to three hours to complete the suggested route.

Site description : The area is located between Saint-Canut and Lachute and is flanked by the Montreal lowlands on one side and the Laurentians on the other. It is characterized by mixed, regenerating forest in various stages interspersed with

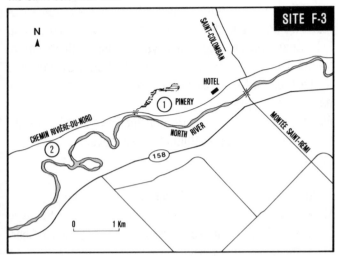

pasture and cultivated fields. Some of the stands of young pine and cedar contain an interesting variety of bird life. In winter, white-tailed deer are very much in evidence. The species that attract birders to the area are warblers and particularly sparrows, ten of which can be seen in the summer. The most sought-after are the Clay-coloured and Field Sparrows.

Suggested route : Chemin Rivière-du-Nord is the only passable road through the area. It is a picturesque, little-travelled dirt road running between the North River on one side and the Laurentian foothills on the other. Head west along this road from Montée Saint-Rémi. Go past the Colford Hotel to a huge stand of young pine in various stages of maturity, to the right

(Site 1). The trail through the stand begins exactly 1.4 km from Montée Saint-Rémi. This is where the many species of sparrows are found during the summer. Clay-colored and Field Sparrows are seen each year, along with the more common Chipping, Vesper, Savannah, Song, Swamp and White-throated Sparrows and Dark-eyed Juncos. The trail leads to a swampy pond north of the plantation. Here there are Wood Duck, Green-backed Herons and Olive-sided Flycatchers. Sometimes a Turkey Vulture will soar over the hills on the horizon.

Continue west on Chemin Rivière-du-Nord towards Lachute. About 3 km west past the plantation, you will come to a field crossed by Hydro-Québec power lines. Grasshopper Sparrows are occasionally seen here in the summer *(Site 2).* Further west, Chemin Rivière-du-Nord goes through mixed woodland inhabited by an abundance of warblers including, at times, Pine Warblers. In the evening, the oft-repeated call of the Whip-poor-will is heard on every side, especially in May and June. During the full moon in April, you might hear a Northern Saw-whet Owl calling – a mechanically-repeated single-note whistle. You might easily chance upon white-tailed deer as well.

When you reach the west end of Chemin Rivière-du-Nord, you can continue on to Site F4 (the Lachute area), along Highway 329 south and Highway 158 east.

Field Sparrow

The Lachute Area

What to look for : passerines. *Special species :* Pine Warbler, Red Crossbill, White-winged Crossbill, Gray Jay, Boreal Chickadee.

Where : Northwest of Montreal, about a 60-minute drive from downtown.

How to get there : Take Autoroute 13 north, Highway 640 west and Highway 148 west at Saint-Eustache (Exit 11). Go past the Centre éducatif forestier Le Bois de Belle-Rivière (15 km) and turn right onto Chemin des Sources. You can also take Autoroute 15 north and Highway 158 west to Chemin des Sources.

When to go : Spring and early summer are the best times to visit this area. Some of the boreal species, however, such as Gray Jay and Boreal Chickadee, are only seen in winter. The site can normally be visited in a few hours.

Site description : The Lachute area is between the Laurentians and the Montreal lowlands. Its abundance of coniferous trees and proximity to the Laurentians make it a likely spot for boreal species.

The Lachute Area

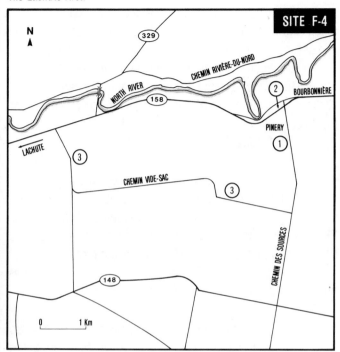

There are numerous land birds but few water birds. Warblers species are well represented and include the Pine Warbler, which has a very uneven distribution in southwestern Quebec.

Boreal Chickadees, Gray Jays and both crossbill species inhabit the pines throughout the area, especially in winter.

Suggested route : Begin your tour at the junction of Highway 148 and Chemin des Sources. In June, make several stops along Chemin des Sources to look for the many species nesting in the woods and surrounding fields. Just before you reach Highway 158, you will see a large plantation of red pine and spruce. Here there are nesting Yellow-rumped Warblers, Golden-crowned Kinglets and Hermit Thrushes. In winter, you will find Gray Jays and Boreal Chickadees. There are trails all through the pine woods, but the snowmobile trail makes for the best walking. It is 3.4 km from the intersection with Highway 148 *(Site 1)*.

North of Highway 158, turn left onto Chemin Bourbonnière. This will take you through a residential park with charming little wooden houses surrounded by magnificent white pines. Pine Warblers nest here, and both crossbill species can be seen throughout the year. These nomadic birds cannot, of course, be counted on to appear with any regularity. Sometimes Gray Jays come here in winter *(Site 2)*.

Take Chemin Bourbonnière back to Highway 158, and go west to Chemin Vide-Sac (3.8 km). You will find yourself in an area of farmland. Eastern Meadowlarks and Bobolinks are among the several grassland species found here during the breeding season *(Site 3)*. Chemin Vide-Sac will bring you back to Chemin des Sources. From here you can take either Highway 148 or Highway 158 to go back to Montreal.

If you wish to continue on to Saint-Colomban, you can do so by driving west on Highway 158 from the junction with Chemin Bourbonnière. Turn right onto Highway 329 north (2.9 km) and right onto Chemin Rivière-du-Nord (1.2 km).

This is a very picturesque road winding through an area of mixed forest. Birds are plentiful here, as are white-tailed deer. Follow this road and eventually you will come to Site F3.

Gray Jay

Mont Tremblant Provincial Park and the Rouge Matawin Wildlife Reserve

What to look for : warblers and other nesting species. *Special species :* Osprey, Spruce Grouse, Black-backed Woodpecker, Olive-sided Flycatcher, Yellow-bellied Flycatcher, Gray Jay, Common Raven, Boreal Chickadee, Lincoln's Sparrow, Rusty Blackbird, White-winged Crossbill.

Where : Mont Tremblant Park and the Rouge Matawin Wildlife Reserve are north of Montreal in the Laurentians. It is at least a two-hour drive by car.

How to get there :

Mont Tremblant Park : The park is divided into three administrative sectors, La Diable, La Pimbina and l'Assomption, each of which is approached by a different route. Detailed maps of each sector can be obtained from the park administration office.

The main entrance to La Diable sector is through La Diable visitors' centre, open year-round. To get there, go through Lac-Supérieur (Autoroute 15, Highway 117, Exit Saint-Faustin) or through Mont-Tremblant village (Autoroute 15, Highway 117, Mont-Tremblant village exit and Chemin Duplessis). If you want to go to La Cachée sector, which is the western part of La Diable, go through La Cachée visitors' centre. This is open only in summer. To get there, go through Labelle, which is 28 km north of Saint-Jovite on Highway 117. Note that you can only get from La Cachée to the rest of La Diable on foot, on skis or by bicycle. You can also get to La Diable through La Macaza visitors' centre in the Rouge Matawin Wildlife Reserve.

La Pimbina is approached through Saint-Donat (Highways 25 and 125 from Montreal or Highways 15 and 329 through Sainte-Agathe-des-Monts). In summer, you can reach this sector by taking Route 1 through the park from La Diable or Route 7 from the Caribou visitors' centre in L'Assomption sector. Another entrance is by Route 3 from the Saint-Michel-des-Saints visitors' centre in the Rouge Matawin Wildlife Reserve.

The main entrance to L'Assomption sector is through the Saint-Côme visitors' centre, open year-round. To get there, drive through Saint-Côme (Autoroute 40, Highways 31 and 347 from Montreal to Saint-Côme or Highways 25 and 343 to Saint-Côme). You can also go through Notre-Dame-de-la-Merci. In summer, you can enter by the Caribou visitors' centre via Saint-Donat or through the Rouge Matawin Wildlife Reserve via the Saint-Michel-des-Saints visitors' centre.

The Rouge Matawin Wildlife Reserve : The reserve, which is located immediately north of Mont Tremblant Park, can be reached through the park or three other visitors' centres.

The Saint-Michel-des-Saints visitors' centre is 26 km west of Saint-Michel-des-Saints village. It is 186 km from Montreal by Highway 131. La Macaza visitors' centre is 16 km north of La Macaza village. It is 182 km from Montreal by Autoroute 15 and Highway 117. L'Ascension visitors' centre is 11 km north east of L'Ascension and 207 km from Montreal by Autoroute 15 and Highway 117.

When to go : The best time to visit the park or the reserve is summer, particularly June and July. During the winter, you can combine cross-country skiing and birdwatching. A trip to this area will take a full day.

Special information : Information on the activities and services at Mont Tremblant Park and road maps for each sector can be obtained by calling the following numbers :

- Centre d'accueil La Diable : (819) 688–2281
- Centre d'accueil Saint-Donat : (819) 424–2954
- Centre d'accueil Saint-Côme : (514) 883–1291

You can also write to the Mont Tremblant Park administration: C.P. 129, Chemin de la Pisciculture, Saint-Faustin (Québec) J0T 2G0.

Information on the Rouge Matawin Wildlife Reserve can be obtained from mid-May to mid-November at the following numbers :
- For general information : (819) 424–2981
- Poste d'accueil La Macaza : (819) 275–1811
- Poste d'accueil Saint-Michel-des-Saints : (514) 833–5530

Common Loon

You can also write to C.P. 370, Saint-Donat, Comté de Montcalm (Québec) J0T 2C0.

Site description : Mont Tremblant Park is a huge 1248-km^2 area located in the heart of the Laurentians. Its purpose is mainly recreational. There are scores of lakes, rivers and mountains, all situated in the Yellow Birch-sugar maple stand and the fir forest. The lakes and rivers in the park are part of three watersheds: Rivière Saint-Maurice, Rivière L'Assomption and Rivière Rouge, which also includes Rivière du Diable. The summit of Mont Tremblant is 960 m high – the highest in the

Montreal Laurentians. There are over 400 km of trails that give access to a wide variety of habitat, mostly forest. Cross-country skiing is very popular in the winter. There are many campsites, 900 of which are mostly around Lac Monroe and Lac Chat in La Diable, and 300 in La Pimbina. L'Assomption has only been part of the park since 1981 and has only 28 campsites and seven cottages. Being much more secluded, its wildlife is more abundant and varied. It includes Moose, Black Bear, Beaver and White-tailed Deer.

The Rouge Matawin Wildlife Reserve, created in 1981, is north of Mont Tremblant Park and encompasses more than 1635 km^2 of forest and 450 lakes. The main activities here are fishing and hunting. The forest is young, the land having been cleared through logging operations a few years ago. It has the highest density of moose in Quebec.

According to the information on Mont Tremblant Park, 193 species of birds have been recorded here. At the height of the breeding season, a single observer can sight 40 to 50 species in one morning. In L'Assomption and La Pimbina in June 1987, a group of birders identified 96 species in two days! With 20 breeding species present in June, the warbler family always makes the best showing. The male warblers defend their territory by singing unrelentingly for several hours a day. The site becomes a sound laboratory for anyone wanting to study warbler song.

Most of the special species mentioned at the beginning of this section are relatively common. Spruce Grouse and Black-backed Woodpecker, however, are rather rare and difficult to

Mont-Tremblant Provincial Park and Rouge-Matawin Wildlife Reserve

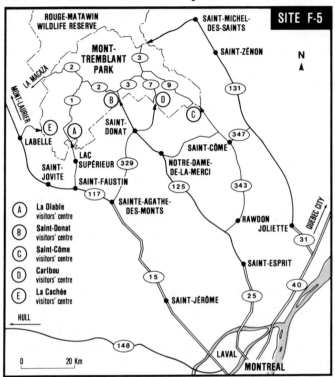

A. La Diable visitors' centre
B. Saint-Donat visitors' centre
C. Saint-Côme visitors' centre
D. Caribou visitors' centre
E. La Cachée visitors' centre

find. In summer, these species, along with Gray Jay and Boreal Chickadee, are more frequently seen in the north of the park and in the wildlife reserve.

Suggested route : It is difficult to recommend one particular route through an area so vast, where so little is known about the birding possibilities. If you camp in the purely recreational areas, around Lac Monroe for example, you will find several trails, such as those to Lac à l'Ours and Lac des Femmes. These offer a good variety of species. The secret for increasing your list, of course, is to bird in several types of habitat: deciduous forest, coniferous forest, peat bogs, lakes.

If you can only spend one day, you could take Route 1 and Route 2 between La Diable visitors' centre and the Saint-Donat visitors' centre. You could stop along the road where trails have been cleared. One of these trails, along Route 1, just before the intersection with Route 2, leads to Lac Tador. Many of the species mentioned above – Spruce Grouse, Gray Jay, Boreal Chickadee – have been seen here. If you have time, you could take a detour up to Lac de la Savanne by Route 2 towards La Macaza visitors' centre. The marshes around this huge lake are inhabited by wetland species.

Chemin Le Boulé, which can be reached from Lac Monroe, is another good route to take. The suggested stops are Lac Racine (colony of Great Blue Herons), Lac de la Fourche (Black-backed Woodpeckers) and Lac Allen (Black-backed Woodpecker and Wilson's Warbler). This route would take half a day.

In winter, you can get to the cross-country ski trails via La Diable and La Pimbina visitors' centres. Gray Jay and Boreal Chickadee are present during the winter months at the latter centre.

Chapter 3

Sites for All Seasons

The preceding site descriptions show that the number and variety of birds at a given site are dependent on the season and type of habitat. In order to help the birdwatcher choose the appropriate destination when planning a field trip, we have listed the sites according to season and species of birds.

The bird species have been divided somewhat arbitrarily into six groups : 1) **water birds :** birds that mainly frequent lakes, rivers, streams and marshes ; that is, loons, grebes, herons, wildfowl, rails and some passerines; 2) **hawks ;** 3) **shorebirds :** plovers and sandpipers; 4) **gulls :** includes terns and jaegers ; 5) **owls ;** 6) **passerines :** land birds and birds that have not been included in the other groups.

The seasons are defined as follows :

- Spring : March through May
- Summer : June and July
- Fall : August through November
- Winter : December through February

For quick reference, the name of each site is followed by its site number.

SUGGESTIONS FOR SPRING BIRDING

Water birds

Nuns' Island (A9), LaPrairie basin (A18), Ile Perrot (B1), Valleyfield-Saint-Barbe (C3), Saint-Paul-de-l'Ile-aux-Noix and Rivière du Sud (D6), Berthierville and the Berthier Islands (E4), Saint-Barthélemy (E6), Baie-du-Febvre (E7).

Hawks

Summit Park (A11), Ile Perrot (B1), Rigaud (B5), Valleyfield (C3), Mount Saint-Bruno (D1), Mount Saint-Hilaire (D2).

Shorebirds

Saint-Paul-de-l'Ile-aux-Noix and Rivière du Sud (D6), Ile aux Fermiers (E1), Baie-du-Febvre (E7).

Gulls

Beauharnois dam (C1).

Owls

Nuns' Island (A9).

Passerines

Morgan Arboretum (A1), Nuns' Island (A9), Summit Park (A11), Mount Royal Cemetery (A12), Mount Royal Park (A13), Ile Perrot (B1).

SUGGESTIONS FOR SUMMER BIRDING

Water birds

Lachine Rapids (A8), Châteauguay (A17), Longueuil shore-line (A20), Saint-Étienne-de-Beauharnois (C2), Dundee (C4), Ile aux Fermiers (E1), Ile du Moine (E5), Baie-du-Febvre (E7).

Gulls

Lachine Rapids (A8).

Passerines

Morgan Arboretum (A1), Châteauguay (A17), Hudson (B3), Saint-Lazare (B4), Rigaud (B5), Huntingdon (C5), Pitch Pine Reserve (C6), Hemmingford (C7), Mount Saint-Bruno (D1), Mount Saint-Hilaire (D2), Philipsburg (D7), Oka (F1), Saint-Colomban (F3), Mont Tremblant Park and the Rouge Matawin Wildlife Reserve (F5).

SUGGESTIONS FOR FALL BIRDING

Water birds

North shore of Lake Saint-Louis (A6), Lachine Rapids (A8), Nuns' Island (A9), LaPrairie basin (A18), Longueuil shoreline (A20), Ile Perrot (B1), Saint-Jean-sur-Richelieu (D5), Ile aux Fermiers (E1), Ile du Moine (E5), Oka (F1).

Hawks

Morgan Arboretum (A1), Ile Perrot (B1), Rigaud (B5).

Shorebirds

Anse-à-l'Orme (A2), Longueuil shoreline (A20), the Coteau-Station turf farms (B7), Ile aux Fermiers (E1), Ile du Moine (E5), Oka (F1).

Gulls

Beauharnois dam (C1).

Owls

Nuns' Island (A9), Mount Saint-Bruno (D1).

Passerines

Nuns' Island (A9), Summit Park (A11), Mount Royal Cemetery (A12), Ile Perrot (B1), Oka (F1).

SUGGESTIONS FOR WINTER BIRDING

Water birds

North shore of Lake Saint-Louis (A6), Lachine Rapids (A8), LaPrairie basin (A18).

Hawks

Brossard (A19), Vaudreuil (B2), Saint-Clet and Sainte-Marthe (B6), Saint-Étienne-de-Beauharnois (C2), Dundee (C4).

Gulls

Lachine Rapids (A8), LaPrairie basin (A18), Beauharnois dam (C1).

Owls

Morgan Arboretum (A1), Nuns' Island (A9), Brossard (A19), Longueuil Regional Park (A21), Hudson (B3), Saint-Étienne-de-Beauharnois (C2).

Passerines

Morgan Arboretum (A1), Nuns' Island (A9), Mount Royal Cemetery (A12), Mount Royal Park (A13), Montreal Botanical Gardens (A14), Châteauguay (A17), Hudson (B3), Saint-Lazare (B4), Mont Tremblant Park (F5).

Chapter 4

In Search of
Rare Birds

This chapter is for the birder who is no longer satisfied with identifying common species but would like to pursue the more elusive birds in the Montreal region. These species are either few in number, have a very localized distribution or are present for only short periods of the year.

The following list of 81 species indicates the sites where they are most likely to be found. It also gives the time of year when they are most often observed.

Most of the species listed here have been designated as rare or irregular in the checklist in Chapter 5. Also included are species whose nocturnal habits make them difficult to find. Others are species relatively common to the Montreal area but irregular in most of the other areas of Quebec.

Red-throated Loon : Nuns' Island (A9), Oka (F1); October-November.

Horned Grebe : Nuns' Island (A9), Longueuil shoreline (A20), Ile Perrot (B1), Valleyfield (C3), Oka (F1); April-May, October-November.

Red-necked Grebe : Nuns' Island (A9), Longueuil shoreline (A20), Ile Perrot (B1), Valleyfield (C3), Oka (F1); April-May, October-November.

Least Bittern : Châteauguay (A17), Saint-Étienne-de-Beauharnois (C2), Dundee (C4), Ile aux Fermiers (E1); late May to July.

Great Egret : Dundee (C4), Ile aux Fermiers (E1), Ile du Moine (E5), Berthier Islands (E4); May to September.

Green-backed Heron : Châteauguay (A17), Hudson (B3), Dundee (C4), Philipsburg (D7); May to September.

Greater White-fronted Goose : Sainte-Barbe (C3), Saint-Barthélemy (E6), Baie-du-Febvre (E7); March to April.

Ross' Goose : Baie-du-Febvre (E7); irregular in April.

Eurasian Wigeon : Lachine Rapids (A8), Saint–Barthélemy (E6), Baie-du-Febvre (E7); April to May.

Canvasback : North shore of Lake Saint-Louis (A6), Ile Perrot (B1), Vaudreuil (B2), Valleyfield (C3), Oka (F1); March-April, November.

Redhead : Dundee (C4), Ile aux Fermiers (E1), Baie-du-Febvre (E7); May to September.

Harlequin Duck : Lachine Rapids (A8), LaPrairie basin (A18); irregular in winter.

Barrow's Goldeneye : North shore of Lake Saint-Louis (A6), LaPrairie basin (A18); winter, especially February-March. Saint-Jean-sur-Richelieu (D5); November.

Ruddy Duck : Saint-Étienne-de-Beauharnois (C2), Baie-du-Febvre (E7); May-August. Saint-Jean-sur-Richelieu (D5); November.

Turkey Vulture : Rigaud (B5), Dundee (C4), Mount Saint-Bruno (D1), Mount Saint-Hilaire (D2), Rougemont (D3), Philipsburg (D7); April to September.

Bald Eagle : Lachine Rapids (A8); irregular in winter. Valleyfield (C3), Baie-du-Febvre (E7); April-May.

Cooper's Hawk : Morgan Arboretum (A1), Bois-de-Liesse (A4), Valleyfield (C3), Huntingdon (C5), Philipsburg (D7); April to September.

Golden Eagle : Morgan Arboretum (A1), Rigaud (B5); October-November. Valleyfield (C3); April.

Peregrine Falcon : Montreal (A10); permanent. Mount Saint-Hilaire (D2); summer. Ile aux Fermiers (E1), Ile du Moine (E5), Saint-Barthélemy (E6), Baie-du-Febvre (E7); April and September.

Gyrfalcon : Port of Montreal (A10); irregular in winter.

Gray Partridge : Dorval (A6), Nuns' Island (A9), Montreal Botanical Gardens (A14), Saint-Constant (A18), Sainte-Marthe and Saint-Clet (B6); permanent.

Spruce Grouse : Mont-Tremblant Park and the Rouge-Matawin Wildlife Reserve (F5); permanent but very difficult to find.

Wild Turkey : Hemmingford (C7); permanent but easier to see in April and May.

Yellow Rail : Dundee (C4), Ile du Moine (E5); irregular from May to August; now rarely reported.

American Coot : Saint-Étienne-de-Beauharnois (C2), Baie-du-Febvre (E7); May to October.

Lesser Golden-Plover : Coteau-Station (B7); mid-August to mid-September.

Purple Sandpiper : Pointe-du-Buisson (C1), Ile du Moine (E5); late October-early November.

Buff-breasted Sandpiper : Coteau-Station (B7), Ile aux Fermiers (E1), Ile du Moine (E5); late August-September.

Wilson's Phalarope : Ile aux Fermiers (E1), Ile du Moine (E5), Baie-du-Febvre (E7); May to September.

Laughing Gull : Lachine Rapids (A8), LaPrairie basin (A18), Beauharnois (C1); irregular in summer and fall.

Franklin's Gull : Lachine Rapids (A8), LaPrairie basin (A18), Beauharnois (C1); irregular in summer (mostly June) and fall.

Little Gull : Lachine Rapids (A8), Beauharnois (C1), Ile du Moine (E5); May, August to September.

Common Black-headed Gull : Beauharnois (C1); irregular from August to December.

Thayer's Gull : Lachine Rapids (A8), Beauharnois (C1); irregular in November and December.

Lesser Black-backed Gull : Beauharnois (C1); irregular in November.

Black-legged Kittiwake : Beauharnois (C1); mostly in November.

Sabine's Gull : Beauharnois (C1); irregular in September.

Caspian Tern : Lachine Rapids (A8), Longueuil shoreline (A20), Ile aux Fermiers (E1), Ile du Moine (E5), Oka (F1); rare but regular in summer.

Arctic Tern : Lachine Rapids (A8), Beauharnois (C1); late May-early June.

Forster's Tern : Lachine Rapids (A8), Beauharnois (C1), Ile du Moine (E5); irregular in spring and fall.

Eastern Screech-Owl : Cap Saint-Jacques (A3), Terra-Cotta Park (A6), Summit Park (A10), Mount Royal Cemetery (A12); permanent.

Long-eared Owl : Nuns' Island (A9); April, November-December.

Short-eared Owl : Nuns' Island (A9), Brossard (A19), Vaudreuil (B2), Saint-Clet (B6); March-April, December, sometimes all winter. Ile aux Fermiers (E1), Ile du Moine (E5), Baie-du-Febvre (E7); summer.

Boreal Owl : Morgan Arboretum (A1), Nuns' Island (A9), Longueuil (A21); irregular in November, also in winter.

Northern Saw-whet Owl : Saraguay (A5), Nuns' Island (A9), Longueuil (A21), Mount Saint-Bruno (D1); March-April, October-November, also in winter.

Whip-poor-will : Saint-Lazare (B4), Sainte-Marthe (B6), Huntingdon (C5), Pitch Pine Reserve (C6), Saint-Colomban (F3); mostly May-June in the evening.

Red-headed Woodpecker : Dundee (C4); May-September.

Three-toed Woodpecker : Nuns' Island (A9), Ile Sainte-Hélène (A10), Saint-Lazare (B4); irregular in winter.

Black-backed Woodpecker : Nuns' Island (A9), Hudson (B3), Saint-Lazare (B4); rare in winter. Mont-Tremblant Park (F5); permanent.

Olive-sided Flycatcher : Summit Park (A11); late May. Mont-Tremblant Park (F5); June-July.

Yellow-bellied Flycatcher : Summit Park (A11); late May. Mont-Tremblant Park (F5); June-July.

Willow Flycatcher : Bois-de-la-Réparation (A16), Châteauguay (A17), Saint-Constant (A18), Brossard and LaPrairie (A19), Dundee (C4), Berthierville (E4); May to July.

Northern Rough-winged Swallow : Châteauguay (A17), Saint-Étienne-de-Beauharnois (C2), Huntingdon (C5); May to July.

Gray Jay : Saint-Lazare (B4), Lachute (F4); irregular in winter. Mont-Tremblant Park (F5); permanent.

Common Raven : Rigaud (B5), Mount Saint-Hilaire (D2), Mont-Tremblant Park (F5); permanent.

Boreal Chickadee : Saint-Lazare (B4), Lachute (F4); rare in winter. Mont-Tremblant Park (F5); permanent.

Carolina Wren : Terra-Cotta Park (A6), Nuns' Island (A9); irregular in winter; may come to feeders.

Sedge Wren : Dundee (C4), Ile du Moine (E5); June to August.

Blue-gray Gnatcatcher : Summit Park (A11); May. Saint-Constant (A18), Brossard (A19), Rivière du Sud (D6); May-July.

Gray-cheeked Thrush : Summit Park (A11); late May.

Northern Mockingbird : Mount Royal Cemetery (A12), Montreal Botanical Gardens (A14), Saint-Constant (A18); summer, also in winter.

Loggerhead Shrike : Bois de la Réparation (A16), Hudson (B3), Dundee (C4). This species has almost disappeared from the Montreal region.

Yellow-throated Vireo : Rigaud (B5), Huntingdon (C5), Philipsburg (D7), Oka (F1); mid-May to July.

Golden-winged Warbler : Huntingdon (C5); mid-May to July.

Orange-crowned Warbler : Summit Park (A11), Mount Royal Cemetery (A12); May, September to October.

Pine Warbler : Hudson (B3), Contrecoeur (E2), Berthier (E4), Oka (F1), Lachute (F4); May to July.

Palm Warbler : Nuns' Island (A9), Summit Park (A11), Mount Royal Cemetery (A12); late April-May, September-October.

Cerulean Warbler : Huntingdon (C5), Mount Saint-Hilaire (D2), Philipsburg (D7); late May to early July.

Kentucky Warbler : Summit Park (A11), Mount Royal Park (A13); irregular in May.

Hooded Warbler : Summit Park (A11), Mount Royal Park (A13); irregular in May.

Northern Cardinal : Cap Saint-Jacques (A3), Summit Park (A11), Mount Royal Park (A13), Montreal Botanical Gardens

(A14), Châteauguay (A17), Hudson (B3), Hemmingford (C7); permanent.

Rufous-sided Towhee : Huntingdon (C5), Pitch Pine Reserve (C6); May to September.

Clay-colored Sparrow : Saint-Colomban (F3); June-July.

Field Sparrow : Huntingdon (C5), Pitch Pine Reserve (C6), Hemmingford (C7), Saint-Colomban (F3); May to August.

Grasshopper Sparrow : Saint-Constant (A18), Sainte-Marthe (B6); mid-May to August.

Sharp-tailed Sparrow : Ile aux Fermiers (E1), Ile du Moine (E5); mid-June to August.

Lapland Longspur : Saint-Constant (A18), Sainte-Marthe (B6); winter.

Yellow-headed Blackbird: Saint-Étienne-de-Beauharnois (C2); irregular in winter, mostly in December.

Red Crossbill : Hudson (B3), Mount Saint-Bruno (D1), Oka (F1), Lachute (F4), Mont-Tremblant Park (F5); mostly in winter.

White-winged Crossbill : Saint-Lazare (B4), Oka (F1), Lachute (F4), Mont-Tremblant Park (F5); mostly in winter.

Hoary Redpoll : Montreal Botanical Gardens (A14); irregular in winter.

Chapter 5

Checklist of Birds in the Montreal and Laurentian Areas

This chapter gives a checklist of species found in the wild in the Montreal area as defined at the beginning of Chapter 1.

A corresponding list is given for the part of the Laurentians situated north of Montreal, this being a resort area much frequented by Montrealers throughout the year. Also, Mont Tremblant Park and the Rouge Matawin Wildlife Reserve, which are representative of the area, are included in this site guide. The part of the Laurentians considered here is between the north boundary of the Rouge Matawin Wildlife Reserve and the north boundary of the Montreal area. The west boundary extends from Montebello to Lake Nominingue and the east boundary from Rawdon to the Taureau Reservoir.

The Montreal list comprises 359 species (including 65 exceptional visitants) and the Laurentian list, 239 species (including 24 exceptional visitants). The name of each species is followed by upper and lower case letters that indicate the status of the species and the frequency of sightings.

Status
The status of the species in the two areas considered is indicated by upper case letters as follows :

MB (Migratory Breeder) : A breeding species that arrives in spring, nests in the area and leaves in fall for its winter quarters, usually further south. Some of these birds occasionally manage to overwinter (e.g., American Goldfinch).

RB (Resident Breeder) : A breeding species that for the most part remains within the area throughout the year (e.g., Black-capped Chickadee).

SB (Sedentary Breeder) : A breeding species that does not migrate at all (e.g., Ruffed Grouse).

(PB) (Possible Breeder) : A species sighted during the breeding season for which there is sufficient reason to support the possibility of breeding, despite lack of actual proof (e.g., Caspian Tern).

M (Migrant) : A species present only during its annual migration between its winter quarters, normally situated to the south, and its breeding grounds, which are usually further north (e.g., American Pipit).

W (Wintering) : A species that is present in winter, i.e., at least in January and February. This symbol is also used for migratory breeders **(MB)**, migrants **(M)** and visitants **(V)** that overwinter in the areas considered; sedentary breeders **(SB)** and resident breeders **(RB)** overwinter by definition. This category covers only those species known to have successfully overwintered at least once, having been present continuously throughout January and February. It is not used in the case of isolated winter sightings.

V (Visitant) : A species not normally found in the areas considered. Such birds may be vagrants, pre- and post-breeding overshoots or migrating strays. They may also be present because of abnormal weather conditions or temporary changes in habitat (e.g., Common Eider).

Relative abundance

The lower-case letters are used to indicate the frequency of sightings. The scale is subjective but based nonetheless on documented sightings and on the author's knowledge of the birds in the Montreal and Laurentian areas. The designation is not intended to reflect true abundance but rather to indicate the likelihood of sighting the species in the area in question, given the appropriate habitat and season. Sizable fluctuations in the frequency of sightings are indicated by a lower-case letter qualifying the status, e.g., "MBr, Mc, Wr" mean that the species is a rare migratory breeder **(MBr)**, is commonly seen in migration **(Mc)** but rarely overwinters **(Wr)**. The following letters are used:

e (exceptional) : five records or fewer; the number of sightings for visitants is given in brackets (e.g., Harris' Sparrow).

i (irregular) :   more than five records but sightings are sporadic and not annual (e.g., Tufted Titmouse).

r (rare) : present annually but in small numbers or in only a few localities (e.g., Northern Mockingbird).

o (occasional) :   seen annually but infrequently during the period when it is normally present (e.g., Eastern Bluebird).

c (common) :   present each year and frequently sighted during the period when it is present (e.g., Great Blue Heron).

a (abundant) : present annually and observed almost everywhere during the time it is present (e.g., Red-winged Blackbird).

v (variable) : presence fluctuates from year to year; either common or rare during the period when it is normally present (e.g., Common Redpoll).

	Montreal	Laurentian
☐ Red-throated Loon	Mr	–
☐ Pacific Loon	Ve (1)	–
☐ Common Loon	Mc	MBc
☐ Pied-billed Grebe	MBo	MBo
☐ Horned Grebe	Mo	Mr
☐ Red-necked Grebe	Mo	Mr
☐ Western Grebe	Ve(2)	–
☐ Wilson's Storm-Petrel	Ve(1)	–
☐ Leach's Storm-Petrel	Ve(2)	–
☐ Northern Gannet	Vi	–
☐ American White Pelican	Ve(3)	–
☐ Great Cormorant	ViWe	–
☐ Double-crested Cormorant	MBe,Mc	Vr
☐ American Bittern	MBc	MBo
☐ Least Bittern	MBr	Ve(1)

		Montreal	Laurentians
☐	Great Blue Heron	MBc	MBc
☐	Great Egret	MBr	–
☐	Snowy Egret	Vi	–
☐	Little Blue Heron	Vi	–
☐	Tricolored Heron	Ve(4)	–
☐	Cattle Egret	Vr	Ve(1)
☐	Green-backed Heron	MBo	MBr
☐	Black-crowned Night-Heron	MBo	Ve(1)
☐	Yellow-crowned Night-Heron	Ve(2)	
☐	White Ibis	Ve(2)	–
☐	Glossy Ibis	Vi	–
☐	Fulvous Whistling-Duck	Ve(1)	–
☐	Tundra Swan	Vi	Ve(1)
☐	Trumpeter Swan	Ve(1)	–
☐	Mute Swan	Ve(4)	–
☐	Greater White-fronted Goose	Vr	–
☐	Snow Goose	Mc	Mr
☐	Ross' Goose	Ve(3)	–
☐	Brant	Mo	Mr
☐	Barnacle Goose	Ve(5)	–
☐	Canada Goose	MBr,Ma,Wi	Mc,(PB)
☐	Ruddy Shelduck	Ve (3)	–
☐	Wood Duck	MBo,We	MBo
☐	Green-winged Teal	MBo,Mc,We	MBr
☐	American Black Duck	MBo,Mc,Wo	MBc
☐	Mallard	MBc,Wo	MBo

	Montreal	Laurentians
☐ Northern Pintail	MBo,Mc,Wr	Mr,(PB)
☐ Blue-winged Teal	MBo,Mc	MBr
☐ Cinnamon Teal	Ve(2)	–
☐ Northern Shoveler	MBr,Mo	Mr
☐ Gadwall	MBo,We	Ve(1)
☐ Eurasian Wigeon	Vr,(PB)	–
☐ American Wigeon	MBc,We	Mr,(PB)
☐ Canvasback	Mo,Wi	Ve(1)
☐ Redhead	MBr,Mo,We	Vi
☐ Ring-necked Duck	MBr,Mc,We	MBo
☐ Greater Scaup	Ma,Wi	Mc
☐ Lesser Scaup	MBr,Mc,We	Mo
☐ Common Eider	Vi	–
☐ King Eider	Ve(3)We	–
☐ Harlequin Duck	Vi,Wi	–
☐ Oldsquaw	Mo	Mr
☐ Black Scoter	Mo	Mr
☐ Surf Scoter	Mo	Mr
☐ White-winged Scoter	Mo	Mr
☐ Common Goldeneye	MBr,Ma,Wc	MBo
☐ Barrow's Goldeneye	Mr,Wr	Ve(1)
☐ Bufflehead	Mo,Wi	Mo
☐ Smew	Ve(1)	–
☐ Hooded Merganser	MBr,Mo,Wi	MBo
☐ Common Merganser	MBr,Ma,Wc	MBc,Wi
☐ Red-breasted Merganser	Mo,We	Mo,(PB)
☐ Ruddy Duck	MBi,Mr	Ve(1)
☐ Black Vulture	Ve(2)	–
☐ Turkey Vulture	MBo	MBo

		Montreal	Laurentians
☐	Osprey	Mc	MBo
☐	Bald Eagle	Mr,We	Mr,(PB)
☐	Northern Harrier	MBc,We	MBo
☐	Sharp-shinned Hawk	MBr,Mc,Wr	MBo
☐	Cooper's Hawk	MBr,Wi	MBi
☐	Northern Goshawk	RBr	RBo
☐	Red-shouldered Hawk	MBo,Wi	MBo
☐	Broad-winged Hawk	MBo, Mc	MBc
☐	Swainson's Hawk	Ve(3)	–
☐	Red-tailed Hawk	MBo,Mc,Wr	MBc
☐	Rough-legged Hawk	Mc,Wr	Mo
☐	Golden Eagle	Mr	Mr
☐	American Kestrel	MBc,Wr	MBc
☐	Merlin	Mr	MBr
☐	Peregrine Falcon	MBr,Wi	MBi
☐	Gyrfalcon	Wi	–
☐	Gray Partridge	SBo	Ve(1)
☐	Ring-necked Pheasant	SBi	–
☐	Spruce Grouse	Ve(1)	SBr
☐	Willow Ptarmigan	Ve(1)	–
☐	Ruffed Grouse	SBc	SBc
☐	Sharp-tailed Grouse	Ve(1)	–
☐	Wild Turkey	SBr	–
☐	Yellow Rail	Vi,(PB)	–
☐	King Rail	Ve(4)	–
☐	Virginia Rail	MBc	MBo
☐	Sora	MBc	MBo
☐	Common Moorhen	MBo,We	Vi

	Montreal	Laurentians
☐ American Coot	MBr	–
☐ Sandhill Crane	Vi	–
☐ Black-bellied Plover	Mc	Mr
☐ Lesser Golden-Plover	Mo	Vi
☐ Semipalmated Plover	Mc	Mr
☐ Piping Plover	Ve(1)	–
☐ Killdeer	MBa	MBc
☐ American Avocet	Ve(2)	–
☐ Greater Yellowlegs	Mc	Mo
☐ Lesser Yellowlegs	Mc	Mo
☐ Solitary Sandpiper	Mo	MBe,Mo
☐ Willet	Vi	–
☐ Spotted Sandpiper	MBa	MBc
☐ Upland Sandpiper	MBo	Vi
☐ Whimbrel	Mr	Vi
☐ Long-billed Curlew	Ve(1)	–
☐ Black-tailed Godwit	Ve(1)	–
☐ Hudsonian Godwit	Mr	–
☐ Marbled Godwit	Vi	–
☐ Ruddy Turnstone	Mo	Vi
☐ Red Knot	Mo	–
☐ ˙Sanderling	Mo	Mr
☐ Semipalmated Sandpiper	Ma	Mo
☐ Western Sandpiper	Vi	–
☐ Least Sandpiper	Mc	Mo
☐ White-rumped Sandpiper	Mo	Mr
☐ Baird's Sandpiper	Mr	–

		Montreal	Laurentians
☐	Pectoral Sandpiper	Mo	Mr
☐	Purple Sandpiper	Vi	–
☐	Dunlin	Mc	Mr
☐	Curlew Sandpiper	Ve(1)	–
☐	Stilt Sandpiper	Mr	–
☐	Buff-breasted Sandpiper	Vi	Ve(2)
☐	Ruff	Vr	Ve(1)
☐	Short-billed Dowitcher	Mo	Vi
☐	Long-billed Dowitcher	Vi	–
☐	Common Snipe	MBc,We	MBc
☐	Eurasian Woodcock	Ve(1)	–
☐	American Woodcock	MBc	MBc
☐	Wilson's Phalarope	MBr	–
☐	Red-necked Phalarope	Mr	Vi
☐	Red Phalarope	Vi	
☐	Pomarine Jaeger	Ve(5)	–
☐	Parasitic Jaeger	Vr	–
☐	Long-Tailed Jaeger	Ve(5)	Ve(1)
☐	Laughing Gull	Vi	–
☐	Franklin's Gull	Vi	–
☐	Little Gull	MBe,Mr	–
☐	Common Black-headed Gull	Vi	–
☐	Bonaparte's Gull	Mo	Mr
☐	Mew Gull	Ve(4)	–
☐	Ring-billed Gull	MBa,Wi	Mo,(PB)
☐	California Gull	Ve(1)	–
☐	Herring Gull	MBr,Ma,Wo	MBr
☐	Thayer's Gull	Vi,We	–
☐	Iceland Gull	Wo	–

		Montreal	**Laurentians**
☐	Lesser Black-backed Gull	Vi	–
☐	Glaucous Gull	Wr	–
☐	Great Black-backed Gull	MBr,Mc,Wo	Vi
☐	Black-legged Kittiwake	Vr	–
☐	Sabine's Gull	Vi	–
☐	Ivory Gull	Ve(3),We	–
☐	Caspian Tern	Mr,(PB)	–
☐	Common Tern	MBo	Vi
☐	Arctic Tern	Mr	–
☐	Forster's Tern	Vi	–
☐	Black Tern	MBo	Vi
☐	Black Skimmer	Ve(1)	–
☐	Dovekie	Ve(4)*	–
☐	Thick-billed Murre	Vi*	–

*Species not sighted for 40 years

☐	Razorbill	Vi	Ve(1)
☐	Black Guillemot	Ve(2)	–
☐	Marbled Murrelet	Ve(1)	–
☐	Ancient Murrelet	Ve(1)	–
☐	Atlantic Puffin	Ve(4)	–
☐	Rock Dove	SBa	SBc
☐	Mourning Dove	MBc,Wo	MBo,Wr
☐	Black-billed Cuckoo	MBo	MBr
☐	Yellow-billed Cuckoo	MBi	Ve(1)

		Montreal	**Laurentians**
☐	Barn Owl	Vi,(PB)	–
☐	Eastern Screech-Owl	SBr	Vi
☐	Great Horned Owl	RBc	RBc
☐	Snowy Owl	Wr	Wr
☐	Northern Hawk-Owl	Wi	Wi
☐	Burrowing Owl	Ve(1)	–
☐	Barred Owl	SBo	SBc
☐	Great Gray Owl	Wi	Wi
☐	Long-eared Owl	MBr,Mo,Wr	MBr,We
☐	Short-eared Owl	MBr,Mo,Wr	Ve(1)
☐	Boreal Owl	Wi	Wi
☐	Northern Saw-whet Owl	RBr,Mo	RBo
☐	Common Nighthawk	MBc	MBc
☐	Chuck-will's-widow	Ve(1)	–
☐	Whip-poor-will	MBr	MBo
☐	Chimney Swift	MBc	MBc
☐	Ruby-throated Hummingbird	MBo,Mc	MBc
☐	Belted Kingfisher	MBc,We	MBc,We
☐	Red-headed Woodpecker	MBr,We	Ve(2)
☐	Red-bellied Woodpecker	Vi,We	Ve(1)
☐	Yellow-bellied Sapsucker	MBc	MBc
☐	Downy Woodpecker	RBc	RBc
☐	Hairy Woodpecker	RBc	RBc
☐	Three-toed Woodpecker	Wi	Wi

		Montreal	Laurentians
☐	Black-backed Woodpecker	Wr	RBr
☐	Northern Flicker	MBa,Wr	MBa
☐	Pileated Woodpecker	SBo	SBo
☐	Olive-sided Flycatcher	Mo,(PB)	MBo
☐	Eastern Wood-Pewee	MBc	MBc
☐	Yellow-bellied Flycatcher	Mo,(PB)	MBo
☐	Alder Flycatcher	MBc	MBc
☐	Willow Flycatcher	MBo	Ve(3)
☐	Least Flycatcher	MBc	MBc
☐	Eastern Phoebe	MBc	MBc
☐	Say's Phoebe	Ve(2)	–
☐	Great Crested Flycatcher	MBc	MBc
☐	Western Kingbird	Ve(3)	–
☐	Eastern Kingbird	MBc	MBc
☐	Scissor-tailed Flycatcher	Ve(1)	–
☐	Horned Lark	MBo,Mc,Wr	MBr,Mc
☐	Purple Martin	MBo	MBr
☐	Tree Swallow	MBa	MBa
☐	Northern Rough-winged Swallow	MBo	MBr
☐	Bank Swallow	MBc	MBc
☐	Cliff Swallow	MBc	MBo
☐	Barn Swallow	MBc	MBc
☐	Gray Jay	Wi	RBo
☐	Blue Jay	RBc	RBa
☐	Black-billed Magpie	Ve(4)	Ve(1)
☐	American Crow	MBa,Wc	MBa,Wr

		Montreal	Laurentians
☐	Common Raven	SBr	SBo
☐	Black-capped Chickadee	RBa	RBa
☐	Boreal Chickadee	Wi	RBo
☐	Tufted Titmouse	Vi,We	–
☐	Red-breasted Nuthatch	RBo,Mc	RBc
☐	White-breasted Nuthatch	SBc	SBc
☐	Brown Creeper	MBc,Wr	MBc,Wr
☐	Carolina Wren	RBe,Vr,Wi	Ve(1)
☐	House Wren	MBc	MBo
☐	Winter Wren	MBo,Mc,Wi	MBc
☐	Sedge Wren	MBr	MBe
☐	Marsh Wren	MBo	Vi,(PB)
☐	Golden-crowned Kinglet	MBr,Mc,Wr	MBc,Wr
☐	Ruby-crowned Kinglet	MBr,Mc,We	MBc
☐	Blue-gray Gnatcatcher	MBr	–
☐	Northern Wheatear	Ve(1)	–
☐	Eastern Bluebird	MBo	MBo
☐	Townsend's Solitaire	Ve(1)	–
☐	Veery	MBc	MBc
☐	Gray-cheeked Thrush	Mr	Mr
☐	Swainson's Thrush	Mc,(PB)	MBc
☐	Hermit Thrush	MBo,Mc,We	MBc
☐	Wood Thrush	MBc	MBo
☐	Eurasian Blackbird	Ve(1)	–
☐	Fieldfare	Ve(1),We	–

		Montreal	Laurentians
☐	American Robin	MBa,Wr	MBa
☐	Varied Thrush	Vi,We	–
☐	Gray Catbird	MBc	MBc
☐	Northern Mockingbird	MBr,Wr	MBi
☐	Brown Thrasher	MBo,We	MBo
☐	American Pipit	Mo	Mo
☐	Bohemian Waxwing	Wv	Wv
☐	Cedar Waxwing	MBa,Wr	MBa
☐	Northern Shrike	Wr	Wr
☐	Loggerhead Shrike	MBi	MBi
☐	European Starling	MBa,Wc	MBa,Wr
☐	White-eyed Vireo	Ve(5)	–
☐	Solitary Vireo	MBr,Mo	MBo
☐	Yellow-throated Vireo	MBr	–
☐	Warbling Vireo	MBo	MBr
☐	Philadelphia Vireo	MBr,Mo	MBo
☐	Red-eyed Vireo	MBa	MBa
☐	Blue-winged Warbler	Ve(3)	–
☐	Golden-winged Warbler	MBr	Vi,(PB)
☐	Tennessee Warbler	Mc,(PB)	MBc
☐	Orange-crowned Warbler	Mr	Mr
☐	Nashville Warbler	MBo,Mc	MBc
☐	Northern Parula	Mo	MBo
☐	Yellow Warbler	MBa	MBc

	Montreal	Laurentians
☐ Chestnut-sided Warbler	MBc	MBc
☐ Magnolia Warbler	MBr,Mc	MBc
☐ Cape May Warbler	Mo	MBo
☐ Black-throated Blue Warbler	MBo,Mc	MBc
☐ Yellow-rumped Warbler	MBo,Ma,We	MBc
☐ Black-throated Gray Warbler	Ve(2)	–
☐ Hermit Warbler	Ve(1)	–
☐ Black-throated Green Warbler	MBo,Mc	MBc
☐ Blackburnian Warbler	MBo,Mc	MBc
☐ Yellow-throated Warbler	Ve(1)	–
☐ Pine Warbler	MBr	MBr
☐ Kirtland's Warbler	Ve(1)	–
☐ Prairie Warbler	Vi	–
☐ Palm Warbler	MBe,Mr	Mr,(PB)
☐ Bay-breasted Warbler	MBe,Mc	MBc
☐ Blackpoll Warbler	Mo	Mo
☐ Cerulean Warbler	MBr	–
☐ Black-and-white Warbler	MBc	MBc
☐ American Redstart	MBc	MBc
☐ Prothonotary Warbler	Ve(1)	–
☐ Worm-eating Warbler	Vi	–
☐ Ovenbird	MBc	MBc
☐ Northern Waterthrush	MBo	MBc
☐ Kentucky Warbler	Vi	Ve(1)
☐ Connecticut Warbler	Ve(4)	Ve(1)
☐ Mourning Warbler	MBc	MBc
☐ Common Yellowthroat	MBa	MBa
☐ Hooded Warbler	Vi	–

		Montreal	Laurentians
☐	Wilson's Warbler	MBi,Mo	MBo
☐	Canada Warbler	MBo,Mc	MBc
☐	Yellow-breasted Chat	Ve(3)	–
☐	Summer Tanager	Ve(5)	–
☐	Scarlet Tanager	MBc	MBc
☐	Western Tanager	Ve(3)	–
☐	Northern Cardinal	SBo	Vi,(PB)
☐	Rose-breasted Grosbeak	MBc	MBc
☐	Blue Grosbeak	Ve(3)	–
☐	Indigo Bunting	MBo	MBo
☐	Dickcissel	Vi	–
☐	Rufous-sided Towhee	MBr,We	MBe,We
☐	Tree Sparrow	Mc,Wo	Mc,Wr
☐	Chipping Sparrow	MBc,We	MBc
☐	Clay-colored Sparrow	MBi	Ve(1)
☐	Field Sparrow	MBo,We	MBr
☐	Vesper Sparrow	MBo	MBr
☐	Savannah Sparrow	MBa	MBc
☐	Grasshopper Sparrow	MBr	–
☐	Henslow's Sparrow	MBe,Vi	–
☐	Sharp-tailed Sparrow	MBr	–
☐	Fox Sparrow	Mo,We	Mo,(PB)
☐	Song Sparrow	MBa,Wr	MBa
☐	Lincoln's Sparrow	MBr,Mo	MBo
☐	Swamp Sparrow	MBc	MBc
☐	White-throated Sparrow	MBc,Ma,Wr	MBa
☐	White-crowned Sparrow	Mc,Wi	Mc
☐	Harris' Sparrow	Ve(4)We	–

		Montreal	Laurentians
☐	Dark-eyed Junco	MBr,Ma,Wo	MBc,Ma,Wr
☐	Lapland Longspur	Wr	Mr
☐	Smith's Longspur	Ve(1)	–
☐	Snow Bunting	Wo	Mo,Wr
☐	Bobolink	MBc	MBo
☐	Red-winged Blackbird	MBa,Wr	MBa
☐	Eastern Meadowlark	MBc	MBo,We
☐	Western Meadowlark	MBe,Vi	–
☐	Yellow-headed Blackbird	Vi,Wi	–
☐	Rusty Blackbird	Mo,Wr	MBo
☐	Brewer's Blackbird	Ve(1)	–
☐	Common Grackle	MBa,Wr	MBa
☐	Brown-headed Cowbird	MBa,Wr	MBc
☐	Orchard Oriole	Vi	Ve(1)
☐	Northern Oriole	MBc	MBo
☐	Pine Grosbeak	Wv	Wv
☐	Purple Finch	MBo,Mc,Wv	MBc,Wv
☐	House Finch	RBo	Vi,(PB)
☐	Red Crossbill	RBe,Wi	RBr
☐	White-winged Crossbill	Wv,(PB)	RBo
☐	Common Redpoll	Wv	Wv
☐	Hoary Redpoll	Wi	Wi
☐	Pine Siskin	RBr,Wv	RBc
☐	American Goldfinch	MBa,Wo	MBa,Wr
☐	European Goldfinch	Vi,Wi	–
☐	Evening Grosbeak	RBi,Wc	RBc
☐	House Sparrow	SBa	SBc

BIBLIOGRAPHY

American Ornithologists' Union. Checklist of North American Birds, 5th ed. Baltimore: The Lord Baltimore Press, 1957.

American Ornithologists' Union. 34th Supplement to the American Ornithologists' Union Checklist of North American Birds. Supp. to The Auk (1982) 90 (3): 1CC-16CC.

Barnhurst, B., and McIntosh, M. "Hawk-watching in Montreal." Tchebec (1976): 67-75.

Barnhurst, R.J., and McIntosh, M. "The 1981 Fall Hawk Migration at the Arboretum, Sainte-Anne-de-Bellevue, Quebec." Tchebec (1981): 100-103.

Bourdages, J.-L., et al. Étude des ressources et des potentiels du parc régional du Cap-Saint-Jacques. Centre de recherches écologiques de Montréal, 1988. 227 p.

Communauté urbaine de Montréal. Parc régional du Bois-de-Liesse : Dossier préliminaire de conception, Mémoire du plan directeur, 1988. 260 p.

Coulombe, D. "L'observation des oiseaux dans la région de Montréal." (map of birding sites) Centre de conservation de la faune ailée de Montréal, 1982.

David, N., et al. "The Ring-billed Gull in the Montreal Area." Tchebec (1977): 64-71.

David, N. "État et distribution des oiseaux du Québec méridional." Cahiers d'Ornithologie Victor-Gaboriault, numéro 3, Club des ornithologues du Québec inc., Québec (1980) : 213 p.

David, N. et Gosselin, M. Observer les oiseaux au Québec. Québec Science, Collection "Faire", 1981. 165p.

David, N. "The Winter Birds of Southern Quebec." Tchebec (1981): 104–112.

de Repentigny, L.-G. Eléments d'histoire naturelle et humaine de la région de la Réserve nationale de faune du lac Saint-François. Canadian Wildlife Service, 1982. 332 p.

Desrochers, A., and Fragnier, P. Étude de l'avifaune nicheuse et de la végétation de la Réserve national de faune du lac Saint-François. Canadian Wildlife Service, Quebec Region, 1983. 160 p.

Dion, J., et al. L'observation des oiseaux au lac Saint-Pierre (Guide des sites). Société ornithologique du Centre du Québec, 1988. 243 p.

Gagnon, N., and Giguère, R. Itinéraire-Nature. Quatre-temps (SAJIB), 11, 1 (1987): 83 p.

Girard, S. Itinéraire ornithologique de la Gaspésie. Club des ornithologues de la Gaspésie, (1988): 166 p.

Godfrey, W.E. The Birds of Canada, rev. ed. Ottawa, National Museum of Natural Sciences, 1986. 650 p.

Holohan, S., et al. "Laridae Migration at Beauharnois, Quebec." Part 1, Tchebec (1984): 28-36.

Houle, G. "Bois de la Réparation, Bois de l'Héritage: Synthèse des données biophysiques et proposition d'un plan directeur." Direction des réserves écologiques et des sites naturels, Government of Quebec, Ministère de l'Environnement, 1981.

Lehoux, D., Bourget, A., Dupuis, P. and Rosa, J. La sauvagine dans le système du Saint-Laurent. Environment Canada, Canadian Wildlife Service, Quebec Region, 1985. 76 p. annex, 72 p.

McIntosh, M., and Barnhurst, R.J. "Fall Hawk Migration at the Morgan Arboretum, Sainte-Anne-de-Bellevue, Quebec." Tchebec (1980): 97-102.

Montgomery, G. "The History of the Philipsburg Sanctuary." Tchebec (1980): 103-107.

Mousseau, P., et al. Evaluation de la valeur écologique de différents bois, ruisseaux et îles du territoire de la Communauté urbaine de Montréal. Centre de recherches écologiques de Montréal, 1984. 235 p.

Ouellet, H., and Lemieux, S. "Contribution à l'étude d'une avifaune nicheuse en milieu urbain : Cimetière Mont-Royal, Montréal, Canada." Tchébec (1971): 49-63.

Ouellet, H. Les oiseaux des collines montérégiennes et de la région de Montréal. National Museums of Canada, 1974. 167 p.

Ouellet, H., and Gosselin, M. Les noms français des oiseaux d'Amérique du Nord. Syllogeus No. 43. National Museums of Canada, Ottawa, 1983. 36 p.

Peterson, Roger Tory. A Field Guide to the Birds of Eastern and Central North America, 4th ed. Boston: Houghton Mifflin, 1984. 384 p.

Pilon, C., et al. Les îles du Saint-Laurent de Boucherville à Contrecoeur: Environnement biophysique. Centre de recherches écologiques de Montréal, 1980. 292 p.

Powe, N.N. The Climate of Montreal. Transport Canada, Meteorology Section, 1969. 51 p.

Rouleau, R. Petite flore forestière du Québec. Ministère des Terres et Forêts. Éditeur officiel du Québec. 1974, 216 p.

Toussaint, D., et al. Guide d'observation des oiseaux de l'Outaouais (Québec). Club des ornithologues de l'Outaouais, 1985. 223 p.

APPENDIX

Birdwatching Clubs in the Area Covered by this Guide

Club ornithologique des Hautes-Laurentides
C.P. 291, Saint-Jovite J0T 2H0

Société d'ornithologie de Lanaudière
C.P. 339, Joliette J6E 3Z6

Club d'observateurs d'oiseaux de Laval
C.P. 46, Succursale Laval Ouest, Laval H7R 5B7

Province of Quebec Society for the Protection of Birds
C.P. 43, Succursale B, Montréal H3B 3J5

Société de biologie de Montréal
C.P. 39, Succursale Outremont, Montréal H2V 4M6

Club d'observateurs d'oiseaux Marie-Victorin
Collège Marie-Victorin, 7000, rue Marie-Victorin,
Montréal H1G 2J6

Nature Illimitée
C.P. 638, Succursale Jean-Talon, Montréal H1S 2Z5

Club d'ornithologie d'Ahuntsic
10640, rue Saint-Hubert, Bureau 11,
Montréal H2C 2H7

Club d'ornithologie de Longueuil
70, rue Lévis, Suite 110, Longueuil J4H 1S5

Société ornithologique du Haut-Richelieu
171, rue Gosselin, Saint-Jean J3B 7J7

Club d'ornithologie Sorel-Tracy
C.P. 1111, Sorel J3P 7L4

Club du loisir ornithologique maskoutain
2070, Saint-Charles, Saint-Hyacinthe J2T 1V2

Club d'observateurs d'oiseaux de Brôme-Missisquoi
C.P. 256, Cowansville J2K 3S7

Société ornithologique du centre du Québec
960, rue Saint-Georges, Drummondville J2C 6A2

LIST OF ILLUSTRATIONS

Song Sparrow, Sylvain Tanguay, 1989, page 180
Collection of Mrs. Francine Noël and Mr. Stéphane Tanguay

Black Tern, René Roy, 1990, page 184

Savannah Sparrow, René Roy, 1989, page 192
Collection of Mr. Jacques Lemieux

Red-headed Woodpecker, Sylvain Tanguay, 1990, page 205

Golden-winged Warbler, René Roy, 1990, page 212

Rufous-sided Towhee, Sylvain Tanguay, 1990, page 216

Barred Owl, Sylvain Tanguay, 1988, page 230

Dark-eyed Junco, Sylvain Tanguay, 1987, page 234
Collection of Mr. and Mrs. Charles Poirier

Upland Sandpiper, Sylvain Tanguay, 1990, page 241
Collection of Mr. Benoit Tassé

Eastern Meadowlark, Sylvain Tanguay, 1989, page 249
Collection of Mr. and Mrs. Charles Poirier

Green-backed Heron, Sylvain Tanguay, 1990, page 252
Collection of Mrs. Francine Noël and Mr. Stéphane Tanguay

Sora, René Roy, 1988, page 264

Common Moorhen, René Roy, 1990, page 267

American Black Duck, René Roy, 1990, page 275

American Bittern, René Roy, 1990, page 286

Wilson's Phalarope, Sylvain Tanguay, 1990, page 297

Marsh Wren, Sylvain Tanguay, 1990, page 305

Ruffed Grouse, René Roy, 1989, page 307
Collection of Mr. Jacques Lemieux

Field Sparrow, Sylvain Tanguay, 1990, page 315

Gray Jay, René Roy, 1989, page 319
Collection of Ms. Sylvie Roy

Common Loon, Sylvain Tanguay, 1989, page 323
Collection of Mr. Michael Branigan